TRADITION VERSUS REVOLUTION
RUSSIA AND THE BALKANS IN 1917

ROBERT H. JOHNSTON

EAST EUROPEAN QUARTERLY, BOULDER
DISTRIBUTED BY COLUMBIA UNIVERSITY PRESS
NEW YORK

1977

EAST EUROPEAN MONOGRAPHS, NO. XXVIII

Robert H. Johnston is Associate Professor of History
at McMaster University

Library of Congress Catalog Card Number 77-071385
ISBN 0-914710-21-4

Printed in the United States of America

TABLE OF CONTENTS

PREFACE

A recent study of pre-war Tsarist policy in the Balkans concluded with the opinion that by 1917, "had it not been for the October Revolution, Russia was much closer to fulfilling her 'historic task' in the Near East" than responsible officials and observers could have hoped three years before.[1] The "historic task" encompassed the securing by Russia of two goals: a strong position, diplomatic if not military, vis a vis the Turkish Straits, and the establishment of her primacy in all important matters affecting the Balkan peninsula. In the nineteenth century Tsarist diplomacy showed itself alert to these interrelated issues; in the twentieth one or the other, when not both, came increasingly to dominate the plans of Russian foreign policy strategists until the new priorities of Bolshevik Russia. Neither objective of necessity implied an aggressive Russian stance in international affairs before 1914; in fact it was not until the changed circumstances of European-wide war that Tsardom could publicly dedicate itself to the solution of these "historic tasks." This struggle was inherited by the regime's successors.

The Tsarist pattern in seeking to solve the "historic task" is, in general, reasonably familiar. Much less so is the coda of the eight months leading up to Lenin's coup. And yet the difficulties experienced by the Provisional Government in addressing itself to the same overall "task" form a microcosm of the whole revolutionary year: its hopes, ambitions, divisions, victors and vanquished. What should be retained of older traditions and what imposed of new ideology? This was a major dilemma for Russia's rulers between Nicholas II and Lenin, as it is for most governments coming to power in revolution. However much those in charge of them might wish otherwise, revolutions must at least begin to build with the materials they inherit. The most successful revolutionary leader of the century acknowledged as much; his immediate predecessors found it far more difficult to make bricks of a new order from the straw of the old. Indeed, those who found themselves vested with the fallen regime's authority in March 1917 were by no means unanimous that new bricks should in fact be made: others were more determined that they would. Their confrontation came to its sharpest point over the campaign to redefine Russia's place and role in international affairs. Within this area Balkan concerns played a vital role, as well they might. Nowhere was the legacy from tsardom heavier or, for those who wished to, more difficult to shake off.

A great deal of archival material relating generally to both the period and subject of this book was published by the Soviets following the October Revolution. These have been extensively used and are listed in the bibliography. Analogous material from South-Eastern Europe is much scarcer and I was unable, while working on the manuscript, to penetrate the several relevant Balkan archives. However, the British Foreign Office and War Cabinet files and the Papers of Baron Sidney Sonnino were rich mines of information that provided many details from observers of and, occasionally, participants in the events under discussion. To a lesser degree this was true also of unpublished American sources in the National Archives and the Edward M. House Papers. I acknowledge with gratitude the assistance given to me by the custodians of these collections. And, as must be the case with anyone working in this area, my especial thanks are due to the staff of the Hoover Institution on War, Revolution and Peace, Stanford University.

Several monographs published in the last few years have taken up questions of revolutionary Russia's international posture and impact in the months between the downfall of tsarism and the Bolshevik coup. The most recent American study along these lines focused on the general foreign situation as seen from Petrograd, particularly as it related to the burning issues of domestic political contention.[2] Soviet studies have chosen a parallel approach, as well as the narrower geographic concentration.[3] The present volume belongs more to this latter category and seeks to analyze how specific, longstanding Russian interests abroad fared during the eight-month hiatus between the death of one Russia and the birth of another.

Considerable attention has been paid in this study to the views, before March and after, of the new regime's first Foreign Minister Paul Miliukov. Since he held office for scarcely two months his prominence in these pages might seem disproportionate to the whole. Yet it seems reasonably clear that the "Cadet Lenin manqué" (to paraphrase slightly one of his most acidulous critics) embodied so much of this difficult legacy in his own person, in addition to his self-proclaimed and uncontested status as Russia's leading expert on Balkan matters, that he by right must occupy an outstanding place in any examination of revolutionary Russia and South-East Europe. At the same time, of course, the influence of the revolutionary events themselves upon Balkan governments and peoples, as upon Great Power planning for the peninsula, has also engaged close scrutiny, particularly for the several months following upon the political demise of the man most dedicated to the principle of unchanging Russian priorities abroad.

In accordance with the pattern customary in subjects of pre–Soviet Russian history, a few words are appropriate on the system of dates and spelling used throughout the book. All dates of days and months conform to the Gregorian calendar, in use in all major European countries save Russia, where the Julian chronology was in use until January 1918. In the nineteenth century the Julian calendar was twelve days behind the Gregorian, in the twentieth thirteen days behind. Where necessary to avoid confusion—footnote citation of Russian newspapers for example—both styles are quoted. Russian personal names are transliterated approximately according to the Library of Congress system. For the sake of consistency this form has been followed even when certain surnames, such as Kerenskii, Izvol'skii and so on, are more familiar as Kerensky, Isvolsky etc. Unless otherwise indicated all Russian newspapers cited were published in Petrograd. Where the year is omitted from dates in the footnotes, it is 1917.

Finally, I should like to record my appreciation to those who gave assistance during my work on this book: to Ivo Lederer of Stanford University, to the Canada Council and McMaster University for financial aid and to Alan Cassels of McMaster University.

ABBREVIATIONS

The following abbreviations are used throughout the book in footnote citations (full publication details are in the Bibliography):

Adamov: Aufteilung	E. A. Adamov et al., eds., Die Europäischen Mächte und die Türkei während des Weltkrieges: Die Aufteilung der Asiatischen Türkei.
Adamov: Griechenland	E. A. Adamov et al., eds., Die Europäischen Mächte und Griechenland während des Weltkrieges.
Browder/Kerensky	R. P. Browder & A. F. Kerensky, The Russian Provisional Government 1917.
Duma: Ochety	Gosudarstvennaia Duma, Stenograficheskie Ochety, 1908-1916.
FO 371	Foreign Office, London, General Correspondence Files.
GP	Die Grosse Politik der Europäischen Kabinette, 1871-1914.
HAA	Hauptarchiv des Auswärtigen Amtes.
KiP	Evropeiskie Derzhavy i Turtsiia vo vremia Mirovoi Voiny: Konstantinopol' i Prolivy.
MOEI	Mezhdunarodnie Otnosheniia v Epokhu Imperializma: Dokumenty iz Arkhivov Tsarskogo i Vremennogo Pravitel'stv.
Ö-UA	Österreich-Ungarns Aussenpolitik von der bosnischen Krise 1908 bis zum Kriegsausbruch 1914.
PRFRUS	Papers Relating to the Foreign Relations of the United States.
Sonnino Papers "Arrivo" & "Partenza"	Papers of Baron Sidney Sonnino, Telegrammi in Arrivo, Telegrammi in Partenza.
VVP	Vestnik Vremennogo Pravitel'stva.
ZRW	Das Zaristische Russland im Weltkriege.

CHAPTER I
THE TSARIST LEGACY

Involvement in Balkan affairs was exhausting and ultimately fatal to the Russian Empire. From Catherine II's fanciful "Greek Project" on, Tsarist attentions were rarely distracted from that turbulent peninsula and its most elusive mirage: the mastery of Constantinople and the Turkish Straits. Through the five reigns of the century following Kuchuk-Kainardzhi, six wars and a score of diplomatic crises provided unneeded reminders to Europe of Tsardom's interest in imposing its favored solutions to that perennial problem of European diplomacy, known to the nineteenth century as the Eastern Question.

In 1878 the Congress of Berlin confronted the latest upheaval in the peninsula and Russian attempts to regulate it. The European settlement which ensued displayed to Russian diplomats and strategists that the Crimean principle still held good twenty-two years later: no unilateral resolution by Russia of Balkan issues would be tolerated by three of her fellow Great Powers. The lesson was clear and, by the Imperial Government at least, accepted for the next three decades as an unpalatable fact of international politics. But in 1878 public opinion in Moscow and St Petersburg thought otherwise. Never before had journalistic views been so fervently expressed on so delicate a matter of foreign policy concern; never again would they be so successful in stampeding the Russian Government into strong and diplomatically disastrous action in South-East Europe. However, once the euphoria of San Stefano wore off, Tsarist authorities were able to terminate Katkov's effusions on behalf of "our suffering Slav brothers" with no significant repercussions.[1] Russian foreign policy would continue to be decided with as little reference as possible (and preferably none at all) to the vagaries of opinion in the newspaper reading public of the two capitals. There was no desire or intention in St Petersburg seriously to challenge the diplomatic decisions on Balkan matters reached in the German capital. Domestic political turmoil and the pressing need to effect reforms in the army militated against adventures likely to renew Austro-Hungarian hostility and bring a British fleet to the Sea of Marmora. For the present Russia's watchwords in foreign affairs were tranquillity and co-operation with those Powers ideologically and geographically closest to her. The Three Emperors' League of 1881 formally consecrated this new relationship. Each empire agreed to refrain from unilateral infringements of the Balkan status quo.

Monarchical solidarity collapsed before repeated challenges in South-East Europe. Every decade from the close of the Berlin Congress to the outbreak of the World War had its Balkan crisis and resultant Great Power tensions. In 1885 the union of Bulgaria and Eastern Rumelia provoked an Austro-Russian confrontation that revealed only too clearly the fragility of their diplomatic truce; more to the point, it demonstrated in a way that would become ominously familiar how rival Balkan nationalisms could draw in the larger Powers in the region. In Bulgaria the lure of the San Stefano frontiers was a constant incitement to adventure; in Belgrade bitterness over the events of 1885 sparked a short, disastrous war with Bulgaria from which Serbia was only saved by Austrian intervention. Nine years later, Armenia, Macedonia and Crete rose in revolt against Ottoman misrule; shortly thereafter Greece and Turkey were at war. These events confronted the Powers with a new and unwelcome fact of Balkan life—the smaller countries of the peninsula could no longer be regarded as the submissive instruments of Great Power diplomacy and dictation. Only the strictest unity of interest could enable Russia and Austria-Hungary to maintain control of events; it was a price each proved willing for the moment to pay. In the midst of the Greek-Turkish imbroglio, the happily surprised British ambassador in Constantinople noted Austrian "docility" toward Russia's lead, no doubt due to their "common fear of European complications, and [their] common determination not to allow the war to spread to the Balkan states."[2] It was an accurate judgment, endorsed by the formal agreement of the two Powers in May 1897 to "freeze" the situation in the Balkans on the basis of the territorial status quo. There was no talk on the Russian side of "historic tasks in the Near East": the Straits should remain closed to foreign warships, as provided in the 1871 Treaty of London, while in South-East Europe the two empires affirmed their intention of pursuing a policy of perfect harmony in defending "the maintenance, the consolidation and the pacific development of all Balkan states."[3] It seemed a hopeful augury for the new century.

The Muraviev-Goluchowski agreement was unquestionably a beneficial step in preserving peace among the Great Powers in Balkan affairs at a time when Russian attentions were shifting to the Far East. It was all the same too much to hope that the two parties might abandon ambitions of improving their relative positions in the several Balkan capitals. In the first half of the decade the advantage on the whole lay with Russia. In 1902 Prince Ferdinand of Bulgaria signed a military pact with the Tsarist government that was specifically aimed at the Danube Monarchy and its Rumanian ally. The following year in Belgrade the incumbent Obrenovic dynasty was replaced in an orgy of bloodshed by the Karadjordjevic King Peter and a Radical Party government under Prime Minister Nikola Pašić. Both men looked to Russia for support in the face of growing Hapsburg intransigence toward their country. The Monarchy's relations with Rumania, its nominal ally, were as bad thanks to Magyar repression of the Rumanian population in Transylvania.[4]

Throughout 1905 the Far Eastern debacle and domestic revolution monopolized all Russian energies. But by the following summer the Tsarist authorities were ready to return to traditional diplomatic concerns, spurred on by the painful memories of several recent humiliations. One of these, in Europe, had been the continued refusal of the British Foreign Office to countenance the passage of Russia's Black Sea fleet through the Straits, a refusal despite the ten-year-old conclusion of British imperial strategists that to exclude Russia from Constantinople was beyond British power or interests.[5] With this particular lesson firmly in mind, the Foreign Ministry on September 7, 1906, submitted a report to the Emperor on the policy tasks of the immediate future. Although the document was unsigned its authorship could scarcely be in any doubt. It bore the sure imprint of the Ministry's new chief, Alexander P. Izvol'skii, whose appointment the preceding May had signalled Russia's reversion to customary diplomatic priorities. The most urgent problem, according to the report, was to end Russian immobility in the Straits region. Such a position was militarily inhibiting, as the war with Japan had shown; more to the point it prevented a "vigorous" Russian policy among the Balkan states.[6] Izvol'skii's submission fixed as the nation's two major diplomatic goals the winning of greater influence among the small nations of South-East Europe and a stronger Russian position at the Golden Horn. Both targets were implicitly seen as complementary, even though events had shown in the past and would show again in the future that this was far from the invariable case. Izvol'skii was not disturbed by such considerations; in any event it was evident which interest was uppermost to him in 1906. If the Straits could be attained only through some sacrifice of Balkan Slavs Izvol'skii would pay that price. There remained the need to square Russia's traditional rivals in all matters affecting Turkey and the Balkan peninsula: Great Britain and Austria-Hungary.

Conversations with London were initiated in March 1907 and continued until the end of April. They settled nothing definite as far as the Straits were concerned, though Sir Edward Grey's convoluted hints of a possible British softening of position evoked an excited response in St Petersburg.[7] Austria-Hungary was a different matter. Under its veneer of co-operation the basic rivalry of the two Powers remained unchanged. In the winter of 1907-08 a severe crisis blew up over conflicting plans for Balkan railroad construction. A head-on collision was only narrowly averted and Austrian Foreign Minister von Aerenthal felt the moment appropriate for a thorough airing of issues relating to South-East Europe. An invitation to Izvol'skii in this sense was accepted with alacrity. The Russian made plain before his arrival that he hoped for a satisfactory settlement of Russia's Straits ambitions and was prepared in return to prove accommodating towards Vienna's wishes in the matter of Bosnia-Herzogovina.[8]

The two men met at Aerenthal's Moravian castle of Buchlau in September 1908. Since the invitation in May the Balkan scene had been transformed by the sudden advent to power in July of the Young Turk regime in Constantinople, bent on effecting serious reforms throughout the Ottoman empire. A revitalised Turkey was equally unwelcome to both Great Powers; its prospect galvanized the Austro-Hungarian government to demand the annexation of Bosnia-Herzogovina before Constantinople's new masters could assert their titular ownership.[9] Incorporation of the two provinces into the Dual Monarchy would bring the added advantage of dealing a heavy, perhaps mortal blow to Serbian aims of westward expansion. Evidently Izvol'skii acquiesced; at Buchlau the two Foreign Ministers apparently agreed that Russia would recognize Austrian annexation of Bosnia-Herzogovina, while Vienna would pose no objection to Russia's wish for passage of her war vessels through the Straits. Whether each was dependent on the other and both on the consent of the remaining Great Powers was afterwards the subject of some fierce polemics and the whole affair could well serve as a useful warning to posterity on the dangers of secret summit diplomacy. Izvol'skii at any rate seems to have anticipated no cause for alarm and embarked upon a leisurely tour of Western capitals. On October 6, with his recent guest still in Paris, Aerenthal announced the fact of annexation. One day earlier, after a strong hint from the Ballplatz, Ferdinand of Bulgaria proclaimed the final independence of his country from Turkey and his own assumption of the title of king.[10]

The annexation announcement set off a major Balkan upheaval during which the never stable Austro-Russian accord was irretrievably shattered. In Paris and London Izvol'skii found there was no support for his designs on the Straits; in Belgrade public outrage reached the point where war seemed possible between Serbia and the Monarchy. In Russia abuse was rampant against the luckless Foreign Minister. The Duma, impotent though it was in most respects, became and remained the natural forum of criticism across the political spectrum of Tsarist Russia. There Imperial foreign policy was periodically subject to hostile examination even though the provisions of Witte's Fundamental Laws had reserved foreign affairs to the government's exclusive competence. Paradoxically, Izvol'skii himself was initially responsible for this intrusion by appearing to take the Chamber into his confidence on matters of Balkan policy. In a speech of April 17, 1908, the Foreign Minister had spoken of Russia's obligations to her Slav co-religionists and of the desirability of maintaining co-operation with Austria-Hungary in Balkan affairs.[11] This was his only hint of current diplomatic preoccupations; not a word was said of his simultaneous schemes for the Dardanelles. These in any case had to be hastily dropped once the bombshell news of the annexation struck St Petersburg; all things considered Izvol'skii could derive little comfort from Russia's consequent diplomatic position abroad or his own political isolation at home.

One lesson above all others emerged from the Bosnian fiasco. Co-operation with the Central Empires in Balkan affairs was no longer practicable, possible or popular in the upper reaches of the Tsarist government. This did not mean that Imperial ministers and diplomats therefore abandoned hopes of advancing Russian interests in the peninsula. The feeling was rather that these might best be served by harnessing Balkan nationalisms against future incursions by the victor of the 1908 crisis. Izvol'skii set the tone, at the same time trying to pacify critics of his ministry's diplomatic ineffectiveness. On December 25, 1908, he appeared once again before the Duma and began his remarks by acknowledging that organizational deficiencies were weakening Russia's diplomatic performance abroad. In the best Parliamentary tradition, the minister promised a more comprehensive statement at a later date on reform proposals. With that safely over, Izvol'skii launched into an elaborate exculpation of his recent behavior, concluding with the counsel he had hitherto preferred not to try: that Russia's future goal in South-East Europe should be the creation of a league of Balkan states and Turkey which would collectively defend the national and economic sovereignty of its constituent members.[12] The speech, with its scarcely veiled anti-Hapsburg motif, went down well with the greater part of his audience. Two future stalwarts of the Provisional Government, the Octobrist chief Alexander Guchkov and his Cadet opposite number Paul Miliukov, accepted the general tenor of Izvol'skii's proposals.[13] Extreme political groupings of right and left were hostile but could be ignored.

For the next three and a half years Russia's Balkan diplomacy pursued the image conjured up by Izvol'skii's Christmas speech. As with him, it never forgot the basic concern with "the keys to Russia's house." Izvol'skii himself, to the end of his ministerial career, put this preoccupation ahead of other aims in the area, whatever indications to the contrary he might lavish on the Duma. His major achievement in international affairs, the Racconigi agreement of October 1909 with Italy, was an echo of the discredited Buchlau tactic of co-operation with a second Great Power against Turkey. It committed Russia to diplomatic support of Italian claims in Libya in exchange for Rome's endorsement of Russian interests at the Straits. Izvol'skii's readiness to accept Turkey's spoliation did not seem consistent with his wish to attract the Porte to a Russian sponsored Balkan alignment in Europe. This ambiguity was most evident in the maneuverings between 1909 and 1912 of Russian diplomats in the field, two in particular, Nicholas Charykov, the ambassador in Constantinople, and Nicholas Hartwig, the minister in Belgrade. Both in theory worked under the direction and coordination of the St Petersburg Foreign Ministry; in fact each was largely free to follow aims that might be quite at variance with those being pursued by the other. Uncertainties abroad were matched at home by insecurity among the Ministry's senior personnel. Izvol'skii himself lasted until September 1910 when he moved to the Paris embassy but his credibility as minister vanished in the aftermath of Russia's "diplomatic Tsushima" of 1909. Two months after the German ultimatum his brother-in-law Sergei D. Sazonov was named Izvol'skii's assistant with acknowledged right of succession to his portfolio. Sazonov in turn was in poor health through most of 1911, a key year of Balkan changes, when the effective leadership of Russian diplomacy fell upon his deputy A. A. Neratov. A diplomatic observer's subsequent condemnation of that "windbag [with] a hardly mediocre mental capacity" and utter lack "of the attributes of a great statesman"[14] might with equal justice have been directed against most senior bureaucrats of late Tsarist Russia, beginning with Nicholas II. In any case the political tribulations of two exceptions to this verdict, Witte and Stolypin, were warning enough to Russian politicians who might think to act more vigorously or with greater initiative than desired by their Imperial master.

In the Turkish capital Charykov's task was the diplomatic equivalent of squaring the circle. He was to win the Ottoman government to the case of Balkan federation and simultaneously seek to strengthen Russia's position at the Straits by securing Turkish consent to the passage of Russia's Black Sea fleet through the Bosporus and the Dardanelles.[15] Charykov's weapons were diplomatic only; they were insufficient. In consequence the ambassador soon found himself and his policy expendable. His instructions prior to his departure from St Petersburg had consisted solely in Izvol'skii's assurance that "you know best."[16] This left Charykov free to attempt his goals as if they were his own private obsession; when they failed to surmount Anglo-French opposition Charykov could be retired without unduly compromising his country's prestige in South-East Europe. Charykov accepted his lot philosophically. His role, as he himself recognized, was limited essentially to glimpses of a high policy directed to ends that were unrealistic in the circumstances of the time.[17] His recall in March 1912 was a signal to Turkish leaders, if they needed one, that Tsarist Russia had abandoned her fanciful schemes of co-operation in favor of the tried and true alternative of an overtly anti-Turkish policy. This all along coincided with Hartwig's views from Belgrade. Rather than seek to preserve Turkey, Russian diplomacy should recognize the obvious by presiding over the partition of her European provinces among the Slavs of the Balkans. On that occasion Russia could fulfil her own secular destiny by placing her foot firmly on the Bosporus at the entry to Russia's sea.[18] These ideas owed nothing to St Petersburg's formal direction and Sazonov for one was to be loud in his complaints at Hartwig's independent intrigues in the Serbian capital.[19] Was he there to promote Russia's interests or Serbia's? Hartwig's assumption was quite evident that the two dovetailed when it came to Austria-Hungary. Hatred of that power lay at the basis of his efforts in Belgrade until his sudden death in July 1914 "after drinking a cup of black coffee at the residence of the Austro-Hungarian minister" according to a Russian colleague who shared his bias.[20] Hartwig was prepared to harness the two larger Slavic kingdoms of the peninsula against Turkey if ultimately their animus might be mobilized against Austria-Hungary. An alliance between Serbia and Bulgaria, with or without Turkey, was thus the keystone of Russian efforts on behalf of Balkan federation in the years immediately following Aerenthal's Bosnian triumph. Unfortunately between the two states lay the most volatile of all Balkan issues, one which Russia herself could not determine, but which would influence the course of her involvement in Balkan affairs until the October Revolution. The problem was Macedonia.

Two questions lay at the center of the dispute: what was the nationality of the Macedonian population and, following from this, which of Macedonia's neighbors should rule it once the Turks were driven out? There was much at stake. The term "Macedonia" covered the three Turkish provinces to the north and west of—and including—the port of Salonika. Through this extremely fertile region ran the chief traffic and commercial arteries from Central Europe to Constantinople and the Aegean. It was evident that the possession of Macedonia would be a valuable addition to any of the three Balkan states who most energetically sought it: Bulgaria, Serbia and Greece. By 1909 the rivalry among the three claimants had produced such a flood of emotion and comment that it seemed impossible to reach any accepted solution for the region's future. While it was easy enough to admit that the principle of nationality should be conclusive, there was no agreement whatever among the three on just how this principle should be applied in Macedonia's ethnic confusions.

Basically there were four criteria for determining nationality: historical traditions, customs, religion and language. By the end of the nineteenth century the third and fourth of these had become the most potent. From the religious viewpoint Greece had the senior claim. Until 1870 the Orthodox Patriarch of Constantinople exercised jurisdiction over the entire region. In that year, however, the Porte responded to rising nationalist clamor and Russian diplomatic pressure by permitting the institution of an autonomous Bulgarian exarchate church.[21] Originally this applied to Bulgaria proper, that is the area between the Danube and the Balkan mountains, but article X of the Sultan's decree provided for the extension of the exarchate if two-thirds of neighboring populations voted to accept it. By 1912 seven such bishoprics had been created in Macedonia. With the church came church schools, and their natural preference for instruction in Bulgarian reinforced that country's growing cultural predominance in Macedonia by the turn of the century.[22] Non-Balkan cartographers of European Turkey generally agreed on the numerical superiority of Bulgarians throughout the area, basing their conclusions on the language factor.[23] Serbian and Greek map drawers counterattacked strongly, all purporting to show their nations' exclusive rights over the Sultan's last remaining Slav provinces. They failed to change cartographic opinion outside the peninsula, but that was the least damaging aspect of the problem. More dangerous was the apparent ease with which national passions on the Macedonian issue could poison attempts to compose differences among the three rivals.

As it had in Russia, the Bosnian affair of 1908-09 led to some sharp rethinking in Balkan capitals. Austro-Serbian enmity compelled the smaller state to repair relations with other neighbors, Bulgaria in particular, for whom also the moment seemed propitious to rapprochement. The Serbian humiliation in Bosnia left Sofia unmoved, but the coincidental Young Turk coup in Constantinople caused alarm that a reinvigorated Turkey might reimpose control over her restive Macedonian subjects. Under these circumstances the two governments began the first of several tortuous discussions, which would ultimately lead to the formation of the Balkan League. The Macedonian issue, which Aerenthal had confidently expected would forever bar the possibility of such an alliance, did not turn out to be an insurmountable obstacle.[24]

It took two years and outside events to bring the parties to a bargaining position. The Italian invasion of Libya in September 1911 was the final incentive to the reluctant suitors to act before they lost a last splendid opportunity to profit from Turkish misfortunes. Hartwig and his colleague in Sofia, Anatolii Nekliudov, did everything they could from behind the scenes to urge the negotiations to a successful conclusion. Their government in St Petersburg acquiesced in the impending alliance, preferring to stress its defensive implications against Austria-Hungary, rather than its offensive certainties against the Ottoman Empire. The former feature was, to Sazonov, the justification of the entire course of Russia's diplomacy in South-East Europe under his administration: "500,000 bayonets to guard the Balkans—but this would bar the road forever to German penetration, Austrian invasion."[25] This continued to be Sazonov's attitude until the outbreak of the First Balkan War. Following the signature of the Serb-Bulgarian alliance on March 13, 1912, he requested his brother-in-law to tell President Poincaré of the outcome of negotiations and that in the alliance Russia had "fashioned a weapon to oppose the extension of influence of a larger Power in the Balkans."[26] Six months later he was still assuring Paris that "if it was a question of starting things, it is Russia which ought to determine the moment and that moment is not yet come."[27] At least part of Russia's "historic task" seemed solved.

Sazonov's several pronouncements on the Balkan situation that summer reflected his unrealistic assessment of the crisis now at hand. Tsarist politicians, headed by himself, still thought of the Balkan Slavs, when they thought of them at all, as "the younger brothers," and put an excessively low value on the several leaders of Balkan governments. They in turn kept St Petersburg largely in the dark on the precise state of the negotiations between them.[28] Public protestations of loyalty to Mother Russia were all very well but privately they had no intention of waiting for a signal that might never be given. The Balkan League would choose its own moment for action; one month after Sazonov's stout words on Russia's control of events it did so. In October 1912 the League's members fell upon the Ottoman territories in Europe and were everywhere victorious. Then Macedonia intruded once more. Barred by Austro-Hungarian intervention from the Adriatic, Serbia and Greece refused to quit the portions of Macedonia assigned to Bulgaria, citing by way of justification that power's unexpectedly large gains in Thrace. Sazonov peremptorily ordered the parties to submit to Russian mediation, as provided in the Serb-Bulgarian alliance. Instead the enraged Bulgarians hurled themselves upon their recent allies. They, with support from defeated Turkey and acquisitive Rumania, crushed their new foe and triumphantly divided Macedonia between them.[29]

The treaty of Bucharest ending the Second Balkan War put the seal on a major setback to Russia's Balkan diplomacy. Not only had the alliance ignored Russian wishes at the test, it had even acted in defiance of them. It had demonstrated to Europe, most especially to the Tsar's French ally, that Russia, far from controlling the situation throughout, was as much a prisoner of events as any. The outbreak of the First Balkan War caught the Tsarist government by surprise; its course was followed in official St Petersburg with mounting apprehension. The progress of Bulgarian troops toward Constantinople raised the unendurable prospect that the small Balkan kingdom, which owed its existence to Russian benevolence, might in a few weeks pull off a triumph that for two centuries had been beyond the reach of Russian arms and Russian diplomacy. Even more obnoxious to Sazonov was the thought that his particular Balkan bête-noire, Tsar Ferdinand, might soon justly don the theatrical costume of a Byzantine emperor that he was rumored to have purchased against the day of his entry into the old capital of Greek Orthodoxy; six white horses and the royal coach were also to be at hand for the great parade.[30] However, typhus and exhaustion proved to be more inhibiting to Bulgarian progress than Russian alarm; the Allied armies failed to storm the Chataldja lines defending the capital and Europe was consequently spared the quixotic spectacle of a Russian intervention to save Constantinople from a Slav army. The Second Balkan War did nothing to retrieve the situation for Russia. Bulgaria burned with resentment at alleged Russian favoring of her neighbors and was dangerously unreconciled to the loss of Macedonia.[31] Yet St Petersburg was not unduly disturbed. Sazonov reported to Nicholas that Bulgarian greed had landed that nation in its current predicament and Russia's policy should now be one of closer cultivation of Serbia and Rumania.[32] Ostentatious gestures were made to both states, culminating in the spring and summer of 1914 with the cordial reception in St Petersburg of a Serbian delegation, headed by Prime Minister Pašić and an exchange of visits between the Russian and Rumanian Courts. Both Balkan governments endeavored to cement this promising state of things by requesting a grand duchess in marriage for their respective royal heirs.[33]

On the eve of the Great War Russia's position in South-East Europe was not reassuring, royal jamborees to the contrary, and was certainly more defensive than the reverse. The Central Powers, especially Germany, were thrusting hard; the Balkan states had shown collectively their willingness when it suited them to flout outside wishes in pursuit of their various objectives. Tsarist diplomatic ineffectiveness must unquestionably bear a share of the responsibility for this: St Petersburg's "rather nebulous purposes in the Balkans" during the previous half-decade had inhibited any real consistency in the formulation and execution of Russian foreign policy tasks.[34] Conservative opinion in the capital dreaded the European outcome of so uncertain a program but outside views, whether pro or con, had no appreciable effect in molding official attitudes to concerns in South-East Europe or anywhere else. This did not, of course, mean that no opinions were expressed. The well known Durnovo Memorandum of February 1914 spoke in the most apocalyptic terms of the direction taken in past years by Russian diplomacy and of its particularly bad effect in the Balkans; the nationalist press echoed Durnovo's judgment with unbridled vituperation. Sazonov duly recorded his indignation over the epithets hurled at his head by the ultra-reactionary *Grazhdanin*, the Emperor's favorite paper, thundering against the minister's treason to the Slav cause.[35] Similar if less frenzied sentiments over Russia's "bloodless and shameful defeats in the Balkans" were expressed by Alexander Guchkov, the Octobrist chief, who saw South-East Europe as the prime arena for the expression of Russian Imperial power abroad and a strong Russian army as the means to make such expression most effective.[36] Simultaneously, Sazonov heard knowledgeable voices from within his own ministry warning against undue sympathy for Balkan Slavs or for "the keys to Russia's house."[37] None of this varied counsel mattered much. Sazonov could rightly take comfort in the fact that Russian foreign policy initiatives, at least from the St Petersburg end, remained in 1914 in the proper hands: his and the Emperor's. Others, including Cabinet colleagues, had no business to interfere or even be informed if the two principals wished to exclude them. They usually did.

When the news from Sarajevo arrived in St Petersburg the twin Tsarist objectives of strength in the Balkans generally and at the Straits in particular were still far from realization. German influence reigned supreme at the Golden Horn; to the north only Serbia could be counted on as reliably in the Russian camp and even that from no doing of Russia's. Determination to prevent that final defection largely governed the Russian response throughout the July crisis. The humiliation of 1908 had been grave; on that occasion an enfeebled Russia had assuaged Serbian outrage with counsels of moderation, military preparation and waiting for an eventual settling of accounts.[38] A repetition of the same tactics five years later could not be contemplated. If the Danube Monarchy and its German ally succeeded in destroying Russia's last Balkan bastion, the Tsarist regime would lose its last foothold in South-East Europe. Worse, it would forfeit the respect of Russia's Great Power fellows and the right to be included in their number. Her survival as an equal of the Central Powers depended on the outcome of the Austro-Serb confrontation: that and not Balkan dominance, still less the desire for Constantinople, was the factor uppermost in the minds of the two irresolute men whose decisions would count the most. Nicholas II promised the

Serbian Prince Regent Alexander that Russia could in no case remain indifferent to Serbia's fate.[39] With greater urgency his Foreign Minister sought from mid-July on to impress upon Vienna Russia's interest in seeing that Serbia's independence and territorial integrity were not fatally compromised by Austrian demands. His famous cry on hearing the terms of the ultimatum—"c'est la guerre européenne!"—conceded the likely result of Russian tenacity but emphasized anyway the determination to persist in it. Articulate opinion in St Petersburg, while not unanimous, was not unsympathetic. Bernard Pares, lecturer at Liverpool University and a British intimate of the Russian liberal circles from which would come several members of the Provisional Government, later remarked that ever since the Bosnian affair Russian intellectuals saw European war as certain and likely to arise from a renewed German challenge in the Balkans.[40] This prospect was more palatable for Pares' friends than for conservatives, to whom the idea of war between Europe's three dynastic empires represented the very summit of national folly. Though at last their worst fears were to be surpassed, at the crucial moment their warnings in Durnovo's Memorandum and elsewhere went unheeded. Sazonov himself, no liberal, made it clear to the Ballplatz that there must be no reliance on traditional sentiment: the days of monarchical solidarity had vanished beyond recall in the aftermath of Buchlau.[41] When war came it was accepted by official Petersburg, embodied in Sazonov and the Tsar, with a fatalistic resignation and a foreboding of trials to come.[42]

August 1914–March 1917

For the first three months of the war Great Power prestige and the existence of Serbia had to suffice as Russia's major war aims since Turkish neutrality put more tangible goals out of reach. As far as Sazonov was concerned there they could stay; if the Young Turks would keep the Ottoman Empire out of the war he was ready to join his Entente colleagues in a guarantee of its territorial integrity.[43] The formal offer in this sense was made on August 18, but even then it had the appearance of a ritualistic gesture without any hope of a positive response. Within little more than a week both Sazonov and Grey had accepted that their fair words were insufficient to overcome the political and strategic facts of life in Constantinople. If any Russian doubts on the matter did persist the Turkish closure of the Straits on October 8 ended them. All that remained to be determined was the actual moment, one of Turkish choosing; the salvos on October 29 and 30 from the *Goeben* and the *Breslau* answered that question too and permitted the Tsarist government to revert to more substantial themes in its war aims policy. The Imperial manifesto of November 2 announcing war with Turkey spoke in terms reminiscent of the late Hartwig: Russia would now finally eliminate the eternal oppressor of Slavic peoples and could now "open a path towards the settlement of the historic tasks bequeathed to her by forbears on the shores of the Black Sea."[44] As if to reinforce the certainty of the eventual settlement Russia's historic adversary in Ottoman affairs ranged herself behind Nicholas' words. On November 9 Sir Edward Grey told the Russian ambassador Count A. K. Benckendorff that the fate of the great city on the Bosporus could not be settled otherwise than in accordance with Russian wishes. Four days later George V repeated to Benckendorff that "Constantinople must be yours." A much gratified Nicholas minuted his satisfaction at his cousin's "significant" remark.[45]

The King of England was willing to see the Ottoman capital in Russian hands but it took a brief and not very severe struggle with its own reservations before the Tsarist government was ready to accept the proferred prize. A committee of military, naval and foreign ministry experts sitting at Sazonov's direction reported exhaustively on the options before the government on the Constantinople question, but the participants were far from being of one voice on the subject.[46] Sazonov wrote of his own initial hesitations: realism rather than sentiment should decide the question of what Russia should seek from a vanquished Turkey. Realism suggested to many that Russian acquisition of Constantinople might bring in its train all sorts of unwelcome ethnic, political and diplomatic problems to complicate the nation's future. The vision of the Orthodox cross on St Sophia should not be allowed to interfere with these more practical considerations. Sentiment carried the day in spite of these brave words, though cloaked in the language of wartime imperatives. Nothing could guarantee more effectively Russia's security at the exit to the Black Sea than Tsargrad's possession; public opinion demanded it, as did strategic necessity dictated by the General Staff: "and one should not quarrel over strategy with the General Staff."[47]

The invocation of public opinion marked Sazonov's revival of the tactic used by Izvol'skii in December 1908 in prompting Duma members to express their views on a vital area of Russian foreign policy. Reaction from that unrepresentative body was much more enthusiastic in February 1915 than seven years before; all but the far left eagerly climbed aboard the Constantinople bandwagon. In a foretaste of the confrontation two years later over the same issue, the Georgian Menshevik N. S. Chkheidze denounced all predatory annexationist ambitions. He was joined by the Trudovik Alexander Kerenskii who went on to rhapsodize on the imminent birth of Russian liberty without coming to any easily discernible point. The Cadet leader Paul Miliukov rather condescendingly congratulated Sazonov and put the whole business on a "moral" basis.[48] This near unanimity came, as the minister had intended, at a time when precise bargaining was about to begin between a now resolved Russia and her Western partners. Two weeks after the Duma's opening session Sazonov cabled Izvol'skii and Benckendorff that Russia was laying formal claim to Constantinople and a "minimum" of its hinterland, plus a slice of the Asiatic side of the Straits. He promised to take into consideration the economic interests of Bulgaria and Rumania, both at the time eagerly courted neutrals, as well as the interests of international commerce. The islands of the Sea of Marmora, as well as Imbros and Tenedos, which guarded the southern approaches to the Dardanelles, should also pass to Russia.[49]

This program considerably exceeded Sazonov's earlier suggestions and provoked in consequence some Anglo-French hesitations. These in turn caused some concern in newly rebaptised Petrograd, already keenly alert to the possibility that the Western allies through their assault on the Dardanelles might get to Constantinople first. Sazonov swung into action. On March 4 he formally requested Russia's two Great Power allies to accede to his earlier approaches; and as a sweetener to the pill, he included the open bribe that the two countries could rest assured that Russia would be sympathetic to plans they might have in relation to other parts of the Ottoman empire or elsewhere.[50]

This brought the British into line. On the 12th the Petrograd embassy took pleasure in informing His Excellency that in the event of victory and subject to British and French wishes being met in Turkey and elsewhere, His Majesty's Government was prepared to accept the Russian position. An accompanying memorandum stressed the magnitude of Great Britain's concession, the reversal of a century-long tradition and the unmistakable proof thus afforded of British goodwill toward Imperial Russia. After three weeks of fencing on precise wording, the French government followed suit on April 10.[51]

Tsarist Russia had thus won the great diplomatic triumph which had eluded her statesmen for so long. In the next two years she and her Great Power partners made further arrangements in the same co-operative spirit in dividing the anticipated spoils of German-Turkish defeat. In March 1916 they partitioned (on paper) the Asiatic provinces of the Ottoman empire, with Russia promised wide new accessions on the Black Sea.[52] Finally, on the eve of the March Revolution, the French and Russian governments agreed that Russia would admit France's full freedom to settle her Eastern frontier in exchange for a parallel Russian privilege in respect of her Western border.[53] A Germany reduced in the West was more important to Paris than a Poland revived in the East. At any rate, by the spring of 1917, diplomacy had done all it could to resolve the "historic tasks" mentioned by Nicholas II on November 2, 1914; the rest was up to Russian arms.

With the conditional promise of Constantinople and the Straits, Petrograd was free to turn its attention to Russia's second major wartime concern in South-East Europe: strengthening her influence among the several Balkan states. Here the record was gloomy indeed. A bare six months after the Constantinople accords, Izvol'skii was reporting on a profound French irritation with Russia. She alone was being blamed for the relentless flow of bad news from the East: Rumania's stubborn neutrality, Bulgaria's adherence to the Central Powers, the ensuing ruin of gallant Serbia and the general failure of the Entente to make significant military or diplomatic headway in the Balkans. French opinion was asking, Izvol'skii went on, why France should continue to bolster Entente efforts in the peninsula when Russia, the main prospective beneficiary there, would not co-operate with her four allies.[54] The ambassador was more than once unduly sensitive to dangers threatening the Franco-Russian alliance, but it could not be denied in September 1915 that his country's prestige with her allies had slumped disastrously since the beginning of hostilities. Balkan developments were mostly responsible. Paris and London both considered that Russia was dragging her feet on the issue of alliances with the Balkan neutrals, a charge which did less than justice to Tsarist diplomacy. Russia's military retreat, rather than her bureaucratic obtuseness, accounted for Rumania's hesitations, domestic division for those of Greece. In Bulgaria's case the lure of Macedonia and memories of the Second Balkan War sufficed to range her on the side of Serbia's enemies.[55]

Though well meant, Izvol'skii's warnings failed utterly to induce a more favorable attitude from his civilian superiors toward the affairs of South-East Europe. Consciousness of military and diplomatic feebleness stimulated an intense resentment inside reactionary Petrograd at the foreign parties deemed chiefly responsible: the Balkan states themselves and the Western allies, conniving to exclude Russia from her rightful role in the peninsula. Empress Alexandra Feodorovna repeatedly expressed her exasperation on the subject in letters to her husband absent at the front: "idiotic Rumania," "rotten Bulgaria," "oh confound those Balkan countries," "beastly false Greeks." As Serbia's martyrdom began she reminded Nicholas that "Our Friend was always against this war, saying the Balkans were not worth the world to fight about . . . ." Nothing in her opinion had happened to reverse Rasputin's judgment; the future only promised a continuation of troubles:

"I foresee terrible complications when the war is over and the question of the

> Balkan territories will have to be settled, then I dread England's selfish policies coming into contact with ours—only to well prepare all beforehand, not to have nasty surprises."[56]

One last nasty surprise from the Balkans came nevertheless the following summer when a richly bribed Rumania finally took the plunge against the Central Powers, only to collapse in a matter of weeks before their vigorous counterthrust. By the time the Empress herself came to pass from the political stage Russia's enemies were in military control of every Balkan capital save Athens.

Imperial fears found an echo inside less exalted levels of political Russia. On December 2, 1916, when Prime Minister Trepov made public the Entente arrangements for Turkey's future, his disclosures did nothing to stimulate enthusiasm for the war effort, but provoked a mixture of indifference and indignation that the country should assume these vast new burdens on top of her many other more urgent problems.[57] The Left maintained its implacable hostility; at the center Miliukov's was now the most insistent voice in favor of war to victory for the Straits and Tsargrad. The Right, which in February 1915 had acquiesced in Tsardom's Turkish goals, had come in the meantime to dislike more than anything else the alliances with the Western democracies that alone could bring Constantinople within reach. Better an honorable peace without the city than the triumph of that Jewish pack in the Duma and its foreign sponsor, British diplomacy.[58] The High Command had long abandoned hope of winning the Straits by direct Russian assault and as early as October 1915, less than a year since Sazonov had "lost" his argument with the General Staff, military leaders were urging the government to make peace with Turkey on the basis of the status quo. That this meant the abandonment of Constantinople was perhaps unfortunate but to Chief of Staff Alexeev unavoidable: "What can be done? One must come to terms with necessity."[59] This was now beyond the regime's power. It could shuffle personnel, Stürmer for Sazonov and Pokrovsky for Stürmer; it had nothing new to offer in terms of policy. Nor did it wish to: to the bitter end the Imperial government insisted that the war must go on because Russia's major prizes were not yet secure. Few observers were deceived. In February 1917 British and French delegates to the Inter-Allied Conference in Petrograd left Russia deeply pessimistic about her immediate military and political prospects. The two resident ambassadors Sir George Buchanan and Maurice Paléologue warned their respective cabinets that an explosion was imminent, though Sir George hoped the regime might somehow muddle through.[60] This sanctified British tradition had, unfortunately, no roots in Petrograd politics: on March 15 the Tsarist structure crashed to the ground and new men stepped forward to assume the government of Russia.

* * *

When Sergei Sazonov came in exile to write his account of Russia's prewar Balkan policy, he summed up its deficiencies in the observation that "between determination of the goal and its attainment lay a vast gulf."[61] If true in 1914, how much more so by March 1917! The military failures of the intervening three years obviously contributed their share to widening the gap but in essence they confirmed the pattern evident before August 1914. Divisions within the government and between it and its agents abroad, alienation between the regime's proclaimed foreign policy goals and elements of informed public opinion, the inability to distinguish between the desirable and the attainable, the ineptitude of individual ministers all at varying times, singly or collectively, characterized Tsarist policy in Balkan matters in the last decade of the Empire. Now the Tsar and his government were gone; the problems they had confronted or evaded remained for Nicholas' successors. Whether their handling of them would be any more successful or better organized was for time and circumstance to tell. The first man officially to address himself to these questions after March 15 had no doubts of the outcome.

CHAPTER II
PAUL N. MILIUKOV

The Leader of the Opposition

On March 16 black headlines in the morning editions of all Petrograd newspapers proclaimed the personnel of Russia's new government. Of the ten names given only a handful were instantly familiar to the newspaper reading public as belonging to prominent critics of Tsarist mismanagement and folly. One, the second listed, stood out from the rest in this context: the new Minister of Foreign Affairs, Paul N. Miliukov.

In describing later the events of March 1917, P. N. Miliukov attributed his appointment to his "former activity in the State Duma."[1] Political friends and foes were much less restrained in their comments on his selection. To his political colleague and close friend Vladimir Nabokov, Miliukov was "the first person of the Provisional Government in intellectual and political greatness."[2] Nikolai Sukhanov, polemical diarist of the events of 1917 and one of Miliukov's bitterest critics, acknowledged the Foreign Minister to be "de facto head of the first revolutionary government . . . without whom there would have been no bourgeois policy . . . the flower, cream and pride of our bourgeoisie."[3] Another sharp eyed observer, Victor Chernov, leader of the Social Revolutionary Party, was unsurprised at Miliukov's inclusion in the cabinet, stressing his many gifts and total unsuitability for the conditions of March 1917: "a superior scholar . . ., a typical parliamentarian, a splendid mediator, a creator of compromises . . . meant for quiet, normal times . . . not for times when irrational popular passions rage, when the entire situation changes constantly."[4] Lenin too was quick off the mark to acknowledge the new minister's pre-eminence, along with his colleague at the War Ministry, in a cabinet otherwise composed of mediocrities like "the balalaika Kerenskii" in the Justice Ministry.[5] Personally acquainted with many Western statesmen, Miliukov came to his new post confident of foreign goodwill and of his own abilities to deal with all problems of wartime diplomacy. None of these were more complicated nor of greater personal interest than the many issues involving South-East Europe. Four years after the Revolution Miliukov wrote that his study of Balkan questions had made him by 1908 "the only competent specialist among Russian public figures" on the intricacies of the Bosnian affair of that year.[6] A simultaneous Octobrist invitation that he help prepare for the Slav Congress in Prague as one "competent in the Slav question" anticipated his judgment.[7] The foreign affairs portfolio must have seemed to him in March 1917 a natural award to Russia's most qualified authority in matters of longstanding national concern. He had been acquiring his credentials over the previous twenty years.

Miliukov first came into direct contact with the Balkans in 1897 when he accepted the offer of a teaching position in Sofia, a job he deemed preferable to the single alternative of a year in Siberia for his political views. He remained in Sofia for two years until official Russian pressure on the Bulgarian authorities forced his resignation. The brief episode was extremely important in the formation of Miliukov's lifelong interest in the history and politics, not just of Bulgaria, but of the peninsula as a whole. He related in his memoirs how the complication of the Balkan situation and its relation to Europe "forced me attentively to study foreign policy questions: in Bulgaria I passed through preparatory school under very favorable conditions."[8] While in the small kingdom he established friendly relations with several local political and intellectual figures, among them Alexander Malinov, a leader in 1917 of the Russophil element in the National Assembly and future Prime Minister. These friendships caused him to take a deep interest in the country and to sympathize with its people in their struggle against what he termed Russia's "clumsy provocations" in their affairs.[9]

In 1899 Miliukov set out to familiarize himself with the thorny Macedonian problem. During that summer he travelled through most of the region with the intention of clarifying the degree of ethnic unity in Macedonia, the very issue then being so fiercely debated throughout the southern Balkans. He concluded that thanks to her pre-eminent position in the exarchate church Bulgaria had the clearest title in the province. Serbian propaganda against this was not conducive to Balkan tranquillity, nor did he care for the support afforded Serbian publicity efforts by local Russian representatives. He enlarged on these and other themes in articles for the Moscow newspaper *Russkie Vedomosti* and in lectures to the Russian Archeological Institute in Constantinople.[10] By the year's end his exile was over and he was free to return to St Petersburg, no less prepared to harass the government than he had been before his enforced departure from Russia.

In 1904 Miliukov again visited the Balkans, concentrating this time on the Western half of the peninsula. His purpose, again in his own words, was "to seek out what could not be found in books: a national Slav movement" among the South Slav populations of the Dual Monarchy. Travelling through Dalmatia and along the Adriatic coast he was struck by the intense national feeling and mutual ill will among the Serbian, Croat, Slovene and Italian subjects of Francis Joseph. He failed to be impressed by Montenegro, Russia's only friend in the region according to Alexander III, but he did find reason for optimism in Croatia, "the only Slav country where the national and political conflict promised to be resolved in a civilized manner." On the whole, however, he could not feel very hopeful about the prospects for South Slav unity, an issue that would much concern him in years ahead.[11] Following the October Manifesto Miliukov began to concentrate his energies on the consolidation of his political party, the Constitutional Democrats or Cadets. 1905 and the years that immediately followed were years of struggle, not Balkan adventure.[12] As befitted Russia's most ardent Anglophile and liberal, he campaigned for the creation of a responsible ministry on the British pattern, even holding discussions with Tsarist officials on the subject. In his own account of these conversations Miliukov unconsciously gives us a glimpse of the features Victor Chernov was to see in the Foreign Minister. Witte invited him as one who possessed "a certain expertise in the general political situation and in possible solutions of it" to submit his ideas for reform. Miliukov, speaking for himself and not his party, recommended that Witte model his draft, Fundamental Laws, on the Bulgarian constitution, presented to that nation by the Emperor's grandfather, or alternatively on the Belgian, the classic statement of nineteenth century political liberalism.[13] When he revealed this advice in 1921 Miliukov came under heavy fire from a member of his old party, Vasilii Maklakov, for his political naiveté: "how could Miliukov have thought that the Emperor would be convinced by a reference to Belgium or Bulgaria?"[14] It is unlikely that he did think so, but Chernov's "lecturer rather than the apostle of a political creed" was not averse to making the point anyway. There could certainly be no question of his political prominence, alluded to by Witte. In a list submitted to Nicholas II in 1906 of the probable members of a party cabinet, Miliukov's name was advanced for the Foreign Affairs or Interior portfolios.[15] Any higher post, specifically the Premiership, would be inappropriate for Miliukov, Nicholas was told, since he was too domineering a chief for any but his own Cadets.[16] At any rate, by the opening of the Third Duma in 1907 Miliukov had become the recognized spokesman for liberal oppositional Russia and was seen as such by at least one foreign politician of note.[17]

The events of 1908 inevitably jolted Miliukov's attention back to South-East Europe. The July Revolution in Constantinople convinced him he should renew acquaintances in the Ottoman capital, make some new ones and learn more about Turkey. All went as planned and more; the main

Young Turk newspaper saw him as a brother in arms and on the train between Salonika and Constantinople he found his travelling companion to be none other than Talaat Pasha, a rising star of the Young Turk movement, destined to serve as Grand Vizier during Miliukov's own period of office. The tourist remained politely skeptical of Talaat's assurances that all Ottoman subjects were now equal, though in general he welcomed the new Turkish order. His tour concluded with stops in Belgrade, Sarajevo and Zagreb. In the first of these cities he was introduced to young officers whose reproaches left him painfully impressed by Russia's much eroded prestige on the eve of the shattering Bosnian crisis. It was to be Miliukov's last friendly welcome to Serbia.[18]

The fiasco for Russia of October 1908 drew from Miliukov his first full length analysis of the Balkan imbroglio. On December 25 he followed Izvol'skii to the rostrum of the Duma and as "the representative of the opposition"—a parliamentary role he maintained for the next nine years—he elaborated for several hours on the errors of recent Russian foreign policy. It was a melancholy tale he had to tell of mistaken priorities and misdirected effort. As a result of ministerial ineptitude Austria-Hungary had succeeded in extending her influence over areas of vital interest to Russia: "from that moment on began the hateful, fratricidal Serbian policy against the Bulgarians in Macedonia." He endorsed Izvol'skii's proposal to further an alignment of the Balkan kingdoms and Turkey. National diplomacy should co-ordinate all efforts to that goal, put an end to fumbling pretensions based on inadequate resources and preserve Balkan tranquillity in the face of Austro-Hungarian provocations.[19]

The view that Russia should pursue a conciliatory policy toward Turkey lay at the root of Miliukov's foreign policy recommendations in 1908. Two years later he published his own study of the Bosnian affair in which he emphasized that Turkey was a Balkan power and that the Young Turks should be given a chance to co-operate in the maintenance of Balkan stability. The outcome of the Bosnian scare also taught Miliukov a major domestic lesson, one he would remember in March 1917 in justifying his approval of Nicholas' enforced departure. This was that no Russian effort to change the diplomatic situation abroad was likely to succeed unless the internal condition of the Empire were improved. A Bulgarian correspondent put it succinctly: "it is impossible to fight the foreign foe until peace has been made between the Russian government and its people."[20]

In 1912 and 1913 events in the peninsula overturned many preconceptions about the state of things in that corner of Europe. Miliukov, no less than other observers, was forced to re-examine his opinions on related questions and his assumptions as to Russia's wisest course in Balkan matters. In doing so, he later wrote, he abandoned "many former illusions and exaggerations."[21] First to be jettisoned was his belief in the potential of Ottoman regeneration. Defeated first by Italy, the weakest of the Great Powers, Turkey immediately faced a hostile combination of four Balkan monarchies prepared to submerge their mutual animosities in a profitable campaign against the Sultan's last remaining territories in Europe. The value of the Balkan alliance was not lost on Miliukov. On April 26, 1912, he told the Duma that Russia ought to protect Turkish integrity "only up to a time when a combination occurs which enables [the Turkish provinces in Europe] to become autonomous and which shows the way to the realization of Balkan ideals."[22] The Serb-Bulgarian alliance had now created this combination; the road was clear for the Balkan states to complete their work of national unification. A visit to Bulgaria after the Duma's dissolution encouraged Miliukov's belief that Russia's stock now stood high in the Balkans. He rejoiced at the triumph of the Allied armies but disapproved, along with Sazonov, of the excessive adulation of the Slav cause in Petersburg nationalist circles.[23] In the Easter recess of 1913 he managed another flying trip and found to his amusement that the government in Sofia was under the delusion that he wielded some influence over Nicholas II. In fact, it was unlikely that Ferdinand genuinely misrepresented his visitor's domestic importance. Flattery cost nothing; the King was never averse to its application or reception and when directed at Miliukov it might conceivably win Bulgaria's ruler a useful friend in days to come. Not for nothing was the King known familiarly outside his kingdom as Foxy Ferdie. In Serb-occupied Macedonia Miliukov received "the best impression" of the Prince Regent but neither touched on "delicate aspects" of future territorial changes in the province.[24]

It could not be expected that the man who regarded himself as his country's foremost expert on nationality issues in South-East Europe would preserve his silence indefinitely. In his by now annual review of foreign policy, on June 19, 1913, Miliukov devoted much of his speech to a discussion of an equitable solution of the Macedonian dispute. He saw three possible answers. Macedonia could either be partitioned between Bulgaria and Serbia, or assigned entirely to one of them, or else become an autonomous Turkish province under a Great Power guarantee. He personally preferred the third way out but conceded it was then impractical. So too was partition, since Macedonia's territorial integrity must be preserved in the interests of European peace. Which, then, of the two claimants should have all Macedonia? In replying to his own question (as he often liked to do) Miliukov asked another. "What do the Macedonians consider themselves to be?" His own answer was prompt. "Since 1870, when the first national Slav church appeared in the Balkan[s] . . . the Slav inhabitant of Macedonia has consistently considered himself Bulgarian." The liberation and defense of Macedonia's nationality was therefore not merely Bulgaria's right, it was her sacred duty.[25]

This address had repercussions that pursued Miliukov to the Bolshevik Revolution and beyond. From then on he was labelled a confirmed Bulgarophile. It was a charge he had anticipated before speaking by insisting that his opinion did not represent any prejudice toward Serbs or Greeks. He argued solely on the basis of his convictions reached after much travel and study. Thirteen years before had he not written of his determination never to be a friend of the Bulgarian people against the Serbian or of the Serbian against the Bulgarian? Only the end mattered, the welfare of the Macedonians themselves: "and I have the right to judge which of the means, the Bulgarian or the Serbian, better serves the realization of this aim."[26] He had now judged and he, more than any other Russian, must have known how his words would forever brand him in the eyes of the disappointed claimants. So it turned out. When Miliukov arrived in Belgrade in November as a member of the Carnegie Commission investigating the conduct of the recent wars, he met an icy reception. Prime Minister Pašić refused to meet "the declared enemy of Serbia"; hostile demonstrations greeted him in Athens. Miliukov's friendship with Talaat spared the Commission embarrassment in Constantinople; in Sofia his presence on it guaranteed it a warm welcome.[27]

The Second Balkan War induced further rethinking. According to the regime's most trenchant Parliamentary critic, selfishness and not ill-considered altruism must now be the order of the day in Balkan policies. Since the nations of South-East Europe had shown they cared only for their own interests, Russia should do likewise and not again go out on a limb for Balkan Slavs.[28] Nothing in July 1914 brought him to abandon this stand. He relates in his memoirs that he regarded it as "inevitable and incontestable" that Austria-Hungary should wish to settle accounts with Serbia; he urged only that the conflict be localized. To claim that Russia must fight in defense of Slavdom or of an aggrieved Serbia ignored the Empire's exclusion from the peninsula at a crucial time by the Balkan states themselves with Serbia at their head. Moreover, the shaky condition of Tsarist Russia made victory unlikely, defeat probable and the consequences incalculable—a retrospective conclusion not dissimilar to, if less clairvoyant than, Durnovo's judgment five months earlier. "No, whatever happened to Serbia, I was for localization."[29] A perusal of the relevant "Orange Books" subsequently led him to modify his stand but his known opposition to Russian intervention brought about the brief suspension of the Cadet newspaper *Rech'* following the German declaration of war.[30]

The war brought conversion in its train. When the Duma reconvened on August 8 for a one-day feast of national unity, the self-styled "representative of the opposition" ranged himself behind Sazonov in a manner no doubt gratifying to that gentleman: "we fight for the freedom of our native land, for the freedom of Europe and Slavdom from German rule." What more tangible aims was Russia fighting for? Again it might be Sazonov speaking: "our first duty remains to preserve our country one and indivisible and to maintain for it that position in the ranks of the world powers which is being contested by our foes."[31] Any lingering reticence on a more specific program vanished in the wake of Turkey's Black Sea attack; it is from November 1914 that the onetime spokesman for a restrained, realistic Russian policy in South-East Europe begins to evolve into the publicist of the most radical war ambitions. He stressed to the re-assembled Duma on February 9, 1915, that complete national unity was now imperative, not only for victory, but for what had become the nation's principal task in fighting, the acquisition of Constantinople and the Straits.[32] A few months later he depicted Russian war aims in the most categoric terms. His contribution to a series of essays on Russia's war expectations duplicated, if they did not exceed, the most extreme demands yet enunciated. He approved plans for a reconstituted Polish kingdom under the Tsar, as well as the incorporation of Galicia into the Empire. Constantinople and the Straits must be Russian "with a sufficient portion of the adjacent coasts to guarantee their defense." Armenia must be wholly Russian as the Turks had proved their unfitness to rule Christians. If Bulgaria, still neutral, would assist Russia against the Straits, the Imperial government should promise an extension of her frontiers toward the south.[33] It was an Imperial program thus presented by Russia's leading spokesman for the cause of political liberalism.

The key to the change of emphasis and direction was surely to be found in Miliukov's intellectual conviction, expressed many times during the war, that Slavdom and the Teutonic Powers were locked in a death struggle throughout Eastern Europe. Constantinople, the Straits, Galicia and Armenia were to be the pledges that Russia's dearly bought victory would not have been in vain. Economic, historical, religious and security reasons added their further sanctions. The disruption of Austria-Hungary would have the practical effect of permanently removing a bitter rival from European politics, to be replaced by a ring of national states linked to Russia, not Germandom. That some of this would later receive the imprimatur of "self-determination" only strengthened his conviction of right.

The second spring of war gave Miliukov the chance to try out some of his ideas on the Allied governments. In April 1916 he travelled west as a member of a Russian Parliamentary delegation to London, Paris and Rome.

Though only one of sixteen, Miliukov acted—and in Britain seems to have been treated—as if he were the delegation's most important member. He defended Bulgaria from British criticisms, informing Sir Edward Grey in rather condescending tones that Serbian megalomania and Entente blundering were responsible for Sofia's partnership with the Central Powers. He was nonetheless certain that military reverses would quickly bring Tsar Ferdinand to his senses when he, Miliukov, might more successfully influence the course of Bulgarian policy. Then he turned to another issue. What did Sir Edward think about the future of Austria-Hungary, specifically its dissolution, "without which the Polish, Serbian and Rumanian questions cannot be solved?" The visitor's own thoughts on the post-victory rebuilding of South-East Europe had now moved strongly in that direction but Grey refused to follow. He did admit that the problem of South Slav unity was one for Russia to raise at the appropriate time. Then he escaped into his inner office while Miliukov met British nationality experts, including two he had recommended to Grey as knowledgeable about and friendly towards Bulgaria: Noel Buxton and Robert Seton-Watson. Buxton was the nearest figure in England to Miliukov as a Balkan expert, especially on matters Bulgarian, though he naturally faced somewhat severer competition than did the Russian for the title of supreme authority on the subject.

These London talks may not have achieved much of a tangible nature and everyone on the Russian delegation was aware that the government at home was not viewing the junketings with any vast pleasure. Yet his meetings with Grey and the others were something of a triumph for Miliukov personally, all the more when compared to the diffident reception he encountered in Paris. He managed to have interviews with some Socialist leaders who would afterwards cause him some difficulties as minister. Rome was another success, perhaps less personally satisfying than London, but one to be savored no less fully. Everything considered, his experiences abroad that spring provided eloquent proof to the esteem he enjoyed in the Allied capitals as the embodiment of liberal Russia and an authority on East European nationality issues. Clemenceau's earlier judgment seemed thus amply confirmed; Miliukov's trip abroad turned out to be a splendid dress rehearsal for the responsibilities in store.[34]

The few months that remained to the Tsarist regime saw Miliukov consolidating and expanding his opinions on questions of war and peace. In December 1916 he felt able publicly to maintain that on the issue of Russia's (and his own) primary war aim at the Straits national opinion was "extraordinarily unanimous." The claim was wildly exaggerated, even if the national opinion so invoked referred only to the non-Socialist, metropolitan press. On the other hand there had been much discussion in pamphlets and the press on the future of European Turkey.[35] Yet the general reaction to Trepov's partial disclosures of the secret treaties showed that enthusiasm about "Tsargrad" was anything but universal. To convince the doubters "and dispel misunderstandings" Miliukov published an elaborate defense of the extreme war program he was pressing. He divided his opponents into "idealists" who felt that the seizure of the Straits was a betrayal of the liberating character of the war, and "realists" who held such plans possibly desirable in theory but diplomatically and militarily unfeasible in practice.[36] The writer denied the validity of both approaches. Annexation would not be imperialism "in the negative sense in which this word is sometimes used," since Russia's strategic and economic future required that Germany be prevented from establishing her power at the Golden Horn. Turkey herself was finished, at least in Europe. Miliukov invoked the powerful aid of Russia's Western Allies in their reply to President Wilson in January 1917 that the Turks must be expelled from Europe as alien to Western civilization. Russia was the obvious heir to the Ottoman legacy; her possession of Constantinople would bring final victory in the Great War which, as far as he was concerned, had started in 1908.[37]

He disposed as easily of Austria-Hungary. There must be a radical reconstruction of the Dual Monarchy, one which would "lead naturally to its final liquidation as constituted at present." Reconstruction would involve the incorporation of Galicia into the projected Polish kingdom, of Transylvania into Rumania, the satisfying of Italian and Czech claims and meeting South Slav desires for unity. To strengthen the anti-German aspect of the future Czech-Slovak and Yugoslav states Miliukov proposed a one-hundred-kilometer-wide corridor connect them, thus cutting off Austria proper from Hungary.[38]

By March 1917 Miliukov's views on Russia's war aims were set. Constantinople and the Straits, portions of European and Asiatic Turkey (as much as already promised Russia by her Allies), Armenia and all Polish and Ukrainian territories must pass under the scepter of the Russian Tsar. The Dual Monarchy should be reduced to its national components and its South Slav subjects join Serbia and Montenegro in a new, Russian oriented state on the Adriatic. The sum of these goals illustrated the vast gulf that separated Miliukov's opinions on Russia's foreign and domestic needs, even if his journalistic musings about a hundred-kilometer corridor are overlooked. His formal war aims program was more extreme than any other Russian's including Nicholas II. Only at home did his liberalism have any relevance. He himself of course did not consider the two aspects as mutually exclusive, rather the reverse, and with his British exemplars leading the way in a world-wide division of spoils, who could find fault with his position? It was one that lent urgency to his insistence by March that the Emperor must go since his incompetence prejudiced the victory that alone could bring foreign goals within reach. With Nicholas out of the way Miliukov could confidently set out to promote all Tsarist ambitions, now those of free Russia, plus some ambitions of his own. With perhaps greater justice he was equally sure that no other Russian in public or private life was a competent as "the representative of the opposition" to defend the nation's traditional interests abroad.

The Foreign Minister

"Who elected you?"—the question shouted at Miliukov on March 15 from the jubilant crowd outside the Tauride Palace went to the heart of the new minister's political position, as to that of the new regime as a whole. His answer "the Russian Revolution" was factually correct and satisfied his audience; his own private scruples were not so easily soothed.[39] Revolution may have wrought what Nicholas II would not but otherwise it should not be allowed to intrude into the government's responsibilities. To Paléologue's query "do you receive your power from the Revolution?" Miliukov's reply was immediate and uncompromising: "No, we have received it by inheritance from the Grand Duke Michael who transferred it to us by his abdication decree."[40] Revolution or inheritance: the conflict was admitted from the start of Miliukov's tenure in his own contradictory versions of the source of his authority. The public wanted the one, the Foreign Minister the other; the issue was joined one week after the government's accession.

On March 22 P. N. Miliukov appeared before representatives of the Petrograd press to clarify his attitude toward his new post. He began by stressing a concept which remained basic to his position throughout: the revolution had changed nothing as far as Russia's foreign policy was concerned. His first action on assuming office was to pledge loyalty to the fallen regime's international obligations. This step he justified with the explanation that "the sharp changes which occur in internal affairs are impossible in diplomacy." What were to be the foreign goals of free Russia? "Only the fulfillment of our national tasks . . . liberation of the Austro-Hungarian nationalities and the liquidation of Turkey's domination based solely on principles of conquest . . . ." Russia, he insisted, had no other duty but that of bettering the lot of small oppressed nationalities.[41] He could see no reason why thoughtful citizens should not agree.

The Left supplied reasons enough. The Petrograd Soviet of Workers' and Soldiers' Deputies found Miliukov's position totally unacceptable. His goals were not only relics of an unworthy past, they also debased the revolution by using its language in favor of ambitions, such as the parition of Austria-Hungary, that not even Tsarism had proclaimed. The Soviet had already crossed swords with Miliukov on the question of the dynasty; now it had a much more important fight on its hands. "They tell us," wrote *Izvestiia*, the Soviet's organ,

> that we must conquer Constantinople and Armenia, take back Poland, annex Galicia . . ., that the Allies together desire the dismemberment of Austria-Hungary and the Balkans to subject them to their own influence . . . . We must resolutely declare that we do not wish to shed our blood in the interests of the ruling classes.[42]

Izvestiia editorials were all very well and clearly indicative of the prevailing mood in a body that had little reason to defer to an ex-history professor who sat in the government with the Soviet's acquiescence. Yet there was no unanimity of action or intent among the several Socialist factions on the attitude to be taken toward the war. The one Socialist in the Cabinet, the Minister of Justice, Alexander Kerenskii, was the first to challenge Miliukov directly on the subject. An unsympathetic Nabokov recorded Kerenskii's discomfiture. His unnatural laughter and nervous finger drumming contrasted sharply with Miliukov's calm self-possession in defending his ideas on foreign policy as those of the whole government. He carried his point. It was agreed that ministers should from now on refrain from private newspaper interviews. This was a concession Miliukov could make to his Socialist colleague without cost to himself, for, whatever the impression given to the contrary, the government's foreign policy had not so much become his, as his policy still remained that of the government.[43] This was precisely the point on which Kerenskii had been repulsed; his allies in the Soviet were prepared to show a greater persistence. On the day before Miliukov's interview the Soviet's Executive Committee, on a motion by the ever suspicious Sukhanov, named a Liaison Commission to serve as a link between Soviet and Cabinet. Its main job was to ensure that Soviet wishes met with a proper respect from a body which in Sukhanov's opinion at least existed only on Soviet sufferance. The last sentence of the Commission's mandate promised trouble for Miliukov's freedom of action; it intended "to exercise vigilant control over the realization of the demands of the revolutionary people."[44] But what were these demands? The future Foreign Minister of the USSR, V. M. Molotov, made an inauspicious debut to his political career in posing his version of the correct answer: all power to the democracy and an immediate end to the Provisional Government and its pretensions. In the days before Lenin's return to Russia these words were thought by fellow Bolsheviks to be rather excessive; Sukhanov noted with pleasure how the "irresponsible critic" was slapped down by his party colleagues.[45] Sukhanov himself saw the main danger to Socialist unity as coming not from the Bolsheviks, but from right-wing Mensheviks under the Georgian Irakli Tsereteli, who were demanding that the Soviet emphasize the need to defend the revolution from the external, i.e. German foe. Their opponents in the Soviet, represented though not led by Sukhanov, rejected this defensism as un unhealthy manifestation of Russian chauvinism and called for a renunciation of Tsarist war aims, as approved by Miliukov. Revolutionary Russia should then induce her Allies to join her in making peace on the basis of no annexations or indemnities.[46]

The Soviet's "Appeal to the Peoples of All the World," published on March 27, reflected both lines, steering an uneasy course between the Scylla of defensism and the Charybdis of capitulationism. The job of composing the first draft had been entrusted to the undoubted literary talents of Maxim Gor'kii. Alas, his version proved too much a work of art and too little a work of politics: Sukhanov took over. He was quite aware of the final edition's liabilities. The document began with the obligatory salute to the revolution, going on to warn readers that "our work is not yet finished against the shades of the old order." The Russian democracy would oppose the policy of its ruling classes "by every means." Very fine as far as it went but not quite the unequivocal repudiation of annexationist policies that Sukhanov had envisaged. The Appeal was more specific on the defense issue: "We will firmly defend our own liberty against all reactionary attempts from without and within. The Russian Revolution will not retreat before the bayonets of conquerors and will not permit itself to be crushed by foreign military force." Then came a call to German workers:

> "Throw off the yoke of your semi-autocratic rule as the Russian people have cast off the Tsar's autocracy; refuse to serve as an instrument of conquest and violence in the hands of kings, landowners and bankers, and then by our united efforts we will stop this horrible butchery . . . ."[47]

The first public Soviet challenge to Miliukov was now open for public discussion.

To the minister himself the slogan of no annexations or indemnities had very little relevance to the crucial issues of the war whether phrased in defensist terms or not. He was honestly unable to see how popular catchwords of that kind related to the vital concerns of the war as he conceived them to be. Still less did he grasp how Socialist foreign policy dilettantes could imagine that an international appeal might sway the German government from its anti-Slav crusade. Moreover, Socialist interference did not cease with the Appeal. One week later the Ex. Com. decided to set up its own International Relations Section with an agency in Stockholm and couriers to represent it abroad.[48] As with the Appeal the Section's main function was to attract foreign Socialists of every hue to the Soviet's position on the war; yet from Miliukov's viewpoint it was just one more proof of that body's lack of realism on complex issues of international affairs. As if to remind the Ex. Com. and its new creation precisely how complex those issues were he took it upon himself to inform the press on April 4 that he did not consider as annexation the endeavors of the Entente Powers to alter the map of Europe "especially in its South-Eastern part" so as to make possible the triumph of the national principle. He went on to repeat his already notorious conviction of the need to rebuild Central and South-Eastern Europe by creating an independent Czechoslovakia, the return of Italians to Italy, Rumanians to Rumania, "the natural unification of the Serbian people" and the union of Western Ukraine (Galicia) with the Russian motherland. What he delicately described as "the more restricted Balkan problem," that is frontier adjustments, would be solved later "in accordance with the results of the war." Constantinople and the Straits remained still the essential goal, one indeed on which Miliukov was more peremptory than ever. Where he had once justified Russian possession on the grounds that Turkey-in-Europe was doomed, he now appeared to demand "the keys to Russia's house" whether the Ottoman Empire survived the war intact or not.[49]

These sentiments, in flat contradiction to the spirit of the Socialist Appeal, spurred the Soviet on to a showdown with the government. On the evening of April 6 the Liaison Commission met with the Cabinet to secure its adhesion to the Soviet's position. The Commission found Miliukov obdurate but most of his colleagues conciliatory. Their reluctance to join him in complete opposition illustrated how isolated Miliukov-"Dardanellskii" had become in country and Cabinet on matters of acute national concern. The Soviet of course had never been behind him, but even non-Socialists for the most part were unenthusiastic about the objectives nearest his heart. Paléologue, ever alert to the nuances of Petrograd society on the subject of the war, reported one unnamed but representative high-born lady's opinion on Russia's official war aims: "Constantinople, Santa Sophia and the Golden Horn—whoever gives that fantastic notion a thought nowadays except Miliukov and he solely because he's a historian."[50] Differences of personality scarcely less than of policy helped to widen the breach in government ranks incipient since the first Miliukov-Kerenskii confrontation. The former thought little of most of his colleagues. Prince L'vov, Premier and Interior Minister, was "not in his place," a surprising statement in view of the role Miliukov had played in putting him there.[51] Still worse was Kerenskii's "ostentatious grandeur" and "dictatorial pose." Michael Tereshchenko, Finance Minister and Miliukov's successor in the Foreign Ministry, a sugar millionaire eighty times over and a pianist of almost professional standing, owed his initial (and secondary) appointments to his connections with fellow capitalists and nothing else that anyone could see.[52] A fellow Cadet, N. V. Nekrasov, completed the list of Miliukov's critics within the Cabinet where he held the transport portfolio.[53] The rest, with one or two exceptions like Alexander Guchkov, were nonentities. They in their turn, while ready to admit his talents, were no longer prepared to give Miliukov free rein in ministerial policy and pronouncements. Their objections came to a head when the Liaison Commission presented its program.

Tsereteli led off. Concerned primarily with the need to protect the revolution from German arms, he told the assembled ministers that Miliukov's actions threatened Russia's newly won freedom "by sowing alarm and discontent over the long-drawn out character of the war for alien goals." The government must commit itself to an official declaration renouncing all aims that might be construed in that manner. Only then could the Soviet devote its energies to what in Tsereteli's judgment was its major external concern: the mobilization of all forces at front and rear in defense of the revolution. What Sukhanov called "a long, boring, fruitless, perfectly verbal polemic" then ensued. Miliukov would not give in, nor would Guchkov. Kerenskii and his fellow "conspirators" insisted passionately that their colleagues' concept of Russia and Europe died with Tsardom. The split in the Cabinet yawned open for all to see; a complete Soviet victory seemed unavoidable.[54]

Miliukov rose to the emergency. The first version of the government's answer, approved by him, conceded that the ideal of free Russia "is not to rule over other peoples, nor the seizure of their national property but the establishment of a stable peace based on national self-determination." So far so good; unfortunately, from the Soviet point of view, there the concessions stopped. The statement went on to promise that "the Russian people will not allow its homeland to emerge from the great struggle humbled, with vital energies sapped . . . . The obligations towards our Allies will be fully observed." To calm Soviet scruples Miliukov allowed that he was contemplating an address to the Allies concerning a revision of the treaties: "just now I consider the moment unfavorable but I see no obstacle to taking this step shortly."[55]

The Liaison Commission still required further assurances. On April 9 the government sent an alternative draft to the Ex. Com., one still couched in defensist-patriotic terms by and large but with the addition of six words "underlined in red pencil" to the earlier version. The key paragraphs now read:

> Leaving to the will of the people, in close union with our Allies, the final solution of all problems connected with the World War and its conclusion, the Provisional Government considers it to be its right and duty to declare that the aim of free Russia is not domination over other nations or seizure of their national possessions *or forcible occupation of foreign territories*, but the establishment of a stable peace on the basis of self-determination of peoples. The Russian people does not intend to increase its world power at the expense of other nations . . . . But it will not permit its Fatherland to emerge from this great struggle humiliated and sapped in its vital forces.
>
> These principles will be made the basis of the foreign policy of the Provisional Government which is unswervingly executing the will of the people and defending the rights of our Fatherland, at the same time fully observing all obligations toward our Allies.[56]

A majority on the Ex. Com. decided that this account represented "a great democratic victory" and "a long step forward in the cause of peace." With the Soviet's endorsement the Declaration of March 27/April 9 was issued to the citizens of Russia as the foreign policy and war program of their government.

Technically the Soviet had won. In its first confrontation with the Cabinet over foreign affairs, the latter body, including Miliukov, had promised that there should be no seizures or domination of foreign lands. The Rightist majority on the Ex. Com. was certain it had clarified beyond any doubt Russia's purpose in the war. Sukhanov was not so confident and saw the Declaration more as a starting point for further demands than as proof of final victory over Miliukov and his ambitions.[57] The minister indeed had some cause for self-congratulation. He considered that the Declaration embodied an incomplete and illusory victory for the Soviet; it is difficult not to share his opinion. What exactly had he abandoned? The Declaration's language was ambiguous and deliberately so. Its author later wrote that he had selected expressions which would not require him to make any changes in Russian foreign policy as he understood it.[58] How, for example, was the promise of no domination over other nations to be reconciled to the refusal to allow Russia to be humiliated and sapped in her vital forces? And what precisely did that nebulous phrase mean? Much more to the point, how did the government propose to abstain from the forcible occupation of foreign territories and still remain faithful to all obligations toward the nation's Allies? Obviously the Declaration was liable to any one of several interpretations depending on the aspect the reader cared to emphasize. Newspapers of the Right and Center were favorable. *Rech'* held that the statement would become "a most essential factor in the future course of events," these last to include decisive military victory. The Conservative *Novoe Vremia* underlined the inviolability of the treaties as the Declaration's most significant feature: "to safeguard the peace it is necessary to pull the teeth and break the back of the [German] brute."[59]

The Leftist press concentrated on the apparent abandonment of annexations. The Social Revolutionary *Delo Naroda* stressed this aspect, observing in passing that loyalty to Russia's obligations "means negatively only the inability to conclude a separate peace and the fulfillment of civic and moral obligations and . . . peace without annexations on either side." The Menshevik *Rabochaia Gazeta* wrote that the Declaration was "an important step toward meeting the aspirations of the democracy," though it was "far from all we can and must demand." The left of center *Den'* concentrated its ire on Miliukov's presumptuous views on the need to re-organize South-East Europe. *Izvestiia*, perhaps sensing the document's chief weakness, criticised the "devious path" of the non-Socialist parties who, it alleged, were trying to capitalize on the Declaration's imprecise language. *Izvestiia*'s perceptibly defensive tone was understandable in the official organ of the body that claimed to speak for the greater portion of assembled Russian Socialists. The Bolshevik *Pravda* alone queried how Miliukov could remain in a government that had officially renounced all annexationist aims in Europe and the Near East; his continued presence in fact proved the Cabinet's hypocrisy on the war aims question.[60]

None of these reservations, doubts or challenges were going to have any impact on the minister in question. He might indeed have fortified himself with the thought later expressed by his friend Vladimir Nabokov that if the circumstances had ever arisen in which the realization of Russian war aims appeared likely, "who would have remembered the words of this Declaration [or] used them to argue against Russia?"[61] Revolution or no, Russian foreign policy remained inviolate to the man in charge of its formulation and execution. His views of March 22 had not changed a whit in the face of strident public disapproval and the efforts of Soviet representatives to bridle his freedom of action and speech.

Satisfied that domestic opposition was for the present, if not actually mute, then at least repulsed, Miliukov turned his attention to Russia's Allies.

It was not a moment too soon. Two days after the abdication they had been assured that the Provisional Government would correct the errors of the past which had up to then paralyzed the enthusiasm and spirit of sacrifice of the Russian people.[62] That was just the sort of language they wanted to hear, though unfortunately its effect was weakened by the obvious lack of agreement in the government on what the revolution meant to the common conduct of the war. Buchanan, an acute observer of the Russian scene, quickly noted Miliukov's isolation in the Cabinet where he was, in Sir George's words, "almost in a minority of one on the subject of Constantinople."[63] What did the new Russia want from the war? It depended on the speaker, and the ambassador was finding it increasingly difficult to decide who spoke for Russia.

The difficulty was as great in Paris and London. On the first full day of the new Russian regime's tenure, the charge d'affaires in England, Konstantin Nabokov, cabled his new chief about Foreign Secretary A. J. Balfour's alarm at "extreme elements agitating for an end to the war." Balfour was in fact rather more realistic than Miliukov in his assessment of Russian political conditions, foreseeing the distasteful possibility that the Soviet's position on the war might spread far beyond the confines of the Tauride Palace wing assigned to that organization. Allied Socialists were pressed into service to keep their Petrograd brothers up to the mark by standing fast against extremism and calls for a separate peace: virtually synonymous offenses to the Western governments.[64] The Miliukov-Kerenskii duel attracted immediate foreign attention. Both Paléologue and Buchanan regarded the Justice Minister as the Cabinet's strongest member and he made a point of telling Knox, the British military attaché, that the Allies should not believe Miliukov when he said that Russia still wanted Constantinople. He, Kerenskii, demanded the internationalization of the Straits and self-determination for Poland, Finland and Armenia. A weary Foreign Office minute testified to the mounting British reservations about the Eastern Ally.[65]

Kerenskii's remarks to Knox, no secret in Petrograd, had immediate repercussions. On March 21 they were reported in the London press which proceeded to speculate on an impending change in Russia's official position on Constantinople. Four days later a second article noted that Miliukov had now "reduced Russian claims in Turkey." A much concerned Nabokov warned Petrograd that unless definite assurances were given, there would be increased public discussion of Russia's "rights" in the Ottoman capital.[66]

The Declaration of March 27/April 9 engaged the close scrutiny of the British press, even though it was addressed to the citizens of Russia, not to Russia's Allies. Most newspapers saw it as a victory for the antiannexationist forces in Petrograd. But the ambiguities that had caused hesitations in the Russian press had a similar impact in Britain. The *Manchester Guardian* welcomed the Declaration as proof of Kerenskii's triumph over Miliukov. England and France, the paper said, must support the non-aggressive designs of the Russian people. The *Daily News* was also pleased that Russia had abandoned an acquisitive foreign policy "including presumably the renunciation of the agreement concerning Constantinople and the Straits." Less sure of the concession, the *Daily Mail* suggested that Russia's Allies ask whether or not she actually desired the city.[67]

This speculation reached into the government. News of the April 9 Declaration arrived at a moment when the Imperial War Cabinet was sifting through various committee reports on European territorial desiderata at the eventual peace conference. Russia emerged from these papers a doubtful and discredited factor in determining post-victory problems in the Balkans. A section of one set of recommendations stated baldly that "unless Russia is more successful in the field and less absorbed in her own internal problems the terms of the peace settlement will certainly be determined by the wishes and interests of the Western Allies, rather than by those of Russia." This was deemed to be in accord with Russia's own preferences. "Her immense bulk . . . [makes her] more truly interested in her own internal reorganization. She is better off without being saddled with Polish and Rumanian problems and this apparently is also the view of considerable sections of opinion in Russia itself." What of Constantinople? The report reflected newspaper doubts about Russian intentions but was convinced that Russian renunciation would be most desirable since it would "at once open the field for the possibility of a separate peace with Turkey and even conceivably with Bulgaria."[68] This vision of Germany's two Balkan Allies being bought off at Russia's diplomatic expense exerted a persistent fascination upon British political and journalistic thinking throughout the summer of 1917. Public comment was much more restrained in Paris and Rome, in part since the censorship of incoming cables from Petrograd made it difficult to know exactly what was going on in Russia. The serious press agreed that Miliukov's presence in the Cabinet remained the best guarantee of Russia's sincerity in the common war effort.[69] Probably reflecting Paléologue's marked preference for Miliukov over Kerenskii, the Quai d'Orsay responded more readily than Whitehall to the Russian minister's overtures. On March 24, only two days after receipt of Miliukov's formal request to do so, Paléologue's government authorized him to commit France to continued recognition of the secret treaties Miliukov valued so highly. Buchanan had to wait six days further before he could make a similar engagement.[70]

Russia's representatives in Paris and London were experiencing a certain difficulty in reconciling their chief's known position with the various pronouncements issuing from Petrograd. On April 11 Nabokov cabled that the British were still anxious to do everything in their power to help Russia since London was "convinced of the patriotism and political wisdom of those now in charge of Russia's destinies." Unfortunately, Nabokov continued, press and public opinion had noted the discrepancy on foreign policy between the Foreign and Justice Ministers. As a result they had become interested "in a vital way" in the Constantinople issue.[71] Two days later Nabokov's Paris opposite number, Matvei Sevastopulo, announced that Kerenskii's remarks on war aims, combined with the April 9 Declaration, had given the impression locally that Russia now definitely renounced her claims on "Tsargrad" and the Straits.[72]

In his replies to these warnings Miliukov showed how little he really understood or cared about the nature and passion of the forces arrayed against him. At a time when public opinion in Petrograd overwhelmingly supported the Declaration's position on war aims, Miliukov, virtually alone as Buchanan had seen, insisted on Russia's right to every promised gain. He continued to deprecate hostile views:

> Except for extreme Social Democratic organs whose agitation at present has been significantly weakened by the Declaration [of March 27/April 9], all the serious press and widespread public opinion supports our . . . viewpoint which has also found a sympathetic response in the army.[73]

Coincidently Sukhanov remarked in his journal that the revolution was now forced in the interests of its own survival to rid itself somehow of "this predatory foe" in the Foreign Ministry.[74] Clearly nothing had yet been settled in the contest between Miliukov and the Soviet but a final showdown could not long be postponed. Until that occasion he would redouble his efforts. For two centuries Russia had been a Great Power of consequence in European affairs. In South-East Europe and Turkey he saw the means to make certain she remained one.

CHAPTER III
BALKAN ENEMIES

Russia and Turkey

Whatever other accusations his critics might justly make, the inheritor of the Romanov diplomatic legacy could not be charged with obscurity on the issue of Turkey. For Miliukov, no less than for his Tsarist predecessors, the material justification for Russia's continued belligerence remained the acquisition of the Ottoman territories conditionally promised the Empire by its Allies in 1915-1916. Entente victory was naturally the surest guarantee of this, even though the new Foreign Minister continued in a half-hearted way Russian attempts to induce Turkey to abandon her partners. His diplomatic program of course made that prospect exceedingly remote; his enthusiasm was understandably much keener over a parallel ambition for Bulgaria, as he had made clear in opposition days to Sir Edward Grey. Achievement of either goal would bring victory appreciably nearer and give much needed reinforcement to Russia's strategic position in South-East Europe and diplomatic standing in the Entente alliance.

The surest method of securing Russian desiderata in Turkey was superior military force. If Russia could wrest Constantinople and the Straits by dint of her own, preferably unaided efforts, her position in both the peninsula and the alliance would be vastly strengthened. So argued the last Foreign Minister of the Empire, N. N. Pokrovskii, in a report submitted to the Tsar one week before the revolution.[1] Showing what under the circumstances seems a surprising optimism in the imminence of Entente victory (perhaps for the benefit of his reader) Pokrovskii argued that Russian troops should at once be sent against the Ottoman capital. If unable to capture it themselves, they could at least put the Empire in a position to exert maximum pressure upon Turkey at the peace conference Pokrovskii felt was at hand. His sense of urgency reflected a distinct lack of confidence in the willingness of his country's Allies to continue the struggle for the sake of "Tsargrad" and he warned Nicholas that if the current offensive on the Western front were successful, there was little reason to suppose that victorious Britain and France would wish to keep on fighting to bolster Russia in the Near East.[2]

Response from Supreme Headquarters to this appeal was discouraging. General M. V. Alexeev, Chief of Staff to the Emperor and effective Commander-in-Chief, thought the proposed expedition impractical and futile as long as the arch-foe remained undefeated. There the matter briefly rested.[3]

On Nicholas' downfall Miliukov reopened the question of a military assault on the city he so greatly desired for Russia. Diplomatic and political factors combined to make the scheme irresistibly attractive to him; he had no appreciation of the military obstacles likely to prevent the plan's implementation. One push, he was sure, would bring success and, just as important, present the parties of the left with a dazzling fait accompli.[4] His pressure became so insistent that Alexeev, now nominally as well as factually in supreme command, reluctantly conceded the possibility of "a small expedition" against the Turkish coastline. Preparations slowly got under way and almost immediately halted. On April 5, N. A. Bazili, Miliukov's representative at Supreme Headquarters, cabled his chief apologetically that the War Minister had ordered all work to be stopped on the preparation of naval transports to participate in the attack. The Russian railway network was in such chaotic disarray that any further strain would lead to its complete collapse. Bazili expressed the hope that the Russian deficiency in barges might be made good by Rumania; in the meantime was there any chance that Miliukov might persuade his Cabinet colleague to rescind his prohibition?[5]

This unpromising start heralded final disillusion. On April 24 Miliukov heard from Bazili once again, this time to the effect that insuperable difficulties lay in the way of a military expedition against the Straits.[6] Reasons given included the anticipation at Supreme Headquarters of an imminent German offensive and difficulties with transport and supplies. These problems were no doubt vexatious enough but a more inhibiting factor to the proposed assault was the inability of local military commands to convince the troops under them of its necessity.[7] Bazili did not himself mention this latter obstacle, yet his message was clear; Russian ambitions in Turkey could not be achieved by force of Russian arms alone. Miliukov's agent saw two possible alternatives. If Russia was determined to have Constantinople and the Straits she should try to bring Bulgaria to her side, so that together they might force Turkey's submission. This, as Bazili knew, was Miliukov's preferred solution, although rather difficult to foresee in Bazili's view. The second possibility, one he recommended to Miliukov, was that Russia content herself with "the necessary factual guarantees" at the Golden Horn and leave actual sovereignty over the city and its surrounding district to Turkey.[8] Above all else, ran Bazili's prescription, the impression must be avoided that Russia's "alleged" renunciation of her war aims on March 27/April 9 meant that she now favored neutralization "as preached by our extreme left circles." If conquest were for one reason or another out of reach, Russia should attempt a bilateral settlement with Turkey. Success here would force quick Bulgarian compliance and leave Germany alone in the field with her battered Austrian ally.[9]

Bazili's telegrams to Miliukov accepted that Bulgaria or Turkey or both held the key to future Russian success or failure in the non-military context of the war. His advice presumed, though refrained from saying, that Russian arms had done all they could; the goals which had proved beyond their capability might be brought nearer by diplomatic maneuver. This counsel came at a time when the tasks facing Russian diplomacy seemed daily to be growing more difficult. By mid-April Miliukov had no trouble in discovering evidence of a growing tendency among Russia's partners to belittle her role in the formulation of Allied war policies. Nor did he need to ascribe this to Entente duplicity, for in spite of his reassurances to the contrary, domestic opposition to his program inevitably cast its shadow over Russia's diplomatic effectiveness abroad. The views of Alexander Kerenskii were by then well known and the Allies were no less likely to have noted the criticisms levelled at Miliukov from other parts of the political spectrum in Russia. Indeed, the specific issue of Turkey and his plans for her "reconstruction" came up in a way perhaps unexpected by Miliukov at the Seventh Congress of the Cadet Party between April 7 and 9. A small group of dissidents among the delegation representing Russia's Moslem population took issue with the majority's endorsement of the Government's foreign policy stance. It seemed clear to the minority that the Cadet Party or at least its head applied one criterion to Christian nations in post-war planning and quite another to Moslem Turkey.[10] Though the thrust was lost in the larger body of support for Miliukov-"Dardanellskii," it added its contribution nonetheless to the rising chorus of criticism which the Cadet leader preferred not to notice. Allied governments were more sensitive, as Konstantin Nabokov quickly pointed out. On April 17 he warned from London that whatever Russia might determine as her policy in territorial questions it was certain that none of her Allies would accept the principle of peace without annexations if this meant, as it assuredly did, the renunciation of lands either conquered or desired. Nabokov advised strongly that the Government make a point of guaranteeing the continued security of the Black Sea if it wished to inspire Allied confidence that the Socialist slogan of No Annexations or Indemnities did not contradict Russia's own "vital interests" in the Near East.[11] Russia's "vital interests" from the lips or pen of any Russian statesman by then had become a euphemism for Constantinople;

the favorable use of the words stamped the speaker indelibly as a member of Miliukov's camp. Nabokov and all other senior Russian diplomats were proud to count themselves of that number.

Miliukov realized as clearly as any diplomat the need for an energetic campaign along the lines proposed by Nabokov. It had, however, become his misfortune—though he would not have seen it as such—to defend a diplomatic settlement for Russia that critics at home and Allies abroad were increasingly coming to question.[12] Even so, he did not allow this to divert him any more than it must from the traditional exercise of diplomacy as he had inherited it. Personal inclination and strategic possibilities suggested Germany's Balkan allies as the most promising areas for a Russian initiative. Well before Bazili suggested he do so, Miliukov had extended feelers to both Constantinople and Sofia. In both cases he was emphasizing again the continuity of Russian diplomatic practice, unbroken by the events of March 14-15.

* * *

Tsarist ambitions at Turkey's expense made any negotiated Turkish withdrawal from the war as unlikely an eventuality as could be imagined in the wartime diplomatic context. For just that reason Petrograd did not at first welcome the suggestion that overtures in that direction be made. In January 1915 Sazonov informed his opposite numbers in Paris and London that in view of Russian designs on the Ottoman Empire he had forbidden his agent in Constantinople to make contact with members of the ruling Committee.[13] In the first wartime session of the Duma following the *Goeben* and *Breslau* cannonades he spoke in the strongest terms of the need to use maximum diplomatic and military pressure to ensure Russia's position at the eventual settling of accounts with Turkey; Miliukov warmly endorsed his observations.[14] As long as the military situation stayed favorable the Tsarist Government held out for a hard Entente line toward the Turks. Thus Sazonov reacted with considerable nervousness to reports current in the summer of 1915 that confidential exchanges were going on between the French Government and various Turkish officials on unspecified matters. On April 9 he heard that the Ottoman Minister of Finance Djavid Bey had arrived in Geneva from Berlin prepared to open discussions with the Entente.[15] Hard on the heels of that piece of news came another rumor of Djavid's conversations with certain unnamed French politicians.[16] When pressed for clarification the French Government, through Foreign Minister Delcassé, evaded giving any precise information, announcing only that approaches had been made but "from a still more authoritative personality" than Djavid—an identification that could only have designated one of the governing triumvirate itself. To Sazonov's annoyance Delcassé refused to be any more specific and proposed that the Entente listen to whatever the Turks might have to say. Sazonov gave grudging consent to this, but stipulated that Constantinople first be told of "the irrevocable Allied decision" to hand over the capital to Russia.[17] Possibly as Sazonov had anticipated, Turkish overtures ceased abruptly, though French hopes still remained high.[18]

The question was taken up again the following spring and this time, probably reflecting the change in Russia's military fortunes, the Tsarist authorities proved more enthusiastic. Delcassé's successor, Aristide Briand, was as interested in a potential Turkish armistice as his predecessor but rather more deft in handling Russian susceptibilities on the issue.[19] He promised that nothing would be done in the matter of a separate peace without Russia's prior consent since she, of all members of the alliance, was the one most directly affected by that prospect.[20] This assurance prompted Sazonov to intervene more energetically in the various intrigues that involved Turkish and Entente political figures. In March 1916 a diplomatic agent, A. N. Mandelshtam, former dragoman at the Constantinople embassy, was sent off to Berne to maintain contact with Turkish emissaries in Switzerland. For the next five months he reported sporadically on the approaches made to him from exiled Turkish dissidents whom he lumped under the general title of "the opposition."[21]

On August 26, 1916, Mandelshtam cabled excitedly that the opposition had at last submitted to the Entente legations its plans for the Committee's overthrow. As reported to Petrograd there was nothing to the plot, apart from the vague hope of inciting civil insurrection in Constantinople, and there was no mention at all of what Mandelshtam's guests thought of Russia's war aims at their country's expense. But they seem to have made the extravagant promises of political "outs" and that was enough for Mandelshtam. It did not suffice for his sovereign. At the foot of the telegram from Berne, Nicholas II wrote: "We must finish with Turkey. There is no further place for her in Europe. We should not therefore enter into relations with the opposition."[22] This appears to have coincided with the general Entente view of the matter. For the remaining seven months of Nicholas' reign neither Russia nor her partners had any further dealings with opponents of Talaat Pasha, Miliukov's erstwhile travelling companion, the fiercely mustachioed "Danton of the Turkish Revolution."[23]

The March events in Russia caught Turkish officials, like everyone else, by surprise. The lack of precise information added to the general uncertainty. On March 18 *Tanin*, quite close to the Committee, observed approvingly that "a deeply rooted system of tyranny" had been overthrown and expressed the conviction that the situation of the Provisional Government was "splendid" and widely supported. *Tanin* shared the widespread impression in the Central Powers that English guile had brought about the Tsar's downfall. The right wing *Sabah* predicted, in a perceptible spirit of wishful thinking, the outburst of a long and bitter civil war between royalists and republicans, a prospect full of favorable possibilities for Turkey. *Ikdam*, the oldest Constantinople daily and a fervent supporter of the German alliance, professed to see little real difference between the new Russia and the old and made a point of rejecting Miliukov's version of the reasons for the monarchy's collapse.[24]

Any initial enthusiasm on a governmental level over events in what *Tanin* called "free and Socialist Russia" was tempered by knowledge of the new Foreign Minister's notorious views on Turkey. In an interview on April 5, clearly designed to set the official line on developments in Petrograd, Talaat evinced the hope that the two countries would now be able to live in peace and friendship. This had been impossible up until then because of aggressive Tsarist designs. Talaat then went on in a warning tone:

> I must however declare with regret that the spirit of the Russian Revolution has not completely overcome the old aggressive tendencies. In his speech [of March 22] about an honorable peace Mr Miliukov mentions the need to solve the Turkish question in Russia's favor. We do not know whether Russian liberals subscribe to these old formulas of hate and lust for conquest. If the Russian people want to pursue this infamous legacy of Tsarism as their own goal, it is superfluous to talk of peace. . . . The Turkish question can be solved only in favor of Turkey.[25]

This was in effect the policy of the Petrograd Soviet and none else on the Entente side, but it was apparently still too early for Talaat to bid openly for Russian Socialist sympathy.

Inside the Ottoman capital, as outside, concern for the security of the city remained the strongest bulwark against the undeniably growing war weariness. Interest in Russia was acute from officialdom and the newspaper reading public. On the day following Talaat's admonition, the German ambassador, von Kühlmann, reported to the Wilhelmstrasse that leading Turkish circles were following the Russian crisis with such excited optimism "that sometimes I find a gentle warning note is necessary." How would Russia's current difficulties affect the future of the Straits? Kühlmann observed that he noted a strong, though not yet dominant belief that Turkey should make every concession to Russia compatible with the security of the

Straits and the capital. Via the Foreign Ministry he had heard that the government had approached Russia confidentially on many occasions about the Dardanelles and that if matters got to the point where the Porte were actually to make concessions to Russia on the question of access to the Mediterranean, Kühlmann counselled that the Foreign Office react "calmly," rather than anticipate an impending Turkish defection from the alliance.[26] Although there is no reflection in published Russian materials of Turkish overtures on the Straits—and the remark may well have been no more than a strong hint to Berlin of an option open to the Porte if it chose to use it—Kühlmann's American colleague, Abraham Elkus, also noted the evident Ottoman willingness to compose differences with Russia. But he was sure, and reported as much to Washington, that the Turks looked to a peace between Russia and the Central Powers, rather than one between Turkey and the Entente. However, after a discussion on this subject "with one of the most influential cabinet ministers," Elkus apparently changed his mind enough to cable his new conviction that a categoric declaration from Russia of her determination to prosecute the war would force Turkey to sue for terms.[27] Elkus did not name his "most influential cabinet minister" but there were only three who mattered: Talaat and his co-leaders of the Committee, Enver Pasha and Djemal Pasha, respectively Ministers of War and the Navy. All three, especially Enver, were heart and soul behind the German alliance, if for no other reason than by 1917 their own political futures depended on its success. Even given the deviousness of Ottoman politicians, it is unlikely that Elkus derived his conclusion from one of these three.

With the diplomatic and political facts of life so unpromising and his own inclinations so inhibiting, Miliukov could hardly have been expected to do much more than go through the motions of putting out feelers to Turkey. Shortly after assuming office he inquired at Berne about the state of Russo-Turkish contacts on the separate peace issue. He learned that not only was there no special Turkish representative in Switzerland but that even the oppositional elements who had once confided in Mandelshtam had by now lost hope in the utility of further contacts with Russia.[28] Their loss of faith was overdue; since the rupture of the previous August the Entente seemed to have gone out of its way to bar the road to separate Turkish approaches. On December 2 came Trepov's speech in the Duma on the Straits and Constantinople agreements; in the following month the Entente publicly informed President Wilson that its fundamental goals in the war included "the liberation of peoples still subject to the bloody tyranny of the Turks" and the latter's expulsion from Europe "as alien to Western civilization."[29] Confirmation of Russian intransigence came with Miliukov's appointment and his immediate endorsement of Tsarist designs on the Ottoman Empire.

On April 9 the Provisional Government issued its Declaration on war aims to the Russian people. Ignoring the document's ambiguities, the Constantinople press seized upon what seemed to it to be the statement's most conspicuous feature: Russia's abandonment of annexationist ambitions. All newspapers saw the Declaration as the deathblow to Miliukov's program. *Ikdam* greeted its publication as proof of Russia's desperate need for peace "even though the Foreign Minister continues to talk in his usual way" about continuing the war. *Tanin* felt that Talaat especially would welcome the Declaration since he had publicly singled out Miliukov as the greatest barrier to the establishment of good relations between the new Russian regime and Turkey. That this barrier had now been dismantled *Tanin* was in no doubt at all. It commented editorially:

> On the basis of the Provisional Government's manifesto, a new Russia has come to meet us, one that has done with questions of the Straits and forgets its claim in Anatolia. Between such a Russia and ourselves there is no ground for enmity.[30]

But by the end of the month the press was having second thoughts. Contrary to the expectations engendered by the April 9 promises Russia remained, if only nominally, in the war; worse, Miliukov was still at his post in the Cabinet. *Ikdam* ascribed his perverse continuity "to the complete subjection of Russian liberals to England . . . so strong that it amounts almost to treason." Of greater interest because of the paper's proximity to the Committee was *Tanin*'s caustic rejection of French speculation that the renunciation of Russian war aims might encourage Turkey's withdrawal from the war. It was ridiculous to suppose, *Tanin* remarked, that a feeble Russia could succeed where a mighty Russia had so often failed. Constantinople and the Straits had ceased to be serious issues of wartime diplomacy and strategy.[31]

Now it became the turn of Russian Socialists to be wooed by the Turks who continued to dangle the possibility of real concessions on the Straits. A new minister, widely announced to be a personal friend of Talaat, was dispatched to Stockholm with the mission, according to von Kühlmann, "of fulfilling the Porte's wish to be as close to Russia as possible." Evidently it hoped to profit by means of "the radical Russian parties," since Miliukov had clearly removed himself from consideration as an instrument of Turkish action.[32] Constantinople's eagerness to be of service to the alliance occasionally misfired, at least when it came to tutoring opinion in neutral capitals. The Turkish representative in Switzerland told a correspondent from the

Berner Tageblatt that in questions of Mediterranean strategy his country had "no further interest in caring for England's affairs" and was prepared to accommodate any Russian wishes as long as they did not contradict Turkey's independence. The ensuing speculation in the Swiss press that Turkey was about to open the Dardanelles to her Russian foe prompted some agitated explanations from the Ottoman legation. Its government would negotiate with a "liberal" but not an "imperialist" Russia and only then on issues "which do not by their nature adversely affect the independence and sovereignty of the Turkish Empire."[33] Opening the Straits to Russian vessels clearly fell into this category. Meanwhile, reports circulated in Constantinople itself that in return for abandoning her designs on Turkey and for her exit from the war Russia would be compensated by access to another open sea in the form of a corridor across Norway to the Atlantic.[34]

Four facts emerge from the welter of rumor and speculation. The first and most obvious was that Turkey very much desired Russia to make peace as the prelude to a general cessation of hostilities that would leave the Ottoman Empire undiminished, if exhausted. To encourage Russia to that end the Porte was prepared to discuss, or at least to announce her readiness to discuss Russia's problems of access to the Mediterranean. But these discussions would not take place as long as Miliukov stayed at his post and if Russian Socialists also proved "unrealistic" Turkey would wash her hands of the question until a strong regime in Petrograd was able to speak and act for the entire Russian nation. Early in May the Turks made their choice. On the 4th Miliukov heard from Berne that local Turkish agents now minimized the chances of a speedy conclusion of peace, since Russia was deemed to be in a state of anarchy "and did not yet have a definite form of government." When she finally acquired one and was ready to do business the minister in Sweden was empowered to open negotiations.[35] The patronizing tone from spokesmen for the hereditary enemy stood in painful contrast to the calm assurance of Tsarist condescension toward Turkey. The unpalatable fact could nonetheless not be denied: less than a year after the Emperor of Russia had decreed her place was not in Europe, Turkey was in a good position to contemplate the ruin of her oldest and bitterest foe.

Russia and Bulgaria

The Russian campaign to woo Turkey was so perfunctory and unenthusiastic as to scarcely merit the name. A change, if there was to be one, would come only when Miliukov and his program had vanished or if Turkey herself contemplated imminent military collapse. Neither moment seemed immediately at hand in early May but it took little ingenuity to anticipate that the first eventuality was a good deal closer than the second. Miliukov himself saw far brighter prospects in Germany's other Balkan ally. She was Slav, indebted to Russia for her liberation, with no "Constantinoples" to complicate relations with Petrograd. Better than these, Bulgaria was sensitive to Russian developments and the Russian Foriegn Minister knew her and was known in her better than any other foreign statesman. Bulgaria's abandonment of the German alliance would break the geographic solidarity of the Central Powers and achieve the same strategic results as a Turkish withdrawal at a fraction of the diplomatic cost. Or so it must have looked from Miliukov's viewpoint on March 15.

Bulgaria's entry into the war in October 1915 as a German ally was on three counts a resounding rebuff to Tsarist Russia. It undermined confident claims of Slav solidarity against the Teutonic hordes; it made the realization of Russian wartime ambitions vastly more difficult and produced the impression, even in Petrograd, that Tsarist diplomatic bungling was responsible for still another Entente debacle in the Balkans.[36] This was less than fair to the Imperial Government; its partners too shared in bringing about Bulgaria's decision. Yet more fundamental than any of these was the unhappy legacy of the Second Balkan War.

The Cabinet of Prime Minister Vasil Radoslavov took office in 1913 two weeks after the disastrous Bulgarian offensive that opened the Second Balkan War. The ensuing debacle, ruinously confirmed in the Bucharest Treaty of August 1913, in effect determined the new government's diplomatic priorities: collaboration with Germany and Austria-Hungary and ultimately the reversal of the 1913 verdict. That the first of these tactics implied a weakening of traditional ties with Russia caused no alarm in official St Petersburg, and the incoming Russian minister in Sofia received instructions to maintain uncompromising hostility toward what Sazonov called "the temporary aberrations of Bulgarian foreign policy." If he could achieve the overthrow of the Radoslavov ministry "without fear of exposure" he was to do so, when friendly relations might be re-established between a solicitous Russia and her refractory Balkan protégé.[37] Savinskii hastened to obey, frequented opposition circles virtually from the day he arrived in Sofia and adopted a hectoring tone toward Bulgarian ministers. Far from restoring friendly relations, these tactics succeeded merely in widening the distance between the Bulgarian authorities and "maternal" Russia's embrace.[38]

On the outbreak of war the Tsarist Government assured Radoslavov and the King that Russia was prepared to overlook past difficulties if Sofia, in return, was ready to make some positive display toward the Entente.

Sazonov realized nevertheless that tangible inducements were likely to be more productive of results than appeals to Slav solidarity, especially when these latter were addressed to a ruler largely impervious to such invocations. There was only one inducement guaranteed to bring success and that was Bulgarian acquisition of a province that was not at Russia's disposal.[39] Within a week of the German declaration of war on Russia, Serbia made clear her distaste at the thought of yielding any part of Macedonia to the recently beaten foe; for the next twelve months Russian, British and French diplomacy worked, frequently at cross purposes, to reconcile minimum Bulgarian demands with maximum Serbian concessions.[40] The chances of their mutual "reasonableness" improved or worsened according to the military situation. In November 1914, when Serbian prospects looked grim, Bulgarian diplomats reported that Pašić seemed "conciliatory" and that the Skupština had not registered any strong indignation when told that concessions to Bulgaria were necessary.[41] But a month later, with the Serbian army back in Belgrade, the Prince Regent publicly promised full civil and political rights after the war "to our brothers liberated from the Turks."[42] Macedonia, in other words, would remain Serbian.

In courting Bulgaria both the Central and Entente Powers knew that the side which could offer more in Macedonia and, simultaneously, come closest to victory would win Bulgaria's allegiance. By the first midsummer of war the case for Germany seemed irrefutable. Up to then the best the Entente could hold out was "just compensations" in Macedonia and Eastern Thrace; on June 5, 1915, Austria-Hungary promised that in the event of an Austro-German victory Bulgaria would receive both the "uncontested" and "contested" zones of Macedonia: all this in exchange for her benevolent neutrality.[43] Such a prize for a policy that Sofia was to all intents already pursuing was an offer that Serbia's allies could not hope to match in the three months of bargaining which followed. On September 13 they nerved themselves sufficiently to guarantee Bulgarian possession of two-thirds of Macedonia in return for an immediate declaration of war against Turkey. How her partners planned to coerce Serbia to accept this amputation was not clear; in any event the offer had been overtaken by military developments. One week earlier, encouraged by the Russian loss of Lemberg and Warsaw, King Ferdinand formally bound himself to the Central Empires. A peremptory demand from Petrograd that he break "with the enemies of Slavdom" encountered protestations of "broken hearted regret" but no alteration of policy. On October 11 Bulgarian troops crossed the Serbian frontier; war with the Entente quickly followed.[44]

The easy initial victories, leading to the occupation of all Macedonia and the virtual extinction of the Serbian armies, served from the Bulgarian viewpoint merely to underline the correctness of the Government's decision. The country as a whole acquiesced. In February 1916 the as yet annexationist Center Party leader in the Reichstag, Matthias Erzberger, observed while passing through Sofia that "few Bulgarians now remain Russophiles" and "many" expressed their wish to him that Germany do more to prevent a return of Russophile tendencies.[45] Erzberger's "many" contacts doubtlessly reflected more the Government's careful selection of its guest's Bulgarian visitors than it did national unanimity on the war or on Russia. All the same the press did what it could to convince the reading public to share Erzberger's impressions. Increasingly, public attention was drawn to the Straits rather than to Macedonia as the issue justifying Bulgarian belligerence against Russia. Thus on April 6, 1916, *Narodni Prava*, the major organ of Radoslavov's Liberal Party, anti-Russian and pro-German, wrote "even children know that the secular goal of Tsarist Russian policy is to seize Constantinople [and] the Straits. It is for this reason that we . . . have shown so much hostility to the Russian monarchy."[46] On July 30 the same newspaper explicitly endorsed the opinion expressed by the minister in Bucharest that the reason Bulgaria entered the war was to keep Russia away from the Dardanelles.[47] This was of course a transparent exercise to mobilize public opinion against Bulgaria's liberators and even traditionally pro-Russian elements fell into line. *Dnevnik* on August 16 declared that though Bulgaria was bound to Russia through gratitude for her liberation from the Turks, "we have become alienated from her as a result of her Balkan policy." *Preporets*, speaking for Malinov, leader of the Russophile Democratic Party and a personal friend of Miliukov, welcomed the Rumanian collapse in December as a development which separated Russia even further from her goals at the Straits. Stephen Danev, Prime Minister during the catastrophes of June-July 1913, asked not to be reminded of his pro-Russian past and acknowledged that all parties now agreed that the Russian friendship was dead.[48] Danev's tractability originated at least in part in apprehension at a threatened government probe into his role during the Second Balkan War.[49]

Concern over Russia's war aims also determined Tsarist attitudes toward Bulgaria, nor did Petrograd ever entirely abandon hope that the King might be persuaded to reverse course. In August 1916 Premier Stürmer wrote to the Emperor that the Government's Bulgarian policy should be elaborated on the basis of two requirements, the same two that had dominated official thinking since November 1914: the winning of "Tsargrad" with a minimum of assistance and the reaffirmation of Russian preponderance in Balkan affairs. With all evidence to the contrary, Stürmer insisted that Russia could bring Bulgaria to terms without being compelled to negotiate with her deceitful sovereign. He expanded on this theme for two pages, the essence of his argument being that the Bulgarian opposition should be offered parts of Macedonia, the whole of which Ferdinand's Government now controlled.[50] Only in his concluding paragraph did the Prime Minister confront the more realistic alternative:

> But if . . . superior military considerations demand that Bulgaria's change of side be accomplished as the only means of conquering Constantinople and the Straits, nothing remains but to enter into an agreement with Ferdinand. In this event we must consider the extremely unfavorable consequences to us of such a step, the exposure of our weakness, our alienation from the Serbs, the diminution of our moral authority among the Balkan nations . . . and the inconvenience to us of a strong Bulgaria.[51]

These distasteful prospects restrained the Imperial Government from any new initiatives, even after the Rumanian fiasco in December might reasonably have suggested that "superior military considerations" were now operative. Russia's internal difficulties and military debility precluded any bold new moves from Petrograd. The Government nonetheless stayed firm in its loyalty to the common cause. Bulgarian feelers for a separate Russian peace, conducted through the minister in Berlin, Rizov, as part of a carefully orchestrated German demarche, met with no response whatever.[52]

When revolution disposed of the Russian Tsar, it found his Bulgarian counterpart in firm control of his kingdom. If foreigners wished to do business with Bulgaria they must, willingly or not, turn to Ferdinand, the only man of political consequence in the state. The several parties had the superficial appearance of conventional European politics, calling themselves Liberals, Progressives, Democrats, Nationalists or Socialists, but for all practical purposes they were scarcely more than uneasy coalitions around an individual head without much effectiveness independent of the throne. The make-up of the National Assembly helped to maintain this state of affairs. A gerrymandered government bloc of 129 faced an opposition numerically only fifteen less. Yet the far Left alone could be counted on as resolutely and implacably hostile to every aspect of the Royal government's policy. Others, like Malinov's Democrats and Danev's Progressive Liberals, disliked Ferdinand's anti-Russian stance but confined their opposition to verbal sniping at Radoslavov. The one man of substance who had gone beyond this was the Agrarian Party leader Alexander Stambuliski. In September 1915 he had challenged the King directly in a famous scene, threatening him with the loss of his head were he to take the nation into war with Russia. He paid for his insolence with a three-year prison term; no

Agrarian or Socialist figure could fill his shoes. The ranks of Bulgarian Socialists were themselves in disarray between "Narrow" and "Broad" factions corresponding to the internationalist and defensist groupings elsewhere on the European Left. Throughout 1917 the "Broads" faithfully echoed the chauvinist line from the Court on Bulgaria's purposes in the war.

With his sympathetic knowledge of Bulgaria, the Provisional Government's first Foreign Minister was sure he could convince that country's ruler of the advantages in free Russia's friendship. On March 20 he alerted the Russian charge in Berne, A. M. Onu, that the right moment should not be missed to further Bulgarian thoughts of breaking with her present Allies and joining the Entente. Onu was directed not to lose contact with representatives of the Bulgarian government "which must surely understand that the new position of things here provides them with favorable conditions for the restoration of former unanimity with Russia." Desultory conversations ensued between Onu and various persons he described as "several Bulgarian figures in Switzerland"; the indefatigable Rizov meanwhile renewed his blandishments from Stockholm and Christiania. As neither side was interested in leading its respective country out of the war the two sets of talks unsurprisingly failed to make any progress.[53]

Even assuming a Bulgarian interest in Russian overtures, the old problem remained from 1915 of reconciling the price Bulgaria would demand, certainly nothing less than the whole of Macedonia and probably a good deal in other adjacent regions, with loyalty to Serbia and Venezelist Greece.[54] Miliukov brushed this to one side; precise conditions to be offered would depend on whether Bulgaria simply dropped out of the war or could be brought into the Entente camp. Buchanan and Paléologue were told they must renounce all sentimental ideas and look at the question from a practical point of view only.[55] There was some irony here, perhaps detectable to Miliukov's hearers; at any rate their governments were willing to cooperate for the time being. Premier Alexandre Ribot admitted Russian primacy in Bulgarian matters and the need for "reasonable" concessions from Serbia and Greece. These were of course the identical issues that had bedevilled the Entente's Balkan dealings for some time already and, in case Miliukov failed to get the point, Ribot went on to stress that French public opinion—not hitherto noticeably voluble on the subject—was "warmly interested" in seeing that the security of Bulgaria's two Macedonian oriented neighbors was not endangered.[56] The British and Italian Cabinets accepted Miliukov's proposals with a better grace though segments in the former body privately doubted the chances of success. Balfour's assessment at the year's end summarized as well as anything his attitude to the Balkan maelstrom throughout 1917. The patrician shrug at remote and incomprehensible feuds can almost be seen:

> "Events must probably still further develop before the path of true wisdom becomes clear, either to friends or enemies. The Balkan peoples with all their admirable qualities are much more faithful to their hates than to their loves and would much rather injure a rival than benefit themselves."[57]

There was certainly little reason for anyone in the know to suppose that Miliukov would succeed where so many had failed. A Foreign Office minute initialled without comment by Balfour deprecated the Russian's confidence in his ability to work miracles upon Bulgaria's ruler: "he has never had much weight with the King."[58] Rome showed a greater interest. The dominant member of the Boselli Cabinet, Foreign Minister Baron Sidney Sonnino, seconded Miliukov's ideas. The Allies should not be discouraged by Bulgaria's record in bargaining with the Entente. Sonnino had none of Ribot's reservations in favor of Greece and Serbia and was far from dismayed at the prospect of their sacrifices to a friendly Bulgaria.[59]

The views of Russia's most prominent Bulgarophil naturally attracted Bulgarian attentions some months before the March Revolution. The Sofia press gladly endorsed Miliukov's Duma criticisms of Tsarism's Balkan policies but varied widely in assessing Miliukov's present attitude toward Bulgaria. Sharpest censure came from each end of the political spectrum. *Narodni Prava* dismissed Miliukov's "empty, liberal phrases." If ever he were to come to power he would soothe Bulgaria with Macedonia so as to take Constantinople "and afterwards, through the process of natural evolution by which the strong triumph over the weak, [he] would find it quite fair that Russia should lay hands on both Bulgaria and Macedonia." *Narodni Prava* in particular objected to the "fawning" of traditionally pro-Russian press organs over Miliukov. This was a slap at *Preporets* and *Mir*, both of whom had asserted that Miliukov's criticisms of his country's errors should justly prompt Bulgarians to admit their own mistakes and degree of responsibility for the present bad state of relations between the two nations.[60] On the far Left, Dimitur Blagoev, head of the "Narrow" wing of Bulgarian Socialism, attacked those of his flock who thought Russian foreign policy would cease to be dangerous "if Professor Miliukov, the well known friend of Bulgarians" were at the helm. "This ideology is as dangerous as it is unjustifiable. A liberal and bourgeois Russia headed by P. N. Miliukov is even more dangerous for the Balkans and Bulgaria than reactionary Russia."[61] Two months later, commenting on the Cadet war program as outlined by Miliukov in the recently published volume *Chego Zhdet Rossiia Ot Voiny?*

[What Does Russia Expect From The War?], *Rabotnicheski Vestnik*, Blagoev's paper, noted that any judgment was superfluous: "these then are Miliukov's wishes, the same Miliukov who, persecuted by Tsarism, found not just an asylum in our midst but a fraternal welcome."[62]

First press reaction to the March Revolution reflected the conviction that a victorious peace was in sight. On March 16 and 17 *Narodni Prava* remarked that everyone saw in the Revolution the nearing end of the war and went on to gloat that "none is now capable of preventing the imminent destruction of Russia." The "Broad" *Narod* agreed: "the revolutionaries will now understand that the hope of victory is irretrievably lost and their only task is to make peace." A week later *Preporets* wrote soothingly that Russian security could be guaranteed without further war and that it was up to the new rulers of Russia to realize this and act accordingly. Meanwhile Rizov, "who knows Russia perfectly," predicted closer Russo-German ties and the triumph of the Russian extremists "under Kerenskii and Chkheidze."[63]

All sections of official Bulgaria welcomed the Russian revolution and disputed its significance for their own country. Radoslavov, mirroring the King's views as he would continue to do until their joint flight to Switzerland eighteen months later, spoke still in the most uncompromising terms of Bulgaria's need to withstand whatever government ruled in Petrograd. Blagoev warned Bulgarian Socialists not to waste any sympathy on the new regime since "aristocratic and democratic Russia" remained the enemy as long as she protected Serbia and coveted the Straits. In the National Assembly, however, the "Broad" Socialist Pastukhov pointed to the Russian revolution as an illustration of the fate awaiting those governments who persisted in ignoring the rights of opposition groups. He congratulated Russian liberalism for helping the people give voice to their grievances. The relevance of his words to the local scene was not lost on his audience, one of whom proceeded to make the point in specific terms. Alexander Malinov greeted the downfall of Russian autocracy. A revolution such as the one in Russia "for constitutional rights, for progress and culture cannot but be welcomed by the Bulgarian Parliament and democracy with profound sympathy," declared Miliukov's correspondent in the name of Russia's Bulgarian friends. Furthermore, he was happy to see in the unanimity of the revolution convincing proof that the dire predictions of an immediate civil collapse were not justified. Malinov was careful in these remarks to stress Bulgaria's need to hold fast to her alliances, yet government spokesmen reacted sharply to his reception of the news from Petrograd. His "Russianism" was unworthy of a Bulgarian patriot and was as much to be regretted as the hopes of "Broads" and "Narrows" in the Russian Left.[64] In fact, Malinov's criticisms were carefully contained so as to make him in foreign eyes "the perfect leader of His Majesty's Loyal Opposition."[65] His sentiments certainly changed none of the political facts of life in Sofia. On April 5 the Assembly was prorogued with the King and his Prime Minister still in firm control of events.

The Provisional Government's manifesto of March 27/April 9 made a considerable impact in Bulgaria. Official hostility in Press and Parliament abated slightly and for the first time there was speculation that Miliukov's position might not totally exclude the possibility of Russo-Bulgarian cordiality. In an obvious gesture to the man now presiding over Russian diplomacy, the official reaction from Sofia appealed to "the best representatives of Russia's liberal intelligentsia" to recognize the justice of Bulgaria's cause against autocratic Russia: "it is a title of honor for Bulgaria and to her governments' merit that they have always granted the promptest hospitality to the persecuted fighters for Russian freedom."[66] On April 14 *L'Echo de Bulgarie*, a semi-official publication representing the Foreign Ministry, hailed "this remarkable, even extraordinary document." The War Ministry organ *Voenni Izvestiia* wished to know whether Miliukov had changed his opinions on Bulgaria since assuming his post. The paper recalled Miliukov's background as a national friend "who has published precious pages in the Bulgarian cause." In the past he had been "the one Russian who supported with the most disinterested loyalty the just cause of our people." But what of the present? *Voenni Izvestiia* saw slight reason for optimism:

> On the one hand Mr Miliukov is at the head of the Russian Revolution which proposes to repair the faults of past Russian policy. On the other he has stated from the first day of his arrival at the post of minister that the revolutionary government will respect all the treaties concluded between Russia and her Allies and that he will carry on the struggle to the complete realization of the Entente's program.

Fearing that this would include Macedonia's restoration to the Serbs, *Voenni Izvestiia* took what comfort it could from Miliukov's failure to say so openly.[67] The hitherto implacable *Narodni Prava* commented that Bulgaria should, after all, be able to come to some agreement with the men "who as martyrs to their country's liberty found hospitable refuge in democratic Bulgaria."[68] Old time pro-Russian elements cautiously took heart. The German minister cabled Berlin that local Russophiles now believed that with Miliukov and Guchkov in charge of Russia's destinies the two peoples would easily be able to come to some arrangement "on a Slav basis."[69] This may have been Malinov's fondest hope—or so he was taunted in the National Assembly—but it struck no echoes from Bulgaria's German-born

King.

As it became obvious that Miliukov attached little importance to the April 9 document these hopeful speculations began to die away. From the far left came *Rabotnicheski Vestnik*'s assurance that the Russian revolution had thrown Tsardom's Bulgarian apologists onto that favorite Marxist depository, the rubbish heap of history. Recent events in Russia, the paper maintained, opened to Bulgaria and to the Balkan peoples generally "brilliant prospects and great new roads, prospects of an approaching peace and roads to a democratic alliance."[70] Some ambivalence was evident in this diatribe. In theory opposed to all imperialisms, alliances and annexations, the "Narrows" accepted the German link perforce as the only way to undo the injustices perpetrated in 1913. They expressed satisfaction with the victories resulting from that link, victories "which have raised Bulgaria to the rank of first Balkan state." Self-determination was also a qualified virtue in *Rabotnicheski Vestnik*'s opinion. It could hardly be universally applied "without seriously damaging the social and economic interests of various countries and of the civilized world as a whole." It must be subordinated to the far more important principle of international federation. The Balkans, Austria-Hungary and Russia herself were not fit areas for the application of the principle so beloved by most Socialists.[71] Possibly the paper had the unspoken thought that "the first Balkan state" would lead the way to the local fulfillment of this dream. Anyway, *Narodni Prava* had no apparent qualms in reprinting some of these views with approving comment that concluded with some rhetorical indignation:

> "Are we supposed to turn yet again toward Russia? When Miliukov speaks of Constantinople and Greater Serbia our Russophiles are utterly quiet. Will it be for ever? No. Just two words were needed, words spoken by the new Russian Government in favor of peace and Bulgarian Russophiles come out of hiding once again. . . . Autocratic or democratic, Russia remains the enemy of all Bulgarians as long as she has not renounced her claims on the Straits and her wish to unite and liberate all Serbs."[72]

That this was not just the viewpoint of the political extremes emerged from the occasionally anti-government *Mir* which announced on May 7 that if Miliukov wanted to create thousands more victims to his policies, that was his business: "our duty is to conquer."[73]

By May it was clear that Miliukov's blandishments and reputation did not suffice to change official opinions in Sofia on the developments in Russia or on the war. While sympathy for the liberator undoubtedly did exist in the peasant population—and Stambuliski's sharing it had led to his outburst at Ferdinand—its presence had not yet seriously affected the government's external policies. Since November 1916, when Monastir had been lost to an Entente attack in which a Russian contingent had distinguished itself, Bulgarian conscripts successfully held their own on the Macedonian front against all assaults, including a spring offensive from the Salonika armies that cost the Entente some 14,000 dead and no progress. War weariness was growing, to be sure, and in a country of low population and economic resources it was bound to increase the longer hostilities continued. Even so, the quadruple combination of Macedonian victory, police repression, a divided and ineffectual Parliamentary opposition and general ignorance of what was going on in Russia gave Ferdinand and Radoslavov a relatively free hand until well after the Bolshevik coup.

On the diplomatic front the revolution provoked a variety of responses from Bulgarian authorities. The first of these reflected the optimism common to the Central Powers that the chances of a separate Russian peace were now much improved and should not be imperilled by any hasty action from Germany or her allies. Rizov, who enjoyed the undeserved reputation in Berlin of a Russian expert—possibly because he had attended university with Miliukov—pushed this view with vigor. He advised State Secretary Zimmermann that Germany refrain from offensive military action against Russia lest the Provisional Government be put in a position to claim that its enemies fought for the restoration of the old regime. Rizov's counsel coincided with German opinion but he was not averse to taking the credit anyway. He made no effort to hide his eagerness for some arrangement that could accommodate both sides; according to reports reaching the German Foreign Office he had gone so far as to remark in Christiania that peace could be had between Russia and the Central Powers on the basis of the status quo ante and that he personally knew of no reason why Constantinople should not pass to Russia.[74] This was certainly in excess of his instructions; in any case Oberndorff, the German minister in Sofia, sent word to Berlin that "local opinion" (i.e. the Court) did not support Rizov's siren song to Petrograd. Zimmermann could rest assured that Bulgaria was still unswerving in its devotion to the German alliance.[75] As long as Miliukov remained in office, the Bulgarian government could use the specter of Russian imperialism to brace those like Malinov who were anxiously scanning the horizon for some sign of Russian softening.

In the face of Miliukov's obstinacy Bulgarian attention, like Turkish, shifted to the Russian Left. Diplomats abroad set out to discover the thoughts of expatriate and obscure Russian Socialists on the question of a separate peace between Russia and her foes. According to von Kühlmann's account from Constantinople, Bulgarian agents concluded from these conversations that the Provisional Government would soon make peace under pressure from left-wing opinion. Terms would include an autonomous Poland under Russian sovereignty, Galicia and Bukovina for Russia and the neutralization of the Straits. Kuhlmann feared that if these improbable conditions were, in fact, met so that Russia dropped out of the war, Germany's relations with her allies would be radically altered and not for the better.[76] The ambassador was generally more sensitive to the security of Germany's Eastern frontiers than her Western and as State Secretary a few months later he would try without success to shift German priorities accordingly. In May, however, Zimmermann saw no need for concern over yet another spate of rumors, even of the kind and in the terms forwarded from Constantinople. He encouraged Rizov to enlist the services of "Broads" and "Narrows" to work on their Russian opposite numbers in a joint campaign to force the Provisional Government to the bargaining table.[77] Rizov's own intervention in Petrograd in the form of a letter to Maxim Gor'kii on the advantages of a separate Russian peace produced nothing but journalistic abuse for the would-be peacemaker.[78]

In spite of German calmness the March Revolution was not without its effect on Bulgaria's relations with her overwhelming ally. She, no less than her partners, fervently wanted Russia to quit the war. With them, Bulgarian authorities lost no opportunity publicly to proclaim devotion to the common cause; privately they suspected the loyalty of their allies to purely Bulgarian interests. Every rumor suggesting a German, Austrian or Turkish willingness to make a deal with Russia was promptly reported back to Sofia.[79] Suspicions hardened whenever allied leaders got together for sessions from which Bulgarians were excluded. On April 1st the minister in Vienna sounded a loud alarm to the effect that the Chief of the German Imperial General Staff, von Hindenburg, and the Ottoman War Minister, Enver Pasha, had just met and agreed to offer "half Rumania" to Russia as bait to leave the war.[80] Details of the "half" to be offered were not provided but the point was lost in a wider issue more galling to the Sofia regime. Since the Rumanian collapse of the previous December, Ferdinand and Radoslavov had been bombarding Berlin with demands that the Rumanian owned Dobruja be handed over to Bulgaria: now came news out of the blue that Rumania's partition was imminent and not to involve her hungry and vengeful southern neighbor. Indignation was all the keener as the southern half of the province had been lost to Rumania in 1913 and the whole of it had been promised to Bulgaria two years later in the event Rumania joined the Entente. In addition, the prospect of revolutionary Russia being brought that much closer to his own borders was not one that Ferdinand could relish at any time. Of course rumors of far reaching moves were and are an endemic feature of wartime diplomacy and it is a matter of record that senior German and Austrian officials held periodic discussions on the post-victory redrawing of Eastern and South-Eastern European frontiers. Russian events quickened the pace of these sessions. On March 16 Chancellor Bethmann-Hollweg and Austro-Hungarian Foreign Minister Czernin heard each other's ideas on land redistribution in Eastern Europe in the light of the Tsar's overthrow. Rumanian partition did come up in these talks, with Bethmann advancing the suggestion of the transfer to Russia of Northern Moldavia. This collided with Austrian dreams of future Balkan expansion. The top level of the German government continued to see the Balkans as an arena where the Great Powers could slake their territorial thirsts. Such seems to have been the tone of the discussions held at Army Headquarters at Kreuznach on April 23 between the Emperor, his Chancellor, von Hindenburg and Chief Quartermaster-General Ludendorff. No time was spent on Bulgarian claims and it in fact appears that throughout all the discussions of far reaching plans two year old commitments to the junior partner in the alliance were simply sidelined.[81]

If it accomplished nothing else the Dobruja question served to remind Bulgarian leaders of their total lack of leverage in the alliance with Germany, a deficiency that Austro-Hungarian ministers could also notice in their own case. All that Radoslavov could do was to wave the possibility of "events such as those in Russia" occurring in Bulgaria unless justice were done.[82] The tactic enjoyed a brief success. Zimmermann diffidently approached the Supreme Command to make at least a gesture in the desired direction; Hindenburg's refusal stiffened his resolve.[83] On April 28 he told a closed session of the Reichstag's Budget Committee that the government had deliberately not given Bulgaria administrative control of the Dobruja "because we did not wish to encourage the hope and appetite that later they could take it all"—this despite a formal Austro-German promise of September 1915 that the Bulgarians could do precisely that.[84] Two weeks later the State Secretary heard that an enraged Ferdinand was going to offer Germany the choice of yielding the Dobruja or facing a separate Bulgarian peace with the Entente.[85] If actually made, the threat was a meaningless bluff. Dobruja may have loomed large in royal calculations but Macedonia loomed far larger and that fact gave Germany complete freedom to respect or ignore Bulgarian wishes in matters of wartime strategy. German civilian and military chiefs alike were confident that the partner referred to in an internal Foreign Office paper (possibly written by a Rumanian) as "only a more savage type of Russian" had bound its fate irrevocably to the Central Powers.[86] The Wilhelmstrasse would eventually release the Dobruja when all Russian and Rumanian options were played out. Until then, nothing remained for the small Balkan ally but to go on fighting in Macedonia and await developments in Petrograd.

CHAPTER IV
BALKAN FRIENDS

By March 1917 Russia's two Balkan Allies were prostrate. Serbia succumbed fifteen months previously to a triple Austro-German-Bulgarian assault; after an epic flight her civilian leaders were now suppliant exiles on Corfu. Nine months after the Serbian catastrophe Rumania entered the war, buoyed by lavish Entente promises and much self-esteem, promptly to meet the same fate. The military burdens consequent to these disasters fell upon a Russia utterly incapable of effecting any real improvement. The diplomatic legacy was equally bleak.

The Serbian Future

In three years of war the non-military price of Russia's intervention on Serbia's behalf had become progressively higher and unpalatable. The first two notes of disharmony, sounded with what was to seem to Russian politicians a maddening persistence, came in the opening months of hostilities: the "sacro egoismo" attendant upon an Italian alliance and a competing cacophony of Slav opinion on Serbia's future.

On September 21, 1914, Prime Minister Pašić made known to Sazonov his country's territorial aspirations. His attention concentrated largely on obtaining a favorable frontier to the north of Belgrade in the Hungarian governed Banat of Temesvar. Pašić was vague about those regions where declared Italian interests were greatest, that is Istria and the Dalmatian coast, though a further message to Petrograd indicated his readiness to concede Western Istria with Trieste.[1] But these were areas with large Slav populations who could not be presumed enthusiastic at the prospect of exchanging Hapsburg for Italian rule. Three prominent Croatian exiles from the Dual Monarchy—Ante Trumbić, a one-time member of the Reichsrat, Ivan Mestrović, a well known sculptor and Frano Supilo, formerly a member of the Hungarian Diet—called upon the Entente ambassadors in Rome to protest Italian designs upon their homeland.

Encountering little but sympathetic noises, the three-man delegation resolved to press its case in the four Entente capitals.[2]

Initial results were discouraging. With the aid of Serbian diplomats, Dupilo interviewed French and British leaders on their attitude toward the Italian position. His alarmed conclusions prompted him to help organize, in January 1915, a Yugoslav Committee whose job it would be to publicize and defend Austrian South Slav interests during the several months of intensive bargaining with Italy. Supilo placed his greatest faith in Russia. His program, as he explained to Pašić and the Russian minister, Prince G. N. Trubetskoi, was entirely straightforward. He sought the liberation of the South Slav nationalities, Serbs, Croats and Slovenes, and their union with Serbia: was Pašić prepared to work toward this end? After a brief pause the Prime Minister replied "for myself and Serbia, we are ready."[3] So too was Trubetskoi. He urged upon Sazonov the usefulness to Russia of a large centralized Slav state "where the dominant role would indisputably belong to the Serbian Orthodox nucleus."[4] It is evident that the minister's vision of the prospective state coincided closely with Pašić's own views on the subject: centralization, Orthodoxy and Serbian direction were features unlikely to recommend themselves to Supilo's countrymen. He was at any rate sufficiently encouraged by Trubetskoi's blessing to depart for Petrograd with an optimism that did not long survive his reception in the Russian capital.

Supilo arrived to open his campaign at the moment when the Tsarist Government was abandoning its resistance to paying Rome's price for the alliance so eagerly desired in London and Paris. They, rather than Petrograd, "where there is no lack of sympathy for the Slav cause," should be the capitals engaging the Committee's attention.[5] To further incautious protests from Supilo's aggrieved colleagues, an exasperated Sazonov snapped that he knew "nothing" about Russia's Croat and Slovene enemies and would be opposed to even half a day's warfare to free them from Austria-Hungary.[6]

By the time of this outburst and doubtlessly contributing to it, the fate of the South Slavs had been decided. The prospect of a million fresh Italian troops was irresistible and though Sazonov argued against replacing Hapsburg hegemony with Italian, he was defending a lost cause and he knew it.[7] The Treaty of London of April 1915 secured most of Italy's territorial desiderata. Trieste, most of the Adriatic islands, a third of Dalmatia, de facto control over Albania—all these and other prizes testified to a smashing Italian triumph and a corresponding defeat for the Yugoslav Committee and Tsarist efforts. The Russian Government itself was gloomy but resigned to the inevitable. The Emperor himself acknowledged that on many points Italy's spoils directly contradicted Slav aspirations but, in Sazonov's words, it was too late to complain, "even though complaints are justifiable."[8] One could only hope that the strategic gains would be commensurate with the diplomatic losses.

With Italy in, the next Entente diplomatic target was Bulgaria. Here Serbian, rather than South Slav interests were at immediate issue and the outcome of six months of frantic cajoling of Tsar Ferdinand was even more disastrous to Russia's Balkan prestige than the London Treaty. Nevertheless Pašić would not repeat Supilo's error; recriminations to Petrograd would clearly be worse than useless. On the contrary, once established on Corfu, the Premier's first priority was to set about refurbishing his government's links abroad. In so doing, the long simmering difficulties with the Yugoslav Committee over the future composition and frontiers of enlarged Serbia were forced into the open.

In the spring of 1916 Pašić and the Prince Regent embarked upon a tour of Entente capitals. In London they found Sir Edward Grey sympathetic to the post-war union of Serbs and South Slavs. His reticence to be further drawn on the subject probably reflected his belief, shortly thereafter expressed to Miliukov, that such a union affected Russia more than any other Power.[9] Pašić himself referred in a restrained way to Britain's great Eastern ally: "in the past our great friend and protectress."[10] What seemed like an overly delicate approach may have resulted from an awareness of the notorious pre-war dislike of British Liberals for anything that smacked of Russian expansion to the South-West. Such reservations did not, however, prevent a warm welcome to the Serbian delegation once it reached Petrograd. At a press conference in the Russian capital Pašić spoke in cordial tones of the Entente alliance and provoked an uproar in Yugoslav Committee circles by admitting publicly Italy's right to preponderance in the Adriatic.[11] It was now apparent to all that a gulf existed between the Serbian government and the Committee on the crucial issue of Italy's role in the South Slav future.

The fears that had induced Pašić to journey abroad and openly defend the Entente treaties were shared by Serbian diplomats. The consul in Odessa, Marko Cemović, drew up a long memorandum, detailing the reasons why Russia in particular should continue to favor her small ally. Cemović was known personally to the Emperor and had managed by his lurid portrait of Serbian sufferings in persuading Nicholas to authorize, in January 1916, the formation of a volunteer division out of Russia's South Slav prisoners of war.[12] Where he had succeeded once he might succeed again; in late November his petition, endorsed by Pašić, went off to Petrograd. It made remarkable reading; nothing illustrated better where Pašić's emotional loyalties lay. At a time when Russia's Balkan position was daily disintegrating, Russian armies in retreat and Serbia herself occupied by the enemy,

Pašić, through Cemović, looked for Russian arms to restore Serbia, "on whom depends the liberation and unification of Serbs, Croats and Slovenes." The document, couched in the most submissive terms and referring to the Tsar as "our dear and merciful Father-Protector," expanded on Serbian sufferings and called for massive Entente aid in restoring Serbian prestige in the eyes of South Slavs "and neighboring non-Slav states," a reference to Italy and Rumania.[13] The memorandum skillfully combined appeals to Russian Orthodox sympathies with the reminder of the strategic value of a Greater Serbian barrier to German expansion in South-East Europe. As such it might well have won over Nicholas II had not anguished telegrams from his wife announcing Rasputin's disappearance at that moment distracted the Imperial attentions.[14] The question was not raised again, but Tsarist Russian relations with the Serbian authorities remained as close as ever. Thus, when Nicholas' system vanished on March 15, a dismayed Pašić faced the uninviting prospect, in the words of one of his ministers, of "begin[ning] our work all over again."[15]

* * *

The Yugoslav Committee had meanwhile of necessity followed quite a different course. South Slav protests after the London Treaty provoked only annoyance from Russian officials, nor would Pašić's supporters accept Committee claims to speak on behalf of all Hapsburg Serbs, Croats and Slovenes.[16] That the Committee did so claim was put beyond any doubt two weeks after Entente signatures were affixed to the London agreement. On May 12, 1915, a Committee manifesto from London announced the decision of all South Slavs to join together with Serbia in an independent nation whose internal organization would be determined later "in accordance with its needs and desires."[17] Vagueness on the future state's internal organization was not duplicated in plans for its external frontiers; three days later a note presented to the British, Russian and French foreign ministers demanded borders for the new Yugoslav state beyond anything yet enunciated. Serbia, Montenegro, Bosnia-Herzogovina, Dalmatia, Croatia, Slovenia with Fiume, Istria with Trieste, the Banat, Southern Carinthia and Western Styria were all included in the Committee's program. These include territories already assigned to Italy; equally important, fulfillment obviously required the dissolution of the Austro-Hungarian Empire.[18]

The Tsarist government followed no consistent policy in questions concerning the post-war future of its great Balkan rival. From August to December 1914 the government and Nicholas II himself swung between favoring a truncated Hapsburg state and one divided into its national components.[19] Neither Sazonov nor his two Tsarist successors ever formally committed Russia to the total destruction of Austria-Hungary, nor to her preservation. Entente victory would cost the Dual Monarchy territorial losses; such was the tradition in Austrian defeats, and Russia herself was pledged in two instances, to Italy and Rumania, to insure the transfer of sovereignty. But Sazonov could not have been blind to the dangers implicit in any more radical solution of the Hapsburg Empire's future. As the astute former Minister of Finance, Sergei Witte, told Paléologue, the proclamation of republics upon the fall of the Central Empires would assuredly entail the death of Tsarism.[20] The nationality principle was a two-edged sword for the Russian government to turn against another multi-national, dynastic state. In fact, once the initial euphoria wore off and victory receded, Tsarist ministers ceased to concern themselves unduly with the future organization of the Dual Monarchy. Minor officials might so amuse themselves but their recommendations had no impact on Imperial policies.[21] Moreover, as Germany extended her sway into the Balkans, feelings in conservative Petrograd circles grew that anti-German barriers should be erected in South-East Europe once the Entente had triumphed. The dismemberment of a large, conservative monarchy was unlikely to appeal to Tsarist ministers as the ideal way to achieve this goal, and Miliukov told Sir Edward Grey during their 1916 conversation that for this reason Sazonov now opposed the dissolution of Austria-Hungary.[22] Exiled Slav subjects of Francis Joseph took note of Russia's failure to endorse their own position. In August 1916 Supilo, discouraged by Pašić's unwavering devotion to Russia, told Eduard Benes in London, correctly, that the Tsarist government "[had] no Slav plan and no anti-Austrian policy."[23] Yugoslav and Czech leaders agreed that there could be no satisfaction of Central and East European nationality problems until the Entente Great Powers accepted their demand for the total dissolution of the Monarchy.

With the Tsarist government disinclined to consider the Yugoslav program, the Committee's Petrograd representative, Dr. Ante Mandić, necessarily occupied himself with his other major concern, the volunteer unit formed in Odessa at consul Cemović's instance. By March 1917 there were two divisions, totalling some 30,000 men, and several contentious problems.[24] The officer corps was heavily Serbian, imported from the Regular Serbian army, and resisted concessions to South Slav sentiment, such as naming the unit Yugoslav instead of Serbian.[25] This was not finally done until 1918; in the meantime national tensions within the Odessa troops tended to lessen Mandić's already slight prestige with the Foreign Ministry, where he would hold "empty conversations with irresponsible secretaries."[26] Since he was not going to find much sympathy in official circles, he had to look elsewhere—with greater success. He established good relations with a number of Russian intellectuals who, in Mandić's later testimony, "gave sincere, friendly and disinterested support" to the Yugoslav cause.[27]

Of especial moment in his contacts with intellectual figures were Mandić's connections with opposition groups in the Duma. At the request of the British historian of Eastern Europe, Robert Seton-Watson, Bernard Pares introduced the young Committee delegate to his friends in the Progressive Bloc.[28] According to his own evidence Mandić impressed his audience sufficiently to be invited to address private meetings, chaired by Miliukov, when the future of the nationalities of Central and South-Eastern Europe was under discussion.[29] Pares admitted later how effective their guest was in presenting his views; "they carried conviction to all of us."[30] The future Premier of the Provisional Government, Prince G. N. L'vov, spoke for a majority in the Bloc in declaring that the new co-operation between Yugoslav Committee members in Paris and London and emigré Slavs in America "was proof of the new times and of the desire and necessity of unification."[31] But the most outspoken convert to Mandić's side was P. N. Miliukov. On March 24, 1916, he demanded in the Duma that, in addition to Turkey, "another parasite state, Austria-Hungary," be destroyed. He left details for the future to decide but the occasion was significant as Miliukov's first public commitment to the goal of Austro-Hungarian dismemberment. He went on to remind his audience—and here Mandić's influence is unmistakable—that some members of the Dual Monarchy's yet unliberated peoples were then in Russia as war prisoners. These were the future citizens of nations allied to Russia by blood and friendship: "let us lighten the serf-like nature of their labors . . ., let us do what we can so that these citizens take back from their involuntary residence here strong and sincere ties with Russia."[32] These words fulfilled Mandić's highest hopes. For the remainder of the year Miliukov continued to endorse and even surpass the most extreme position of the Yugoslav Committee.[33] Whatever else the March revolution meant, to Mandić at least it brought immeasurable encouragement and relief.

On March 22 the Petrograd representative of the Yugoslav Committee arrived at the Foreign Ministry for his first interview with Miliukov as minister. It is not difficult to imagine Mandić's feelings as he entered the familiar building on Palace Square: this time at least he would not be fobbed off on "irresponsible secretaries." The ostensible purpose of his visit was to offer congratulations and thanks for past kindnesses. More urgently, however, Mandić hoped to be able to persuade Miliukov to make a formal statement binding the new regime to the Yugoslav program. While waiting in an anteroom, Mandić spoke to two assistants who proved encouraging. A.

M. Petriaev, counsellor of the Ministry's Second Department which supervised Balkan affairs, himself the author of a 1917 study on the Straits, and his deputy Nekrasov both favored Mandić's aims and expressed confidence that Miliukov could not easily refuse a request from the Yugoslav Committee.[34] Their forecast proved correct. Miliukov assured Mandić that his opinions on Yugoslav unity remained the same and underlined the claim by dismissing Priklonskii from his post and merging its functions with Petriaev's department.[35]

Private assurance was followed by public commitment. Two days later, exactly one year after his Duma speech calling for the dissolution of Austria-Hungary, Miliukov announced *inter alia* the government's intention "to create a solidly organized Yugoslavia . . . around glorious Serbia as an insurmountable barrier to German aspirations in the Balkans."[36] Committee joy was unbounded. From London, Ante Trumbić echoed Miliukov's sentiments, adroitly including a reference to the subject closest to Miliukov's heart:

> We are deeply touched [Trumbic wrote] by the sincere attention of Mother Russia, who in the first days of the new regime, at once showed through you . . . her traditional motherly feelings for Serbia. . . . At the same time Russia has indicated the necessity of uniting the South Slavs in one state with glorious Serbia at its head. . . . It is the unanimous wish of all Serbs, Croats and Slovenes that united Yugoslavia should serve in the Balkans as the prop of a democratic and Slav policy, and that on the Danube, as well as on the Adriatic, there should be a barrier against German pressure in the east and against Constantinople.[37]

Frano Supilo waxed even more enthusiastic, as well he might after his many disappointments at the hands of Miliukov's predecessors: "45 million Slavs, culturally enslaved by Germandom can now have faith and hope in their redemption." He placed himself at Miliukov's disposal to this end, having no doubts of his welcome "from the great friend of the Croat cause." For the Committee the new minister was a last best Russian hope in the face of two dreaded dangers: a negotiated Entente peace with Austria-Hungary or the triumph of the No Annexation formula in Petrograd and the other Allied capitals. Either of these could leave South Slavs under Hapsburg rule and frustrate two years of hard work.[39] Miliukov returned a guarded reply to these effusions, repeating his sympathy for Yugoslav aspirations. He hoped that the revolution would give "just satisfaction to all legitimate desires of small nationalities."[40]

There was a noticeable restraint in this reply, one not entirely in keeping with his pre-revolutionary fervor in Mandić's cause nor with his post-revolutionary willingness to orate on other aspects of his diplomatic program. He may in fact have become aware that that program now contained two irreconcilable elements. It was impossible for the Provisional Government to remain loyal to Russia's treaty commitments and, simultaneously, plan for a Yugoslav state, especially along the lines proposed by the London Committee and endorsed by Miliukov himself. The Treaty of London provided very definitely for Italian control of most of the Adriatic coastline, while agreements with Rumania in 1915 and 1916 had conceded the Banat. Miliukov had no reason to suppose in March 1917 that Italy might yield on territorial questions and in Rumania's case he specifically rejected a Serbian appeal to force Rumanian compliance in revising the treaties relating to her post-victory gains.[41] While it is true that Miliukov's statement, together with his other public pronouncements on foreign policy, were soon to lose their significance as expressions of Russian intentions, his promises on Yugoslav unity remained to symbolize his basically unrealistic assessment of Russia's diplomatic objectives in the summer of 1917.

The downfall of the Tsarist regime came as an unpleasant and totally unexpected shock to the exiled government on Corfu. Most of Russia's new rulers were unknown to it and the new Foreign Minister's reputation augured ill for Serbian interests, as Pašić conceived them. His burning concern at once became to assess how the Tsar's removal would affect Serbia abroad and his administration on Corfu. On March 21, Lyuba Davidović, a member of Pašić's cabinet then resident in Geneva, gave the Prime Minister his view of the altered situation. He was not optimistic. "I fear," he wrote, "for the success of our cause in Russia. . . . In place of those who once determined Russia's stand on foreign policy questions, there have appeared new people, with whom our ties are weak or non-existent." Pašić must act quickly to make contact with Russia's new government. Miliukov, "today one of the most influential men in Russia," was clearly the key man. Ruefully Davidović acknowledged that no one in the Serbian cabinet had foreseen the possibility of Miliukov's appointment. This neglect must now be remedied, even though relations with the new minister up until then had been "if not unfriendly, then not quite friendly." The letter admitted that Miliukov's opinions on Macedonia and Bulgaria gave cause for concern but Davidović used this fear to urge his chief to greater speed in sending a reliable representative to Petrograd. Otherwise the Bulgarians, "capable of anything," would get to Miliukov first.[42]

Then followed Miliukov's promise on the future Yugoslav state. According to Mandić's not unbiased account, the minister's remarks caused "consternation" among Pašić and his colleagues, who regarded the statement as "an unfriendly act" and a "national calamity."[43] While perhaps exaggerated, Mandić's impression of Serbian reactions was far from wholly unfair. Pašić could easily see in Miliukov's promise the unwelcome possibility that post-war Serbia might be merged into a Yugoslav federation under the aegis of a republican Russia. Moreover Miliukov possessed liabilities in official Serbian eyes that were extremely difficult to overlook. As Davidović pointed out, the new minister's recorded views on Macedonia, known Bulgarophilia and close associations with the Yugoslav Committee made him a less desirable occupant of his post than, for example, Sazonov. Only time would tell if the first two of these fears were justified; as to the third, Miliukov's cautious answer to Trumbić suggested that his earlier enthusiasm for the Yugoslav cause might now be undergoing some dilution. Other signs in the same direction were not lacking. Miliukov emphasized to the Serbian minister Spalajković that the continuity of Russian foreign policy applied as much to his country as to any of the larger allies. Five days after his promise on Yugoslavia he reiterated this point, underlining that Serbia could count on the support of the new Russian regime in the realization of her national aspirations.[44] This would be music to Pašić's ears: even more pointed were his remarks at the government's formal reception of the Allied representatives on March 24. For one participant the ceremony evoked painful memories of vanished Tsarist splendors. Reflecting on the reaction of Imperial flunkeys to bourgeois mismanagement, Paléologue followed Miliukov through the various empty suites of the Mariinskii Palace in search of suitable quarters for the Cabinet's baptism of international legitimacy. One finally located, the "sacramental declarations" could be safely delivered.[45] Spalajković at least had no occasion for gloomy thoughts. Miliukov, addressing him directly, spoke of Russia's affection for her Slav Orthodox brother and promised Serbia "everything" she had lost and the fulfillment of all her national ambitions. "The interests of Europe," the Foreign Minister proclaimed, "require that a new, free, great and united Serbia emerge from this war. . . ."[46] Sazonov himself could have said no more. The initial isolation of the Serbian legation was soon at an end. Spalajković continued his pre-March practice of participation in the regular conferences between Miliukov and the Entente ambassadors, and obtained the former's aid in alleviating the wretched condition of Serbian civilian refugees in Southern Russia.[47]

The response from Corfu to these overtures was one of gratified relief. Pašić made no secret of his nervousness over a pro-Bulgarian orientation of Russian revolutionary diplomacy.[48] This did not now seem a likely prospect. It was not of course to be expected that Miliukov should ever publicly account for, or even admit, his increased warmth toward the Pašić regime: several reasons suggest themselves nonetheless. It is not improbable that he quickly realized the incompatibility of his early ideas about a Yugoslav state with Russia's treaty commitments. Close scrutiny of his public pronouncements as minister as recorded in his party's newspaper does not reveal any occasion after March 24 when Miliukov referred to Yugoslav ambitions, save for his laconic acknowledgment of Trumbić's note on April 10. In that same month he declined to make a statement in favor of South Slav unity on the grounds that it might embarrass the government's relations with the Petrograd Soviet and provoke criticism from the Socialist press. In an unconscious paraphrase of Sazonov's advice to Supilo two years before, he recommended that his petitioners turn to the British Socialist delegation then in Petrograd with the request that it might exert a calming influence over its Soviet comrades on behalf of the Yugoslav cause.[49] One may well challenge the minister's sincerity in invoking the Socialist bogey, though it was real enough to members of the Committee, as on the far more explosive Constantinople issue he had never bowed to fears of Soviet opposition. Yet at no time was he specific on the delimitation of Serbia's future frontiers; the promise of secure borders and "the natural union of all Serbian people" was the furthest he would go in giving substance to the tantalizing vision conjured up for Spalajković on March 24.[50] Bosnia-Herzogovina and Montenegro would assuredly pass to Serbia but there could be no certainty about other coveted territories. Least of all was Miliukov going to commit himself on Macedonia. Quite apart from his earlier opinions on the subject, his plans for a Bulgarian defection were maturing by the beginning of April and it is certain he would not have wished to tie his hands on a matter of such vital interest to Tsar Ferdinand and Radoslavov. A final factor which should not be overlooked in accounting for Miliukov's concern for Serbian susceptibilities was that Pašić did head a legitimate allied regime with whom Miliukov's predecessors had maintained the very closest relations. Given his emphasis on the unbroken continuity of Russian foreign policy, it is unsurprising that he should have gone out of his way to reassure Pašić of Russia's continued benevolence. If he failed to reconcile the exiled leader to the new order of things in Petrograd, the fault was less Miliukov's than it was that of the revolution itself.

In Serbian emigré circles there were mixed feelings about the events in Russia. Nationalists regarded the Tsar's downfall as a disaster, one mightily compounded by the identity of revolutionary Russia's new spokesman on foreign affairs. One illustrative reaction, extreme in language but not in depth of feeling, was that of Svetolik Jakšić, onetime editor of the Belgrade *Štampa* and in March 1917 a member of the Serbian press bureau in Geneva.

On March 21, while Davidović was preparing in the same city his own more measured assessment of the situation, an article appeared over Jakšić's signature in the *Argauer Volksblatt* sharply critical of the Provisional Government. The author singled out Miliukov for special censure. He stressed at some length the Russian's friendly feelings for Bulgaria and tried to prove that Miliukov's entire Balkan policy was directed "in the service of Tsar Ferdinand." The article created a sensation in the small Serbian community. The press agency hastened to disassociate itself from such embarrassing charges, intimating that Jakšić was little better than a German puppet. The Russian press bureau accepted the denials with satisfaction: Miliukov had always been aware of "the justice of the greater Serbian ideal."[51] But Serbian chauvinists remained unconvinced. If Miliukov were not in Bulgarian pay, then he was too friendly to Italy, "our ally and . . . our enemy." He and his assistants had encouraged the revolution; "they may end by being punished by it." Miliukov's intellectual credentials were no less suspect. Why have "our intellectual Jews" joined Russia's Jews in considering Miliukov "a man expressing their own ideals?" This turned into open gloating once the minister fell. "Thus the man who paved the way for the present chaos in Russia is now fleeing the responsibilities for the unfavorable results of the revolution. Now he will have the chance to write his memoirs."[52]

This absurd vituperation represented an extreme opinion which Pašić did not share. All the same, he could take no comfort from the fast moving panorama of Russian events. The ally on whom he had hitherto counted to the virtual exclusion of all others was gone; its successor was an unknown quantity tainted by its revolutionary origin. In Odessa and at the Salonika front the revolution threatened, through the medium of committees set up to maintain contact with the Petrograd Soviet, to undermine the precarious discipline of Serbian military units.[53] Worst of all, many officers and men of the volunteer force were calling for a democratic and federated Yugoslavia after the war "along the lines of Switzerland or the United States."[54] Nobody had to remind the Prime Minister of the republican structure of both examples. Nor was the picture much more reassuring in the remaining Entente capitals where Serbian diplomats had to compete with Yugoslav Committee members for Great Power attention. In London the success of Yugoslav propaganda obliged the legation to co-operate with Committee efforts to the point where, as far as public and Parliamentary opinion was concerned, there was nothing to distinguish between "Serbian" and "Yugoslav" programs for the future reorganization of the eastern Adriatic coastline.[55] With one opponent, Italy, and one dubious, potentially hostile quantity, Russia, Pašić was left with little option but to come to some accommodation with the rival body that enjoyed such prestige in the capital of Serbia's most powerful European ally. In March his closest political collaborator, Stojan Protić, met Trumbić in Cannes for exploratory discussions. Both men concluded that a settlement was imperative and public squabbling inadmissible between the two spokesmen for Serbia's future.[56] Developments in Petrograd only lent urgency to that conviction, whose ultimate expression was to be the momentous meeting on Corfu in July between the Premier and the Committee's head. But by the time that confrontation took place Miliukov had vanished from power and left behind a government that had much less reason than he to favor Russia's onetime Balkan client.

The Rumanian Kaleidoscope

On September 20, 1916, Nicholas II received his daily letter from his wife. Sandwiched between the usual jumble of gossip, denunciation and advice was the line "Our Friend wld have liked if we had taken the Roumanian troops in hand to be surer of them. [sic]"[57] Though not the first Imperial reflection on Rumanian prowess (her correspondence is studded with uncomplimentary references to that country), this one was an unusually accurate foreboding on Rasputin's part. All three regimes that governed in Petrograd through 1917 found Russia's nearest Balkan Ally fully as exasperating as any enemy. Rumanian politicians were, if possible, in even greater need of being taken in hand than Rumanian soldiers; unfortunately that campaign went as ingloriously for Russia as the other. In the context of Russo-Rumanian relations the Provisional Government inherited a legacy of dislike and resentment which it passed on greatly fortified to its successor. Of all Russia's Allies it was Rumania who bargained the hardest, was promised the most, delivered the least and collapsed the quickest. Under the leadership of her wily Prime Minister, Ioan C. Bratianu, she progressed slowly from nominal alliance with the Central Powers to neutrality, to the verge of intervention on the Entente side, back to neutrality and finally, in August 1916, to actual belligerence. One hundred days later Bucharest lay in enemy hands and the Bratianu government was in full flight eastward. The debacle was the culmination of two and a half years of rising Russian fury and frustration.

Within two months of the war's outbreak Bratianu had won Russian recognition of his country's substantial claims in Austria-Hungary. On October 2, 1914, the two governments agreed that in exchange for her benevolent neutrality Rumania should receive Transylvania and that part of

Bukovina populated by Rumanian speaking majorities.[58] This promise of a reward for a policy that was the very least he would have followed handed Bratianu the diplomatic initiative that he did not relinquish for the next two years. As the months passed and Entente desires for a Rumanian alliance grew more insistent, Bratianu's territorial ambitions mounted correspondingly. Russia was first to feel the effect. By the spring of 1915 the Bucharest government was demanding not merely Transylvania and slices of Bukovina but also—peculiarly repugnant to Serbia's principal defender—the Banat of Temeszvar. Ownership of this region would place Belgrade practically under Rumanian guns. Bratianu's proposals were therefore rejected with some asperity.[59]

Throughout 1915 negotiations with Rumania continued in Petrograd. They followed a regular pattern. Russian military successes would induce Sazonov and the Supreme Command to take a hard line toward Rumanian requests; Russian reverses would encourage Bratianu to raise his price ever higher. Unfortunately for Russia defeats were by now more frequent than victories. By mid-June the Supreme Command had so far reversed itself as to urge Rumanian intervention as "extremely desirable, more valuable than ever." Izvol'skii added his weight from Paris with the warning that French public opinion (a regular scarecrow he liked to flaunt) would hold Petrograd to blame if Rumania failed to join the Entente. Sazonov gave way on July 15. In return for her immediate declaration of war on the Dual Monarchy Rumania should have, in addition to Transylvania and most of Bukovina, the entire Banat plus the Rumanian populated counties of Hungary proper. Success seemed imminent when Warsaw fell to the Germans on August 7. Bratianu prudently concluded that the opportune moment had not yet arrived and withheld his signature. His prospective partners nevertheless decided that their promises should stand, pending a more propitious occasion for decisive Rumanian action.[60]

The great moment arrived in July of the following year as Brusilov's armies stood poised on the crests of the Carpathians. A renewed invitation to the Entente Powers from Bucharest led to a draft convention incorporating all former promises and guaranteeing extensive supplies through Russia of war materiel. In return Rumanian intervention was required not later than August 21. After last minute hesitations and doubts that provoked a final outburst of Russian irritation, Bratianu consented to sign.[61] Two clauses, in addition to the territorial engagements, were to be of some future importance. Article V pledged that neither party would seek a separate armistice or peace, Article VI that Rumania would enjoy "the same rights as the Allies in all that concerns the preliminaries of the peace negotiations." The first brought the new Entente member into line with her partners' own commitments to each other; the second was Bratianu's insurance that his country would be protected in the backstage bargaining to go on between the eventually victorious Entente Powers. Unknown to him, two of his foreign colleagues had no intention of permitting such pretensions to pass unchallenged. On August 11 Stürmer and Briand agreed privately that the gains promised to Rumania would be conceded "only to the extent allowed by the general situation at the end of the war." In particular Stürmer reserved the right for his country to raise the question of the Serbs in the Banat should future circumstances require it.[62]

On August 27, 1916, a specially convened Crown Council heard Bratianu exhort the King to imitate the glorious seventeenth-century example of Stephen the Brave. An ultimatum to Austria-Hungary followed at once. On December 6 Austro-German troops under von Mackensen entered Bucharest. King and government fled north-east to Jassy, capital of the province of Moldavia, where they remained in precarious exile for the ensuing two years. It had all been a total fiasco whose appalling swiftness moved Bratianu to an unwonted humility. Early in January 1917 he arrived in Petrograd, no longer a demanding creditor, eager to convince the Tsarist government of the need to place Russo-Rumanian relations on more lasting foundations. His motive was evident enough. As a realist—the characteristic which most impressed Paléologue—Bratianu knew that Rumania's salvation depended on the renewed success of Russian arms. The Inter-Allied Conference that opened in Petrograd on February 1st gave him a chance to remind the Entente's military and diplomatic strategists of their newest Ally's desperate plight. If he were lucky, there was also the possibility that Bratianu might win some needed prestige at home should he return with evidence of Russian goodwill. The Premier won his hearing but nothing more. He failed completely to impress the delegates whose attentions were fixed elsewhere, mostly upon Russia's domestic political griefs.[63] In his report to the Emperor on the conference's work Pokrovskii made one brief reference to Bratianu's appearance.[64]

During the talks Allied leaders heard the first strains of a Rumanian lament to be repeated with rising stridency as the year wore on: the alarming deterioration of conditions on the Rumanian front. The position was indeed exceptionally unpromising. Three Russian armies of forty-four divisions stood side by side with some six hundred thousand demoralized Rumanian troops along a five-hundred-kilometer front, ravaged by epidemics, shortage of supplies and intense mutual ill will. The nominal Commander in Chief of the joint armies, King Ferdinand, possessed no visible talent for his responsibilities, which in practice devolved upon the Russian commander General Sakharov. He in turn made it plain to the assembled military chiefs in Petrograd that his forces were in no condition to re-open offensive action "this year"; his message was duly passed on to Bratianu.[65] According to Paléologue the only promise that the Rumanian leader managed to win in Russia was the Emperor's assurance that he would not oppose a marriage between his eldest daughter and Crown Prince Carol.[66] A month later even that prospect lost its appeal.

News of the March revolution fell with shattering impact on the hard-pressed Jassy regime. The King burst into tears; the Queen preferred to confide her fears to her diary, asking the question Balkan royalty elsewhere were doubtlessly asking themselves: "What influence will it have on the war, on our fate?"[67] The question was crucial for Rumania. Her neighbors were either enemies to whom the revolution promised a victorious peace, or allies dependent in the main on Anglo-French support. Neither Pašić nor Venizelos depended exclusively on foreign troops whose loyalty grew more suspect by the day. Relations between revolutionary Russia and Rumania in fact existed on two levels: the official ties between Bratianu and the Provisional Government and the unofficial, grimmer and far more important reality of the dissolving Rumanian front.

The Rumanian political picture in March stood in sharp contrast to the confident image of the previous August. The dominant figure still remained the Prime Minister, less because of any outstanding talents than as a result of the absence of any serious rivals. The Court posed no challenge to him. The King continued to follow his lead because he had no other choice; in any event Ferdinand was temperamentally quite unlike his slippery namesake south of the Danube. The British military attaché in Jassy, who knew Ferdinand well, characterised him as popular and weak, possessing no vices "save for a taste for rather indiscriminate fornication."[68] This failing was not likely to be politically fatal either to Ferdinand or, in the fullness of time, to his equally venturesome heir. Ferdinand's English-born Queen, much the stronger character of the reigning couple, was of necessity Bratianu's closest ally since both were the most zealous proponents in Rumania of the disastrous Entente alliance. Political rivals Bratianu had in plenty, but defeat and flight had reduced them for the present to manageable proportions. His bitterest critics in the reactionary wing of the opposing Conservative Party, Petru Carp, Alexander Marghiloman and Titu Maiorescu, chose to stay in Bucharest and take their chances with the Austro-German alliance they failed to secure for their own country. The one Conservative of stature who followed Bratianu to Jassy, Take Ionescu, entered the Cabinet on December 12, 1916, in a demonstration of national solidarity.

Military disaster required a reshuffling not only of the Cabinet but, more urgently, of its immediate political priorities. Prominent in the speeches of

Bratianu and Ionescu before the rump Chamber of Deputies had been their insistence that the government truly did intend to institute agrarian and electorial reforms—but after the war was won.[69] The news from Petrograd forced these issues to be faced sooner than anticipated; the King led off with a public promise to his peasant conscripts that they would get their land: "I shall myself set the first example."[70] His personal emissary from Nicholas II, General Mosolov, whose usefulness was now clearly at an end, cabled Miliukov that Ferdinand feared more than anything an upsurge in Rumania on the Russian model. Mosolov's British colleague heard a more personal royal worry. Rumors had reached the Court of Sir George Buchanan's role in dethroning the Tsar; was it likely that Rumanian Socialists might be looking to the British legation for a parallel favor?[71] The query emphasized a major liability of Jassy's marooned position: none really knew what was going on in Petrograd. The wildest rumors were in consequence current and found a credulous audience. Mosolov assured Miliukov that censorship was keeping out the most volatile material but was making him dependent on Bratianu for information. Anyway, with the Russian border only a few miles off and Russian troops everywhere at hand, censorship was unlikely to be very effective. Would Petrograd please keep him posted on political developments so that he might relay all "correct" news on to his hosts?[72]

Bratianu had proclaimed his wish to press for universal manhood suffrage and land redistribution as early as January 1914. Any reforms along these lines would certainly encounter strong resistance from the Conservatives and from within his own National Liberals, nor indeed did his own sincerity on these issues pass unquestioned. There can be little doubt that, if the question had to be faced, Bratianu would have preferred to postpone the inevitable Parliamentary battle until invested with the laurels of military victory. Now the combination of defeat, isolation and Russian revolution threatened to take matters out of his hands. That had at all costs to be avoided. As King Ferdinand earnestly explained to the regular Russian envoy, Poklevskii-Kozell, it was better to start reforms "from above" so as not to give the people grounds to act on their own "by means of revolution."[73] If Poklevskii knew his own country's history he might have recognised an echo in the King's words of Tsar Alexander II's identical conclusion in circumstances not unlike those Ferdinand faced.

Protestations of Bratianu's good intentions encountered some cynicism in local political circles. Coincident with his promises there emerged a fraction of the Premier's National Liberals proclaiming itself a Labor Party which could be relied on to carry the necessary reforms into effect. Bratianu could not be trusted; "only the great events in Russia" forced him out of his customary immobility in all social questions. Such at least was the considered opinion of the fraction's leader, Dr. Nicolae Lupu.[74] British observers of the Jassy scene suspected that the Labor group's sudden emergence on the political stage owed more to the Prime Minister than appearances might suggest. Perhaps, ran their thoughts on the subject, the new party represented an intrigue on his part to stave off attacks from local Soviet organs at the front.[75] If so, it did not entirely succeed in its purpose. A meeting in May of a Congress of Front and Odessa region Soviets listened incredulously as Dr. Lupu's delegates expanded on the good will and dependability of King Ferdinand as an instrument of serious social improvement.[76] The Labor fraction in fact fulfilled the same function in Jassy as the "Broad" Socialists did in Sofia. Salutes to the Russian revolution, criticism of government repression and demands for reform were matched by devotion to the war effort, to the official diplomatic program and to the person of the King. The Laborites at no time threatened Bratianu's majority which remained high in the Chamber and the Senate, based as both houses were on the narrowest of electoral franchises.[77]

Rumania was the Balkan state least known to the new Russian Foreign Minister. He had visited it once briefly in 1913 in order, so he relates, "to observe the last trace of [General P.] Kiselev's administration of the Danubian Principalities under Nicholas I." A ride down Kiselev Boulevard in Bucharest with a cab driver dressed *a la russe* sufficed to satisfy his historical interest in Rumania.[78] A year later, in describing the events of the Second Balkan War, Miliukov barely mentioned Rumania's role and did not include Bucharest in his tour of Balkan capitals with the Carnegie Commission. He was cautious in his assessment of Rumania's relations with the Entente, recognizing that the Serbs of the Banat and Ukrainians of Bukovina made Russian concessions difficult.[79] Rumania was not, however, a Slav state, nor involved in the Macedonian dispute; she consequently engaged less of his interest and attention than did Bulgaria, Serbia or Greece. As minister he might regret the disagreeably large concessions made to Bratianu but his Straits ambitions precluded any denunciation of Russia's treaty obligations. On April 4 he included the return of "Rumanians to Rumania" among the Entente's war goals, this a phrase capable of generous interpretation.[80] The Jassy regime reciprocated the gesture. It agreed, in reply to a Russian request, to supply naval transports in support of Miliukov's cherished plan for an expedition against the Turkish coastline.[81] The plan fell through; yet as long as Miliukov stayed at his post Bratianu had nothing to fear from Russian diplomacy. Miliukov had set his heart and career upon obtaining the Straits; he would not compromise his chances of success by forcing changes in other, less desirable engagements.

First to feel the impact of Miliukov's loyalty to Rumania was the exiled

Pašić government on Corfu. On April 17 the Serbian military representative at Stavka suggested the time had come for the Entente Great Powers to revise their undertakings to Rumania. What he specifically had in mind was a concerted Allied effort to force Bratianu's renunciation of the Banat and its eventual transfer to Serbia. It was the Serbian government's opinion, wrote Miliukov shortly thereafter, that the Rumanian crisis was so acute that Bratianu would be unable to resist Russian pressure on Serbia's behalf. Miliukov refused to encourage this belief, a strange one for the beleagured Pašić regime, and he requested the Supreme Command to do likewise.[82] Bratianu was himself present in Petrograd throughout these exchanges and may well have learned at first hand of their favorable outcome. If so, it was one of the few agreeable impressions he had of the unsteady Russian regime. Paléologue recorded on May 11 a lunchtime encounter with the Rumanian Premier. The latter, "in a woebegone tone, with tears in his eyes," lamented to the ambassador "we shall lose Miliukov before long . . . . It will be Guchkov's turn next, then Prince L'vov . . . . After that the Russian revolution will sink into anarchy and we Rumanians will be lost."[83] Four days later his first two predictions were fulfilled to the letter.

The decisive voice in 1917 in shaping the direction of Russo-Rumanian relations belonged neither to Bratianu nor Miliukov but to the one and a half million Russians immobilized on the Rumanian front. At the Petrograd Inter-Allied Conference Bratianu had not been able to stir them into renewed offensive warfare. His success was no greater after the Tsar's removal when military discipline began seriously to worsen. The Premier's early hope that the Provisional Government might infuse new energy into the army faded away when it became obvious that military commanders, to say nothing of the civilian authorities in Petrograd, exercised little control over affairs at the front. The new regime's sole gesture in that sense was to replace Sakharov with a more conciliatory figure, General D. G. Shcherbachev, later to be a painful thorn in the Bolshevik side. He was no more successful than his predecessor in bringing order; Russian troops roamed more or less at will through unoccupied Rumania with desertions taking on epidemic proportions. Particularly obnoxious to the Supreme Command and the two governments was the growing eagerness of Russian soldiers to interfere in what they judged to be reactionary aspects of the bourgeois Jassy regime. Prison doors were flung open to free the several "martyrs to the people's cause," be they Bratianu's political foes or the *Potemkin* mutineers, interned in Rumania since their flight in 1905.[84] From the prisons the troops moved on to the palace where they celebrated the May 1st holiday by demanding the overthrow of the Hohenzollern dynasty. Fortunately for King Ferdinand that was as far as matters went: his complete helplessness was underscored by his Cabinet's decision, communicated to a sympathetic but equally powerless Miliukov, to offer no resistance even if the building were actually attacked.[85]

In opening Rumanian jails Russian troops succeeded in one instance where Miliukov had failed. Among those liberated was the founder of the Rumanian Socialist Party, Christian Rakovsky, a strong opponent of Rumanian entry into the war. He had in consequence been under confinement since that date. His imprisonment made Rakovsky something of a celebrity in Socialist ranks and after the March Revolution the Petrograd Soviet urged Miliukov to do something to help. He responded—with what little enthusiasm one can imagine—and was suavely snubbed by Bratianu for his pains. Rakovsky lost no time in hurrying off to Petrograd to thank the Soviet in the name of all Balkan Socialists for its concern. He ignored the Provisional Government.[86]

Rakovsky was the Balkan embodiment of Socialist internationalism. By birth he was Bulgarian, forced to turn Rumanian along with his native Dobruja by the fortunes of the Second Balkan War. His upbringing was comfortably middle class, but his political loyalties were devoted at an early age uncompromisingly to the Socialist cause. This and his extensive travels in Central and Western Europe had made him an intimate of emigré Russian revolutionaries and an especial friend of Trotskii. Under the Soviet regime he would serve as Chairman of the Council of Peoples' Commissars of the Ukraine. His association with Trotskii started his decline, which would pass through the Soviet embassies in Paris and London finally to end in 1938 with his return to prison and death as a convicted member of "a counter-revolutionary bandit, espionage diversionist organization of traitors."[87] In 1917 all that mercifully lay in the unknown future: if anyone then had the right to speak on behalf of Balkan Socialists, it was Rakovsky. He had been the guiding spirit behind the organization in July 1915 of an "Inter-Balkan Socialist Federation," consisting of a handful of Bulgarian "Narrows," one Greek Socialist, himself "and the telegraphic adhesion of the Serbian party."[88] This body seems to have led a rather shadowy existence, though its aims, as expressed by Rakovsky to the Zimmerwald Conference in September 1915, embraced the Socialist panacea current since the Balkan Wars: peace and a republican federation of Balkan states.[89] He invoked this image in his address to the Petrograd Soviet on May 19: "we Balkan Socialists have learned from you and we think that the great Russian revolution will give impetus to the creation of a Balkan federated republic."[90] This sort of pronouncement, coupled with his veteran status, helped to earn for Rakovsky a position of respect and attention from the Russian Left not accorded any other Balkan Socialist and few foreign ones.

From Petrograd Rakovsky headed back south, not to Jassy where Bratianu's police would be waiting, but to Odessa. This Black Sea port was in the process of becoming the major local source of revolutionary inspiration to Russian and Rumanian radicals. Unsurprisingly, the Jassy authorities came to regard the city with a dread whose depth was not always appreciated by Entente diplomats who kept urging the King to avoid Jassy's tensions by moving his headquarters to Odessa.[91] Royal disinclination soon received powerful ammunition. On May 10 there opened in Odessa a congress of regional military and naval Soviets, rejoicing in the acronym *Rumcherod*.[92] The congress reflected the complexion of the Petrograd Soviet. Mensheviks and Social Revolutionaries predominated, along with the desire to continue the war in defence of the revolution. On one important matter of local strategic interest a Black Sea fleet congress resolution of a few days earlier had laid down that Russia must have guaranteed freedom of all straits, the Dardanelles must be closed to hostile fleets and an international treaty should enshrine these principles. This sort of approach brought a wide measure of consensus; Shcherbachev himself was a delegate to *Rumcherod*'s opening session.[93] In Bolshevik eyes these features made *Rumcherod* a suspect body but they coincided closely with Rakovsky's own views at the time. He settled down in Odessa to write on Rumanian affairs for the *Rumcherod* organ *Golos Revoliutsii*. His inflammatory articles kept nerves in Jassy stretched taut throughout the summer.[94]

Other than diplomatic protest there was nothing Bratianu could effectively do to combat attacks from the Russian Left. His country's allies were of little help. In Petrograd Paléologue's interim successor, Albert Thomas, protested to the Minister of War against assaults on a monarch "who has loyally stood on Russia's side." Guchkov was sympathetic; he was already on public record as having labelled Rakovsky a German agent. Yet by himself he could do nothing. On May 14, in the face of conditions in the armed forces which by his own admission he was powerless to alter, Guchkov resigned. He left an appalled Bratianu to deal as best he might with the man on whom Rumania's fate now depended, the new War Minister Alexander Kerenskii.[95]

At no time during the life of the Provisional Government was there any official Russian enthusiasm for Rumania, her government or her cause. Bratianu was quite correct in seeing in Miliukov the one friend he possessed in the regime. After Miliukov's resignation his old colleagues hardly bothered to conceal their dislike of that country.[96] It was not enough for Bratianu to proclaim his desire to strengthen ties with Russia and promise overdue reforms in Rumania's social structure. His government had driven a very hard bargain with Russia (just how hard the Socialist press would shortly reveal); its demands were excessive, its complaints endless. From the Russian viewpoint Rumania's main contribution to the war had been to lengthen Russia's already overtaxed front by another five hundred kilometers.[97] And as if all this were not reason enough for a grudge, a new factor had appeared since the revolution: separatism in Bessarabia. The Imperial government had successfully withstood hints from Bucharest and Jassy that the province, or part of it, be ceded to Rumania. The Provisional Government could not afford to be any less resolute and Kerenskii for one believed Bratianu was encouraging irredentist sentiment at Russia's expense.[98] To do him justice, Bratianu was not at that moment intent on raising the Bessarabian issue. The most vociferous Rumanian supporters of annexation, Carp, Marghiloman and their following, were still in Bucharest. For the Provisional Government, however, it was one more reason to distrust the Rumanian Premier, and from May onwards his wishes and complaints ceased to command much attention in the Russian capital.

CHAPTER V
CONFERENCES AND DELEGATIONS

April opened the season of conferences and delegations. All concerned themselves to varying degrees with "the latest events in Russia," an expression which started to crop up with doleful frequency in inter-Allied communications. The conferences wrestled with the problem of determining what effect those events would have on the conduct of the war and the planning for the peace; the delegations busied themselves with the job of turning the energies of newly free Russia in directions profitable to the common cause. Balkan and related issues were fundamental to all these encounters.

Miliukov had staked his political life on the preservation of Russia's diplomatic solidarity with the three other Great Powers of the alliance; two meetings in April severely tested his confidence in their reciprocal good faith. Twelve days after the April 9 Declaration's seeming rejection of all acquisitive Russian war aims, he heard from Rome that his foreign colleagues had met on the 19th at St Jean de Maurienne on the Franco-Italian border to discuss major questions of policy in the Balkans and Turkey. From a private and completely secret source, Giers, the ambassador in Italy, learned that the three Western Entente Powers had come to an understanding on issues relating to Asia Minor and Greece.[1] Russia's opinions had not been solicited although the subjects under discussion presumably concerned her as closely as any of the actual participants. Further details from Izvol'skii only made matters worse by revealing that a recent Austro-Hungarian feeler to Petrograd had been included on the St Jean agenda.[2]

The meeting in the small French frontier town was the first Entente summit conference since the March Revolution. No Russian delegate was present, yet all those in the closely guarded railway car were aware of the preponderant influence that the uninvited ally might exert upon their deliberations. The most apprehensive on this score was Baron Sonnino. One question tormented him and his diplomats more than any other through the summer months now ahead: would Russian opposition in the name of some lofty principle imperil the attainment of Italian territorial ambitions, including those already conceded and those still hoped for? Sonnino knew better than anyone that he had no reason to expect Russian graciousness on the point. Italy had not spared Russian sensibilities in the past, as practically every line in the Treaty of London showed, and Sonnino himself had made difficulties over Tsarist aspirations at the Straits. After months of telegramming to and fro between the several capitals, he had finally granted recognition, but his consent formula indicated very clearly where the next Italian thrust would be now that the rich meal of the London Pact had entered his bloodstream. The statement of December 2, 1916, committed the Boselli-Sonnino ministry to acceptance of Russian possession of the Ottoman capital and the Dardanelles "provided that Italy achieve her objectives in the East and in other places . . . and that she benefit from all the advantages to be guaranteed to France and Great Britain."[3] These objectives, spelled out during the bargaining that autumn, centered on a dominant Italian position in Southern and South-Western Anatolia with control over Turkey's second port, Smyrna, and its hinterland.[4] Since this would put an expansionist Italy uncomfortably close to the Straits, Miliukov had no difficulty in maintaining the continuity of Tsarist hostility to Rome's claims in Asia Minor.[5]

The March Revolution had two effects on the St Jean talks as far as Sonnino was concerned. It raised a question mark over the future of the treaties—whatever Miliukov might claim to the contrary—and in a lesser but not unimportant way dealt a blow to the monarchical principle that Sonnino treasured. The first effect was not an immediate disaster for Rome, though it could easily become one unless the appropriate precautions were taken. Along with the Foreign Office and the Quai d'Orsay, the Consulta noted the contradictory opinions out of Petrograd on the subject of the treaties and rather than seek clarification Sonnino preferred to settle outstanding issues "à trois."[6] He was not averse to employing the same tactic as the Bulgarian King before a stronger ally: threats of an Italian withdrawal from the alliance became a standard ploy of Sonnino's diplomacy.[7] He used it with some success at St Jean, recalling afterwards the "stormy scenes" as Lloyd George stamped out of the railway car in a fury at Italian stubbornness. Naturally that was a price well worth paying; on balance Sonnino had reason for satisfaction at the meeting's outcome. A qualified acceptance of the Smyrna claim; no Entente propaganda in Greece in favor of a republic which, according to the Italian leader, "would lose [the three Powers] the strong conservative support they now enjoy, particularly important in view of recent events in Russia"; and finally, no separate conversations with Vienna on a negotiated Austrian peace. This last was a project much to Lloyd George's liking and Italian objections to it were the occasion of his angry departure for London.[8]

One cloud remained. A condition of the St Jean agreement on Italy's plans for Asia Minor made the terms subject to Russian consent, this being the least Messrs. Lloyd George and Ribot could do for their absent partner whose veto might save them much later trouble. None concerned with the formulation of Italian policy, certainly not Sonnino, could have any illusions on the likelihood of Russian compliance. The Italian ambassador in Petrograd, Marquis Carlotti di Riparbella, had his doubts even of Miliukov's co-operation, but at least the Straits were a lever to his good will. If Kerenskii were to triumph (which he, Carlotti, thought doubtful) the matter would become delicate, "since we have always been suspected of not sympathizing with Russian [Socialist] aspirations"—an understatement of classic British proportions.[9] Italian diplomacy in consequence worked until the November Revolution to dilute the obnoxious clause or, better still, to delete it altogether.

Back in Paris, Premier Ribot hastened to head off the inevitable complaints from Petrograd. He summoned Izvol'skii to his residence so that together they could survey the current military and diplomatic picture in South-East Europe, as seen from the Quai. Both men agreed that there was no worthwhile possibility of a separate peace with Austria-Hungary, as suggested in the letters of Emperor Charles to President Poincaré.[10] In Balkan affairs the Prime Minister showed some skepticism of Russia's chances of bringing Bulgaria to terms, but his major preoccupation in the peninsula lay further south in Turkey. Ribot alluded to the "agonized" Turkish desire for peace and, in the same breath, to the fact that Russia's insistence on her war aims constituted the greatest barrier toward soothing that particular Turkish agony. Of course France would continue unconditionally to respect her obligations toward Russia, but (and here Ribot revealed his own uncertainty over what exactly Miliukov had conceded on April 9) "even if Russia renounces Constantinople and Germany were to return all her seized territories" France would not, could not, make peace. Her sufferings and sacrifices had been so immense that not even the return of Alsace-Lorraine could satisfy Paris any longer. On that note Ribot terminated the interview, expressing regret that "circumstances" had not permitted the Russian Foreign Minister to join his colleagues at St Jean, none of whose decisions could go into effect without Russian consent.[11]

Ribot's disingenuous remarks failed to calm ruffled feelings in Petrograd. On April 26 Miliukov informed his foreign colleagues of his own "extreme astonishment" that he had received no invitation to the Savoy meeting, nor yet to participate in the Entente missions to the United States, due to take place in late April and early May. These slights to Russia, he warned, could have a most unfavorable impact in Petrograd where they could trigger "undesirable talk" about the differences between free Russia and her partners.[12] As could have been expected, his attention was still very much fixed on the Dardanelles. Ribot found to his chagrin that Miliukov continued to exhibit "ill temper" at the possibility of further Italian expansion in the Eastern Mediterranean.[13]

Miliukov read the foreign scene more accurately than he did the local one. The tone of the French and Italian press went far toward justifying his uneasiness at Allied intentions toward Russia's "vital interests." The magisterial *Le Temps*, Bismarck's "sixth Great Power," enthusiastically welcomed the communiqué issued at the end of the St Jean discussions. It reminded its readers that such inter-Allied conferences were "the only really practical means of maintaining full unanimity of view and action" in the military and diplomatic efforts of the Entente, small comfort to the absent partner in that alliance. There were crucial questions, *Le Temps* went on, "notably in the Near East," where French, British and Italian interests were most closely bound together. The article concluded in tones of measured satisfaction "that the Conference of St Jean de Maurienne should permit a clear determination of our goals and a precise definition of the diplomatic and military means by which these may be most safely reached."[14]

In Italy some inspired leaks enabled the nationalist press to exult over the gains won from Britain and France. On April 27 a lead editorial in the Milan *Corriere della Sera* remarked:

> It is no longer a secret that at the Conference . . . there were examined some of the most important of inter-Allied political questions . . . concerning the regulation of the Mediterranean and the Turkish East. . . . For the Allies gathered at St Jean de Maurienne it was not only questions of *common* interest in the Turkish East that were discussed, but also [those] of *individual* interest.[15]

Mussolini's *Popolo d'Italia* commented approvingly on Eastern problems "solved" at the Savoy sessions and of the benefits that must now accrue to Italy "in proportion to her sacrifices." Most other newspapers concurred and demanded national support of Sonnino's successful diplomacy.[16] It was all too much for British nerves. Angry cables shot off to Rome protesting publicity given to an agreement whose terms, besides being secret, were conditional upon Russian support and—though this failed to win equal time in the Italian press—upon a more vigorous Italian offensive spirit at the front.[17] Despite profuse apologies there was a distinct feeling in London that the breach of confidence was perhaps not entirely the fault of the official villain, "the really quite dreadful Italian censorship."[18] As a means of building up to a fait accompli and thus neutralizing Russian objections, press publicity was too useful a tool to be overlooked by the Consultà.

As Miliukov anticipated, the British and French delegations to the United States in April-May again emphasized Russia's drift to the sidelines in the Entente camp. The secret treaties were not the occasion for the journey but it required little effort in Petrograd to foresee that a prominent item on the Washington agenda might well be an examination by the Entente's new associate of the principal Allied undertakings in areas of interest to Miliukov's Russia.[19] Expecting more complaints, Ribot cabled assurances that nothing had been promised and no negotiations had taken place; copies of the cables from America accompanied his message, together with reiterated regret that "circumstances of time and distance" precluded Miliukov's own attendance in Washington.[20] Balfour's deputy, Lord Robert Cecil, performed a similar function in London in his chief's absence.[21] Yet neither man gave any hint of what the American Government thought of the treaties Miliukov prized so highly. Possibly they were themselves not yet clear on the point.

When the Great War broke out the United States Government knew almost nothing of the complex nationality and frontier issues at stake; American representatives were not qualified to enlighten it.[22] Efforts to correct this deficiency received some impetus in January 1916 when President Wilson's confidant, Colonel E. M. House, arrived in Europe to explore the possibilities of a negotiated settlement. While in London, House discussed with Grey and Balfour Lloyd George's idea for the total dissolution of the Ottoman Empire, all three men "stand[ing] before a large map of South-Eastern Europe and Anatolia."[23] Evidently House was still feeling his way around the maze of wartime diplomatic concerns, so said little; one month later, after his return from Paris and Berlin, he proved ready to show his hand. On February 10 he told Grey that should the President demand a peace conference to bring an immediate end to the war and Germany were to reject its reasonable terms, the United States would at once join the Entente. Reasonable terms appeared to include the cession to Italy of Italian speaking regions of the Hapsburg Empire, which would otherwise remain intact, the restoration of Serbia and the turning over of Constantinople to Russia.[24] In the days following, House continued his talks on these weighty issues; in the course of them his opinion on one key subject shifted. The entry in his diary for February 17 runs:

"We all[25] cheerfully divided up Turkey, both in Europe and Asia. The

> discussion hung for a long while around the fate of Constantinople. [Lloyd] George and Balfour were not enthusiastic over giving it into the hands of Russia, Grey and Asquith thinking that if this were not done, material for another war would always be at hand. I suggested the neutralization of Constantinople. . . ."[26]

This jaunty account of the honorary Texas colonel counselling British leaders on diplomatic strategy provides an interesting glimpse of what the next Prime Minister and Foreign Secretary thought of their country's principal diplomatic commitment.

For all his advocacy of neutralization, House turned out to have more thoughts to offer on the subject of Russia's major war aim. In his own version of their discussions, Sir Edward Grey noted that the Colonel subsequently expressed an opinion "decidedly favorable . . . to the acquisition by Russia of an outlet to the sea." On March 7, 1916, Grey's memorandum, with House's latest views, received Wilson's approval with the single insertion of the word "probably" in reference to American action in the event Germany failed to accept "reasonable terms."[27] In the year that remained of American neutrality, the President did not elaborate further on the nature of Russia's "outlet to the sea." His later agreement with House that Turkey-in-Europe "should cease to exist" admitted no more than the neutralization of Constantinople, and House claimed some years afterward that this all along had been his own preferred solution.[28] There could certainly be no justification for Miliukov or anyone else to believe that Wilson favored annexations by Russia in South-East Europe, however "democratic" the language of annexation might be. As a young man some thirty years earlier Wilson had written sympathetically of the national aspirations of Austria-Hungary's subject peoples; as President he was forthright in his statements on behalf of national and democratic principles as the only bases of a just peace.[29] The Ottoman record toward national minorities in the Empire no doubt contributed powerfully to Wilson's distaste for the Young Turk regime, but his acceptance (according to House) of the principle of Turkish expulsion from Europe by no means admitted a willingness to see the Tsar replace the Sultan at the Golden Horn.

Whatever the assurances to Petrograd, Foreign Secretary Balfour arrived in Washington on April 22 ready to discuss the sensitive political question of the Allied treaties.[30] House had briefed him to that end. Virtually from the hour Balfour stepped ashore in New York, House began tutoring him for his American appearances, not least the all-important confrontation with Wilson.[31] Once in the capital, Balfour met House again to take stock of the various agreements so that the Colonel could "convey our conclusions" to his friend in the White House. The two quickly came to grips with Russian and Balkan concerns. They agreed that Serbia should receive Bosnia-Herzogovina and, in return, cede to Bulgaria that part of Macedonia promised the latter by the 1912 Serb-Bulgarian treaty. Rumania "should have a small part of Russia which her people inhabited [Bessarabia] and also a part of Hungary [Transylvania] for the same reason." A brief argument followed over Italian claims in the Adriatic. Then came Constantinople: "we agreed it should be internationalized." Balfour then touched on the spheres of influence in Asiatic Turkey assigned by the four Entente Powers to themselves. His approach to the whole question called for some circumspection in view of the highly unsettled state of the matter; at any rate Balfour either would not or could not provide enough clarification to satisfy House. The Colonel reported to the President that his guest seemed "hazy" and "not altogether clear" whether the Powers envisaged permanent occupation or merely exploitation of their respective Anatolian shares.[32]

On April 30 Balfour met the President. According to House the same ground was covered as between himself and Balfour two days before. When discussion got around to Constantinople, House, "while thoroughly agree-[ing] with the general idea of internationalization," pointed to the dangers this precedent might create for other international waterways such as the Skagerrak and the Suez and Panama Canals. The two others thought these had little in common with the Turkish Straits. Balfour promised to provide the President with copies of all the treaty texts and took his leave, full of admiration (carefully expressed to House) at "the wonderful combination of human philosophy and political sagacity" evident in Wilson.[33]

On May 18 Balfour duly handed over to the President copies of the London Pact with Italy and the Constantinople and Asia Minor agreements.[34] They made little impression. From House's account it is quite clear that Wilson attached little significance to the treaties once the United States entered the war. England and France, he wrote later to House, did not have the same views with regard to peace as the United States, but the latter, thanks to her economic might, could, if she chose, impose her will on the others regardless of their prior engagements.[35] Consequently he did not concern himself closely with the details of the several accords, though he was familiar with and ill-disposed to their general drift.[36] House in contrast took a direct personal interest in plans for European territorial redrafting, but for all the Colonel's influence and importance in the American scheme of things in 1917, the British Foreign Secretary for one never lost sight of the fact that the United States Government remained "the President and nobody but the President."[37] Conversations with House were congenial enough and it did no harm to Balfour to allow the Colonel his head in their diplomatic excursions. Much of the success for the visitor's favorable impression upon the President must go to his close cultivation of the President's most intimate adviser. Balfour himself was unenthusiastic about the treaties. Several years later he explained to his niece-biographer that at their 1917 meeting he and Wilson were only interested in the present and the future: "those treaties had no importance by that time."[38] Neither he nor René Viviani, the head of the French delegation, exerted themselves on behalf of Russian interests, whether as interpreted by Miliukov or by the Petrograd Soviet. The Foreign Secretary professed to accept with complete equanimity the internationalization of Constantinople and the cession of a Russian province to Rumania, who already stood to double her size should the Entente be victorious. On May 4 Viviani's Washington host, the diplomat Henry White, wrote to his half-brother William Buckler at the American embassy in London that his guest had assured him Russia no longer wanted Constantinople. If Germany ceded Alsace-Lorraine and adopted a more democratic form of government, France would make peace. Viviani was sure that "other problems" would present no great difficulty in realizing this hope.[39] His statement is hard to reconcile with Ribot's remark to Izvol'skii of April 24 to the effect that not even Alsace-Lorraine or the return of occupied territories would satisfy France, but White naturally knew nothing of that. The Francophile American was probably told what Viviani knew he would most like to hear: peace in Europe upon restitution of the plundered provinces of France and the institution of political democracy *à l'américaine* in Germany. At any rate neither the St Jean nor Washington meetings offered encouragement to Miliukov's confidence in Russia's Allies, even if their spokesmen in the American capital had been speaking on the war in the language they knew their hosts would find most palatable.

While the Washington talks were in progress the British and French Governments came to a decision that struck at the foundations of Miliukov's position on inter-Allied diplomacy. It was as well for his peace of mind that he did not know, though he probably suspected, that the two Western Powers had concluded by early May that Russia should be overlooked and downgraded in Entente planning for South-East Europe. Thus, on May 19, Lord Robert Cecil was obliged to divert his attention from weightier matters to pacify Baron Sonnino, outraged because the Italian ambassador in Paris had been excluded from Anglo-French discussions on May 4 and 5 about Greece. Abjectly apologetic, Cecil wrote to Rennell Rodd, the ambassador in Rome, that it all boiled down to a question of diplomatic etiquette. Much as the British and French ministers would have wished Sonnino's representatives present, an invitation to the Italian ambassador would have necessitated one also to the Russian envoy. This was now out of the question; "in view of the excitable condition of Russian opinion and still more in view of the breakdown of the Russian precautions against spying, it would have been madness to have discussed with a Russian representative . . . plans of importance."[40] A second May conference on Greek affairs, this one in London, used this pretext again to exclude Russia. Also again kept out were the Italians, whose touchy dignity, mounting demands and diminishing military performance were becoming as vexatious to the Foreign Office as the failing Eastern Ally.[41] The combined experience of these April and May sessions was to demonstrate yet again the truth of the diplomatic adage that *"les absents ont toujours tort."*[42]

Opinions in London

Until May 1, Russia's Allies could take no official note of the April 9 Declaration on war aims to the Russian people. Yet on an unofficial level, the March Revolution stimulated widespread discussion of the likely effect on major wartime questions of the Tsar's downfall. In a war commonly proclaimed by one side to be one of defense of the rights of small nationalities, the most crucial of these questions was the future of Central and South-East Europe. So little was known in the West about the non-Germanic peoples living in those exotic regions that it was first necessary to publicize their cause among the intellectual and policy-influencing elements of the Entente Powers. Most of the effort concentrated in London. Thomas Masaryk, perhaps the best known of all the exiles from the Dual Monarchy, saw little hope of advancing the cause of the nationalities in Rome or Petrograd if Great Britain should fail in her aid to oppressed nationalities.[43] He encouraged his English sympathisers to present their case in such a manner "as to lead the public opinion . . . the Government and the [General?] Staff. What I would wish," he wrote to Seton-Watson, "would be the embodiment of the English conscience and political and strategic thinking."[44] The result was the *New Europe*. First appearing in October 1916, it included among its contributors, besides Masaryk and Seton-Watson, Wickham Steed of the *Times*, J. L. Garvin of the *Observer*, the Rumanian Conservative politician Take Ionescu, historian Nicholas Iorga and the expatriate Russian historian Paul Vingradov. The periodical looked to the eventual emancipation of the subject peoples of Central and South-Eastern Europe from German and Magyar control.[45] It amply fulfilled Masaryk's hopes and acquired a considerable influence in official circles, including the Foreign Office which did not regard all the *New Europe*'s writers with equal favor. Seton-Watson ran afoul of the Foreign Office for his attacks on Grey's policy on nationality questions, or lack of one. His punishment was an official veto against any form of public employment, a prohibition that forced him to decline an offer from Buchanan to serve as an embassy liaison officer between Hapsburg and Balkan Slav emigrés in Russia.[46] Counter-propaganda to the *New Europe*'s position came from one of Miliukov's colleagues on the 1913 Carnegie Commission, Henry Noel Brailsford, in occasional articles for the *New Republic* and the *Nation*. He was joined by the Buxton brothers, Noel and Charles. Noel was Miliukov's English equivalent in terms of his Balkan interests and affection for Bulgaria. He had helped to found the Balkan Committee in 1903 and was strong in his condemnation of recent British policy in the peninsula. Both Buxtons and Brailsford resisted the *New Europe*'s thesis, ardently shared by Masaryk and Miliukov, that the Hapsburg Empire must be destroyed to satisfy the aspirations of its constituent parts.

The March Revolution provoked fresh discussion of these themes. The *New Europe* led off. On April 19 a long article by "Belisarius" analysed the revolution's likely impact in the Balkans. The author was sure that no part of Europe would be more quickly and more permanently affected than South-East Europe. The pull of geography, history and race must necessarily draw the Balkans into line with "the new orientation of Russian policy." "Belisarius" went on:

> Stronger than all of this will be the direct political effects of the Revolution on Russian policy in the Balkans and on the Balkan countries' attitude to the new Russia. The Russian Revolution, then, means . . . that the criteria of democracy are to be applied to the Balkan states from both within and without . . . . The new Russian Government will instinctively take the side of democracy everywhere.

Neither Serbia nor Greece need any longer fear Miliukov's pro-Bulgarian feelings; "essential considerations of justice" would be his only guide in formulating his Balkan policies.[47] Obviously the sympathies of "Belisarius" were with Miliukov as the most fervent Russian exponent of the *victoire intégrale* demanded by the *New Europe*. This vanished within a few weeks. Rex Leeper, writing under the pseudonym "Riurik," urged the need for the Western Powers to meet Russian Socialist demands on war aims. Because British and French ambitions were "not imperialistic" according to Leeper, he felt the Petrograd Soviet might easily be persuaded that Entente victory meant also the triumph of the democratic principle.[48]

The *Nation* and the *Saturday Review* stood out in the periodical press opposing the *New Europe*. Both journals agreed that the revolution removed the Pan-Slav menace from Europe and thereby strengthened the chances of a separate Austrian peace, a possibility endlessly denounced in the *New Europe*'s columns.[49] The point was vigorously taken up by the ultra-radical Union of Democratic Control which had been trumpeting since 1914 the dangers to European nationality causes from rampant Muscovite expansionism. That this put the U.D.C. on the side of those who wished to preserve in some form the Hapsburg Empire was a paradox that could not be helped. The Union naturally wasted no time on Miliukov but thrilled to the pronouncements emanating from the Soviet.[50] Brailsford shared this opinion. He saw Russian liberalism, embodied in Miliukov, as much less inclined to compromise on war aims than Tsardom had been on the eve of its fall. If Miliukov were to pursue a dream of conquest in the Balkans, he would imperil the foundations of Russia's newly won freedom. In fact Brailsford did not hide his preference for what he called "the reasonable and liberal program" of Miliukov's rival in the Justice Ministry.[51] An even stauncher supporter of the Russian Socialist position generally and its lone Cabinet representative in particular was the *Manchester Guardian*'s Petrograd correspondent Morgan Philips Price. He became something of an inspired leak from the Russian Cabinet to the British newspaper reading public via Kerenskii and passed on the latter's early admonition to disregard all individual statements on territorial questions "whatever the authority on which they are based."[52] There was no need to specify whom Kerenskii had in mind in issuing the warning.

Radical views on South-East Europe commanded attention in London from others than Englishmen. Thomas Masaryk reacted with delight to the news from Russia, all the more since his friend Miliukov was the first foreign minister of the Entente on record as favoring the total break-up of the Austro-Hungarian Empire. Masaryk's glowing reports on Russian developments quickly appeared in the *New Europe* and, as soon as circumstances allowed, he took himself off to Russia to promote his cause at first hand. To his chagrin he arrived in Petrograd to find Miliukov had resigned the day before and the Provisional Government itself distinctly less of an asset to his program than he had hoped.[53] Back in London meanwhile the American embassy was turning its attention in the same direction. William H. Buckler, a counsellor at the embassy, reported to Colonel House on April 27 that he had been seeing something of Brailsford, Noel Buxton and other contributors to the *Nation*. They had questioned him whether it was true that the United States proposed to take a share "only in the neutral settlement of Constantinople and the Straits," and leave other "inland" problems to the European nations concerned. Buckler evaded the question, as well he might, but was sure it illustrated a strong British desire to ascertain American attitudes "to Austria, the Balkans &c."[54] These were all issues of great complexity but Buckler, a newcomer to every one of them, felt equal to the challenge. His correspondence with House continued through the lifetime of the Provisional Government and beyond: the Colonel quickly admitted "how helpful your letters and papers sent with such regularity are to me."[55] Buckler's growing familiarity with these territorial issues was doubtless useful enough, but his most valuable function lay in keeping House, and through House Wilson, informed of Radical opinion on questions of war and peace. The U.D.C. in particular lost no opportunity to profit from this pipeline to the White House; their appeals met a sympathetic response.[56] The exchange of letters between House and Buckler gave initial impetus to what ultimately developed into the American task force on questions of post-war reconstruction, known as the Inquiry.[57]

Buckler's reports in the early summer months of 1917 devoted most attention to the deteriorating Russian situation and its Balkan impact. Lloyd George, an occasional member of the discussion group, evidently passed on diplomatic information from Petrograd, since Miliukov's conversations with the British ambassador were sometimes the subject for comment. Russian overtures to Bulgaria, for example, "surprised and impressed" Noel Buxton, who briefed a "much interested Lloyd George" on the value of a Bulgarian defection. Buxton thought an American agent would be more suitable for serious business with Sofia than Miliukov's agents, if only because the United States still retained its Sofia legation. Buckler advised caution. "Various Asia Minor hands" had told him that Russia and Turkey were both on the point of leaving the war. A Russian withdrawal might, in turn, set off what Buckler referred to distastefully as "an all round make peace quick movement based on no conquests, i.e. practically the status quo," a colloquial but not inaccurate summary of what was in fact the Soviet's program.[58] Nobody present at Buckler's gathering, least of all the Prime Minister, wanted that. To forestall the dread possibility, London and Paris had some weeks previously embarked upon the task of stimulating a faltering and war weary ally to fight on to final victory. Apart from Miliukov, there was nothing in Petrograd to suggest that their efforts would be successful.

Miliukov's Last Campaign

In the days immediately before and after the St Jean de Maurienne Conference, delegations of various sorts and nationalities began descending on Petrograd. First to arrive was a combined team of six Socialists, three British—Will Thorne, William Sanders and James O'Grady—and three French—Marcel Cachin, Marius Moutet and Ernest Lafont. Maurice Paléologue sourly noted their arrival and its likely embarrassments for himself: Moutet was a barrister, Cachin and Lafont professors of philosophy, O'Grady a cabinet maker, Thorne a plumber: "theory on the one side, practice on the other." Clearly his heart was on the side of practice.[59] Hard on their heels, on the same day that Arthur Balfour arrived in Washington on his very different mission, Albert Thomas, Minister of Munitions in the Ribot cabinet, stepped from his train at the Finland Station. Also disembarking from the same train was a rejoicing throng of returning Socialist exiles that included the Grand Old Man of Russian Marxism G. V. Plekhanov. The seven foreign guests shared a single purpose in coming to Russia at this moment: to arouse by their presence and exhortations the enthusiasm of their fellow Socialists in Russia for the sacred cause of the war. They came at their governments' instigation and with the support of their patriotic press at home. Their equivocal status prompted warnings to both Miliukov and the Soviet that the first six arrivals were not to be relied on either to support Miliukov on the treaties or to join the Soviet in urging their repudiation. All six in consequence received a reserved welcome from their Russian hosts.[60]

The frigidity of their reception at fraternal Socialist hands came as a shock to the three Frenchmen who showed themselves much more sensitive to Petrograd's political subtleties than the more proletarian Britons. Paléologue took it upon himself to tutor his countrymen for their public appearances, above all for the critical encounter with the All-Russian Congress of Soviets. This body sat in more or less continuous session from April to mid-July and was certain to query the visitors on the war aims assue. Paléologue's own priorities were unyielding. In the West, on the sacred blue line of the Vosges, there could be no compromise. If "certain ambitions" had to be abandoned in the interests of Allied unity, better that these be confined to Eastern Europe and Asia Minor, "where the sacrifices would not cost France too much." Unhappily, and to the ambassador's intense disgust, Cachin's eagerness to win the Soviet's applause was so great that included in the ballast thrown overboard was the untouchable prize of Alsace-Lorraine. The readiness of French Socialists to jettison or call into question their country's war ambitions contrasted vividly with the British reply given a few days later to protests from the Moscow Soviet that Constantinople was not and never could be Russian: "if you don't want it, then, damn it, we'll take it." Morgan Price, who was present during the exchange, noted the long silence which greeted this jovial remark, "then handshaking and withdrawal of the Soviet deputation from the representatives of British 'Labour.'"[61]

The presence of the Allied missions prompted the Socialist press to urge more than ever the renunciation of territorial aggrandizement throughout Europe. Lenin, who arrived back in Petrograd on April 16, proclaimed in his April Theses on the war and the revolution that the former remained "under L'vov and Co." what it had been under the tsar, predatory and imperialistic. As far as the Balkans were concerned he had not changed the view he expressed during the First Balkan War that a federated republic was the only consistently democratic solution of the national problem in the peninsula. That the proletariat there was small in number and the peasantry downtrodden, disunited and illiterate was all undeniable but did not alter the formula's validity.[62] The leftist press generally agreed. *Den'* was unresponsive to pleas from the Serbian intellectual Alexander Belić that the revolution make it possible for the Hapsburg nationalities to form their own states. *Den'* also decided that Constantinople was "too dainty a morsel" for Russia to swallow at the price of the permanent hostility of Balkan neighbors. The only answer was neutralization, "a solution which might be contentious."[63] So it already was, as *Den'* knew very well, even within Socialist ranks. On April 15 Plekhanov addressed the Congress of Soviets immediately following the departure from the rostrum of Cachin and O'Grady on behalf of their respective delegations. In Sukhanov's words "a friendly reception was certain [for] the father of Russian Social Democracy" and even the Bolsheviks joined in the ovation. Plekhanov was careful on this festive occasion "to skirt the most dangerous reefs"; even so, by ostentatiously joining hands with Cachin and O'Grady, he left his audience in no doubt where his sympathies lay on the war aims question. In fact Plekhanov was so much the Social Patriot by the time of his return to Russia that his views were not merely defensist but apparently approached Miliukov's on the Straits issue. Certain of his followers were not far behind.[64]

On April 23 the Ex. Com. reassembled after a brief visit to the front. The most pressing item on its agenda was the need to determine the next steps in the field of foreign policy.[65] This referred to the Ex. Com's wish that the government officially communicate its statement of March 27/April 9 to Russia's Allies and thus bind itself within the alliance to a non-annexationist program. In a cordial interview all members of the Cabinet but one agreed to fulfill the Soviet's request. Miliukov was the inevitable holdout. He argued that transmission abroad of the April 9 manifesto would increase Allied fears of an imminent Russian withdrawal from the war. On this basis the long deferred showdown, so eagerly sought by Sukhanov and the Soviet left, was joined.

The specter of a separate Russian peace was not one dreamed up by a cornered Foreign Minister but was very real in the capitals of Russia's partners. Paléologue spoke in the same language in his cables to Paris, though Albert Thomas, who had been sent out to relieve the Third Republic's too aristocratic representative, chose to see reason for optimism in Kerenskii and the Soviet. Thomas turned out to be even more susceptible than Cachin to the excitement of the place and the moment; in Paléologue's sardonic phrase "it touched him in his revolutionary fibers." These continued to be stimulated throughout the weeks of his visit. When requested by Ribot to summarize their recommendations, the outgoing ambassador urged formal adoption by Paris of his suggestions to Cachin. There should be the quickest possible revision of all engagements relating to Eastern questions. Constantinople, the Straits, Turkey, the Balkans, Austria—all these were Russian interests, not French, and the sooner they were abandoned the better the chances of detaching the Ottoman Empire and striking at Germany from the South-East. Thus spoke the diplomatic Westerner, fearful of the war's outcome, impatient with the new men, French and Russian, who presumed to know better than he, and with no backward look at the torrent of Russian blood soaking the battlefields of Galicia and East Prussia. For his part Thomas, "while not opposed to the idea of a strictly secret attempt to induce Turkey to propose peace to us," felt the time inopportune "for great, new diplomatic combinations in the East." Unlike Paléologue, Thomas was sure Russia might still be saved for the alliance by announcing a democratic policy.[66] Thomas did not then explain what he meant by this expression, one which had a quite specific meaning for Russian Socialists that summer in the context of the war. He later privately rectified the omission for the benefit of Paléologue and Buchanan: "I know my Socialists. They will shed their blood for a formula. You must accept it and alter its interpretation."[67]

Miliukov's Cabinet colleagues were no less determined than Thomas, and with much the same motive, to stamp free Russia's diplomacy with the new cipher. Under their relentless pressure and, as he himself explained it, "so as not to compromise the position of the government," the Foreign Minister was obliged to promise the Declaration's immediate dispatch abroad. On May 2, after still more prodding from Kerenskii and Thomas, the long heralded note to the Allies, bearing the date of the previous day, appeared in the Russian press.

The communication to the Entente governments of April 18/May 1 consisted of the March 27/April 9 document and a commentary by Miliukov, expressly designed (so he told Paléologue) "to eliminate the possibility of interpreting the Declaration to our detriment."[68] His text denied emphatically that Russia planned to leave the war; decisive victory was still "the general aspiration of the entire people." Then came the two key paragraphs:

> It goes without saying . . . that the Provisional Government, while defending the rights of our motherland, will fully observe the obligations made with respect to our Allies.
>
> While continuing to have complete confidence in the victorious conclusion of the present war, the Provisional Government is quite certain that the questions raised by the war will be solved by the creation of a solid foundation and that imbued with similar aspirations the leading democracies will find a way to establish those guarantees and sanctions which are required to prevent new and bloody encounters in the future.[69]

The commentary was Miliukov's last throw and it was hopeless. Unqualified fidelity to the treaties, guarantees and sanctions by the victors against the vanquished and war to total victory were all words from a vanished Russian lexicon. With them, Miliukov had challenged the Left in a manner it could not ignore and had chosen to do so on the one day of the year that celebrated the international solidarity of the working class. "They" had thrown down the gauntlet, commented Sukhanov; it was for "us" to pick it up.[70] Tsereteli, at the head of those in the Soviet most willing to co-operate in the prosecution of the war, believed that if Miliukov had consciously striven to provoke a rift between the Cabinet and the Soviet, he could not have hit upon a surer method than his explanation of May 1st.[71] The streets coincided in that opinion. Through May 3 and 4 demonstrators paraded outside the Mariinskii Palace with banners demanding Miliukov's dismissal. His supporters organized counter-parades addressed by Miliukov from the palace balcony, expressing his fears "not for Miliukov, but for Russia."[72] His Russia differed from the Russia of the capital's working masses; to prevent an irreparable breach between the two, negotiations opened on the evening of May 2 between spokesmen from the two bodies vying for control of Russia's destiny.

On the Cabinet side all participants but Guchkov opposed Miliukov, some, like Prince L'vov, less firmly than others. Miliukov himself argued that the Soviet misunderstood his position. If he had sent off the April 9 Declaration without any explanation Russia's Allies might have taken it as a sign of her impending departure from the war. Nor could he accept that a second message be sent off modifying the first: that too would alarm the

Allies. But the Soviet's agents were unmoved by the possibility of Entente confusion. They were far from desiring that the government endorse the idea of a separate peace nor did they wish to humiliate the non-Socialist ministers. What they did insist on was the imperative necessity of explaining to the Allies in unambiguous terms that Russia had renounced all territorial ambitions in this war and recognized national self-determination as the only basis for peace. Over Miliukov's protests the Cabinet accepted the Soviet's viewpoint. Together Tsereteli and N. V. Nekrasov worked on a resolution that would be palatable to the majority of the Left and yet not leave the government's helplessness totally exposed. The end result had therefore a rather lame look about it. The wording ran that "it goes without saying" that decisive victory over the enemy meant, as the March 27/April 9 manifesto had laid down, the creation of a stable peace on the basis of self-determination of peoples. By "guarantees and sanctions," mentioned in the May 1st note, the government had in mind "the limitation of armaments, international tribunals etc." Approved by a majority on the Ex. Com., the government's newest explanation went to the Congress of Soviets for final and demonstrative ratification. Amid scenes of frantic enthusiasm the motion for adoption passed by a large majority, though with the Bolsheviks and Sukhanov's Menshevik-Internationalists in opposition. On May 5 the note was published in the official gazette, accompanied by *Izvestiia*'s congratulations to the revolutionary democracy on its great victory. The Soviet firmly believed, its organ said, that the peoples of all belligerent countries would scatter their governments' opposition and compel them to begin peace discussions on the basis of no annexations. The Russian comrades had shown the way. But perhaps the last word belonged to Miliukov after all: the new note that *Izvestiia* so proudly endorsed seems never to have been formally transmitted abroad.[73]

Miliukov's political effectiveness was at an end. The Soviet had established beyond any possibility of challenge that it controlled the capital, for the time being at any rate, and with it the direction of Russian policies at home and abroad. It was hardly surprising that in the aftermath of the events of May 4 proposals became more insistent that Soviet representatives enter the government. On May 9 the Cabinet appealed through Prince L'vov for Soviet assistance in averting civil collapse; on the same day Kerenskii called for Socialist additions to help him defend the interests of Russian democracy. He more than hinted that, if reinforcements were not forthcoming, his own continued presence in the Cabinet could be in jeopardy.[74] That particular threat was perhaps remote but the need was real, as *Izvestiia* acknowledged, to end the anomaly where the government had responsibility but no power and the Soviet power without responsibility.[75] All the same it was a hard decision to make. Even Tsereteli feared that co-operation might diminish the Soviet's influence over the non-Socialist ministers and taint the purity of the Left with the smear of ministerialism. Besides, it was difficult to contemplate Soviet representatives entering a Cabinet as colleagues of the incumbent Ministers of Foreign Affairs and War. On May 13 a motion for a coalition was defeated in the Ex. Com. by one vote. The door being thus closed, the idea had to seek readmission through the window.[76] This it gained the next day on receipt of the news of Guchkov's resignation. Negotiations then commenced on the distribution of portfolios. The Soviet was unyielding that Miliukov quit his ministry, though its delegates were agreeable that he move to the Education Ministry where his talents could find less contentious employment. After frenzied bargaining the two sides reached eventual accord. At 2 a.m. on May 18 a new Cabinet took office with four Socialist additions and one conspicuous absence. Spurning all other offices, the man who, in Sukhanov's mordant phrase, "would have had to be called the Cadets' Lenin if he hadn't been a professor," resigned upon being told that his post was required "for other purposes."[77]

It now only remained for Miliukov to justify his stewardship; not to himself, for he had no personal doubts, but to the party faithful. On May 23 when the Eighth Congress of the Cadet Party convened the ex-minister found himself under mild public criticism from a colleague, N. V. Nekrasov, who had stayed in the Cabinet after Miliukov's resignation and had been partly instrumental in pushing him out.[78] Nekrasov suggested that the sacred formulas of Constantinople and the Straits were unrealistic and ought now to be given up in favor of a firm peace in full co-operation with Russia's Allies. Nekrasov was no threat to Miliukov's pre-eminence in the party but his remarks touched the latter on a sensitive nerve and provoked from him a long, carefully argued refutation of Nekrasov's position. He subjected Entente policies in South-East Europe to not altogether friendly scrutiny, his first public indulgence since his fall from office. He took note of the past lack of Allied enthusiasm to see Russia mistress of the Straits and commented ironically on the scarcely concealed relief in Britain and France that she was now "returning the gift." Putting himself in Lloyd George's shoes Miliukov observed that "we will now carry on the war for the sake of the West, for colonies etc. and we will forget about South-Eastern Europe which of course is really more interesting to Russia and Slavdom than to us." This was of course unacceptable. For Miliukov, the reconstruction of South-East Europe, meaning the liquidation of the Ottoman and Hapsburg Empires, constituted still the Entente's major purpose in the war. Any modification, such as now demanded by the parties of the Left, opened the door to renewed German aggression. Least of all could he forget Russia's chief loss on May 15. To great applause he uttered the boast that might well serve as a synopsis of his ministerial career and as the reason for its termination:

> I admit quite freely and stand firmly by it that the main thread of my policy was to get the Straits for Russia. . . . I would say and say it proudly and regard it as a distinct service to the nation that until the last moment I was in office I did nothing which gave the Allies the right to say that Russia has renounced the Straits.[79]

Others had now done this for him; it remained yet to be seen whether Russia would profit thereby.

On that point many had their doubts, among them Sukhanov, utterly dejected by the prospects for Russian democracy under a Soviet-bourgeois hybrid. The appeal of a loudly inebriated citizen, overheard a few evenings later when he was on his way home, seemed to Sukhanov to underscore all his pessimism about the new coalition regime and the program to which it was by Miliukov-"Dardanellskii's" ouster now committed: "let us pra-a-y to the Lord, for pea-a-a-ce for the wo-o-rld, without annexations or inde-e-mn-ities."[80]

CHAPTER VI
COALITION GOVERNMENT

On the day after what Sukhanov was pleased to call "the legal nuptials of the big and petty bourgeoisie,"[1] the Soviet's Balkan guest appeared on the rostrum of the Tauride Palace. First Rakovsky paid tribute: "We Balkan Socialists have learned from you and we think that the great Russian Revolution will give impetus to the creation of a Balkan federated republic." Next he turned to reassure the dubious. They should not fear bourgeois contamination of the Soviet members of the Cabinet. True, Socialist ministers elsewhere became "the tails of their governments [so much for Albert Thomas], but here I see something different. This government will be the tail of the Revolution. Russian ministerialism differs from the Western variety."[2]

The Socialist ministers took office with this their most profound conviction. Tsereteli, the Soviet's leading "defensist" who had campaigned the hardest on behalf of coalition, put his stamp on the new Cabinet's first announcement to the Russian people on the priorities of the day. New departures in foreign policy were the most pressing of these; the opening and longest clause of the ministry's public manifesto of May 5/18 addressed itself to the question:

> In its foreign policy the Provisional Government, rejecting in concert with all the people all thought of a separate peace, adopts openly as its aim the re-establishment of a general peace which shall not tend either toward domination over other nations, or the seizure of their national possessions . . . a peace without annexations or indemnities and based on the rights of nations to decide their own affairs.
>
> In the firm conviction that the fall of the regime of tsardom in Russia and the consolidation of democratic principles in our internal and external policy will create in the Allied democracies new aspirations toward a stable peace and the brotherhood of nations, the Provisional Government will take steps toward

> bringing about an agreement with the Allies on the basis of its Declaration of March 27 [April 9].[3]

No withdrawal from the war, revolutionary "defensism," eventual general peace on the basis of national self-determination without annexations or indemnities and Allied endorsement of these principles were now the stated objectives of Russian foreign policy, each in turn more elusive than the one before. The Petrograd press divided along predictable lines. Newspapers of the right and center stressed unity in the war effort and the smallness of any substantive change in the Government's program.[4] Only *Rech'*, ever alert to Miliukov's interests, sounded real alarm. Treaty revision, *Rech'* prophesied, would end up "not with an equal renunciation of all serious tasks envisaged by the Allies, but a unilateral renunciation of the tasks envisaged in South-East Europe in favor of those planned, not by us, but by our Allies in other regions."[5] The Menshevik *Rabochaia Gazeta* on the other hand saw as "deeply significant the fact that P. N. Miliukov, the most brilliant and doctrinairely stubborn champion of imperialist tendencies among certain strata of our upper bourgeoisie," had fallen. It therefore behooved the widest levels of democratic Russia to support their new Government.[6] Only the Bolsheviks, under their leader's firm tutelage, held fast in opposition to the unsurprising ideological apostasy of their Socialist fellows.[7]

The Soviet voice spoke on May 18; on May 19 the other half of the hybrid was heard. Prince L'vov, still titular head of the Cabinet, warned the nation that

> when one speaks of peace "without annexations or indemnities" one should at the same time declare unequivocally that this must not be understood as passive defense. Free Russia will not consent to leave under the domination of German militarism the lands which have been given away because of the old Government's criminal negligence toward the Fatherland and the army. Valuing highly its alliance with the great democracies of the West . . . the Russian people cannot remain indifferent to the fate of Belgium, Serbia and Rumania or forget its obligations toward them.[8]

His statement concluded with an appeal for unity and discipline in the army; no further details were provided of the new Government's foreign program.

This omission was made good later that day by the man who formally inherited Miliukov's responsibilities. In getting rid of "the Cadet Lenin," the Soviet's team negotiating with the Cabinet spent little time thinking about the identity of his successor. It had been decided in Soviet circles, wrote Sukhanov, to leave this, the most important ministerial post, in the hands of the bourgeoisie. As an afterthought he acknowledges that "the bourgeoisie had also firmly decided to hang on to it."[9] His evident belief that the policy was of greater moment than the executant of that policy may have been justified in theoretical terms, but a non-Socialist entrusted with the Socialist program was a solution unlikely to add to the strength of the political marriage entered into on May 18. One thing at any rate seemed clear. The new minister, whoever he was, would not give the problems to the Russian democracy that his predecessor had. What Kerenskii was later to call "the romantic period of the Provisional Government" ended with Miliukov's removal.[10] The almost simultaneous resignations of Ambassadors Paléologue and Izvol'skii underlined that officially at least a new era was at hand.[11]

The man on whom the bourgeoisie's choice settled was the one whose vast private fortune made appear more genuinely capitalistic than anyone else in the Government.[12] Michael I. Tereshchenko, Finance Minister in the first Cabinet, came to his new post with much less of a reputation than his contentious predecessor. He had little training in foreign affairs and was a complete novice in the complicated nationality issues that so interested Miliukov. One recommendation to the left was his rejection of the Constantinople mirage;[13] far more attractive to it were his obscurity, inexperience and lack of political base. If the new minister had to be from the bourgeoisie, better Tereshchenko than any other. Both wings of the political spectrum saw him as a nonentity. Sukhanov gibed at "our new Talleyrand," while to Miliukov's friend Vladimir Nabokov Tereshchenko was the merest political dilettante, *"ce n'etait pas un caractere."*[14] Nabokov may have owed his theme to Miliukov, patronizing to a degree about his successor. He conceded that for all Tereshchenko's weaknesses, he was not utterly illiterate in foreign affairs "and might even be able to talk with ambassadors."[15] Eventually Miliukov came to bestow a grudging approval when it became evident that many of Tereshchenko's policies in office paralleled his own.[16] At no time for the next six months did Tereshchenko emerge from the background as an important figure in his own right. He remained Kerenskii's protégé and owed his retention of office to his usual willingness to accept the initiatives and serve the policies of the charismatic War Minister.[17]

In his May 19 statement Tereshchenko reaffirmed Russia's desire for a general peace on the basis of no annexations or indemnities. But as if to give the lie to those who foresaw a Russian withdrawal from the war, he went on to speak of liberated Russia's ties with the Allied democracies. He stressed this point at some length in terms designed to appeal to the Petrograd Soviet:

> revolutionary Russia cannot and ought not break those ties sealed in blood; for her it is a question of revolutionary honor which is so much the more precious to her now . . . . The Allied armies of whom the great mass is composed, as with us, of peasants and workers, has carried on without stopping the struggle against the enemy, diverting his strength and by their heroic efforts are saving the Revolution from an external defeat.[18]

There would be no Russian denunciation or publication of the secret treaties while Germany and her Allies were waging aggressive war. Tereshchenko felt it was ridiculous to speak "at the present moment of the annexationist plans of the Allies as a real menace to peace when Russia, Belgium, France and Serbia are themselves occupied wholly or in part by the enemy." Yet the future was radiant with promise: "It is not for nothing that Russian liberty comes to the world and that its consequences and influences are spreading in a large and powerful wave across the civilized world."[19]

The Left concurred in the minister's obeisance to the no annexations program but wanted to go much further. The Soviet now intended to put its political primacy in Petrograd to good use. On May 15 the Ex. Com. issued its second major international appeal, this one addressed more specifically than the first "To the Socialists of All the World." It called upon Entente Socialists to force their governments "to state definitely and clearly" that the platform of peace without annexations or indemnities on the basis of national self determination was also their program. German and Austrian Socialists were summoned "not to allow the armies of your governments to become the executioner of Russian liberty." The manifesto then proclaimed the Soviet's intention to convoke an international conference of all Socialist parties and factions to co-ordinate tactics toward these goals.[20] Three weeks later the Soviet repeated its plea and invited the conference to meet in Stockholm on July 8 "in order to realize an agreement among the representatives of the Socialist proletariat to liquidate completely the policy of 'national unity' . . . which excludes the possibility of a struggle for peace."[21] For the next two and one half months European Socialists, headed by a committee of their neutral Dutch and Scandinavian confreres, argued interminably about the strategy, attitudes and agenda to be adopted at the planned meeting in the Swedish capital.[22] In these polemics Balkan issues as such earned less attention than the overriding imperative to bring an end to the bloodletting. Nevertheless, in both Socialist and non-Socialist circles of Western Europe, the growing power of the Russian left forced re-examination of all important wartime concerns. Of these not the least important was the future of South-East Europe.

Foreign Repercussions

Miliukov's resignation, coming on top of the Provisional Government's note to its Allies of May 1 and the Socialist Appeal two weeks later, had an immediate impact in two key capitals of the Entente. On May 16 the House of Commons discussed third reading of the Government's Consolidated Fund Bill in the light of the Soviet pronouncement on annexations and self-determination. For seven hours members concentrated their oratorical energies on the relevance of the Socialist formula to the affairs of, among other areas, Austria-Hungary, Turkey and the Balkans. Radical and U.D.C. speakers made a powerful contribution to the debate, whose generally cogent and informed level revealed how attentive most members were to Russian revolutionary influences on European nationality questions and the war.

The occasion for the debate was a motion proposed by the spokesman and chief of the Independent Labour Party group in the House, Philip Snowden, associating the British Government in Russian repudiation of annexations and indemnities. Snowden was perhaps the most jubilant man in England at the news of Tsardom's fall. Fearing Russian imperialism, hating the thought of Britain in league with Eastern despotism and detesting a war without any apparent end, Snowden and his fellow Labour Radicals leaped at the March 27/April 9 manifesto as the model on which Britain's own war program should be based. "It has given us a new hope in democracy and revived our faith in internationalism. It has given us a hope that the war aims . . . of the various countries—the maintenance of civilization and the triumph of democracy—are going to be realized in the only way [possible] . . . by the peoples of the different countries." Snowden saw a new dawn coming, one ushered in by Russians, chiefly Kerenskii. Miliukov championed the old order with all his talk of partitioning Austria, but his slogans could be ignored in favor of the "Workmen's Council" in Petrograd and its juster solutions for the world's ills. So passionately did Snowden believe in his cause that he proclaimed Italian Socialists were "practically united in [their] opposition to the war" and Bulgarian Socialists to be en route to Stockholm to fight the battle for peace—both claims, especially the first, far wide of the truth, as Lord Robert Cecil later pointed out.[23]

Speaking for the viewpoint of the *New Europe* of which he was a founder, the Liberal member for Perth, A. F. Whyte, queried the utility of applying the Soviet's ideas to Central and Eastern Europe. Take Bulgaria. Was she to be permitted to get away with the seizure of Macedonia just because her seduction from the Central Powers might be advantageous to the Entente?

Balkan passions made the rigid application of formulas impractical, particularly when in Macedonia there was "no particular national right in the case," did not his friend Mr Noel Buxton agree? That zealous defender of Bulgarian interests did not agree, but Whyte pressed on regardless. Just as "No Annexations" was an unrealistic slogan to parrot in all questions of Balkan settlement, even more so was it when applied to that great bugbear of *New Europe* readers and writers: Austria-Hungary. Whyte turned to the small band of U.D.C. and I.L.P. members imploring them to see it his way. How could they use the Socialist formula to defend a dynastic monstrosity? Whyte insisted that he had no wish to raise the nationality principle into a fetish, "but until you have settled these nationalities, especially in Eastern and Central Europe and have released them from alien rule, you cannot possibly recognize the international world of your dreams."[24] Whyte obviously held self-determination on an anti-German and anti-Magyar basis to be far more important than No Annexations and Indemnities. A fellow Liberal, Halford Mackinder, took up the theme. He accounted for British entry into the war in terms that few of his hearers would have accepted but which accorded with his unique views on the world's "Heartland." The destruction of the Dual Monarchy must be the first priority, "having been compelled to go into this war by that great threat constituted by the German system of empire in South-Eastern Europe." The fear of annexations must yield to the greater and nobler purpose of Britain's war effort. Regarding Germany's two remaining allies, backbencher opinion differed as to whether Russia's war aims renunciation offered the Entente worthwhile opportunities for intrigue. Where one speaker would counsel against it on the grounds that "Bulgaria is so iniquitous and Turkey so full of infamy," another urged it since Turkey's capital was now safe from Russian seizure "and Bulgaria can be bought or sold."[25]

Lord Robert Cecil rose on behalf of the Government. Invoking Turkish atrocities in Armenia, German misdeeds in East Africa and the dying words of Nurse Edith Cavell, Cecil managed to convey the distinct impression that the No Annexations cry played straight into enemy hands and its British advocates were little better than German dupes, if not worse. As for the treaties,

> there is no doubt about [them]. It is of course possible for the new Russian Government to say it does not wish that any particular engagement which we have undertaken on behalf of Russia shall be fulfilled. They can release the rest of the Allies from any particular undertaking, but until that is done we are bound in honor to carry out our engagements not only with Russia, but with the rest of our Allies.[26]

Since British engagements included carving up much of Austria-Hungary and most of the Ottoman Empire, as well as the restitution to Serbia of her Macedonian provinces, those who were listening for some hint of Balkan initiatives heard nothing of comfort.

The Government's majority in the House permitted no doubt but that Cecil's interpretation would carry the day. Even so, the most eloquent critics of the official line were determined that their few voices would prove that the Soviet's position had made some impression on the Mother of Parliaments. Winding up the debate, Charles Trevelyan and Arthur Ponsonby, both of the U.D.C., ranged themselves behind Snowden and his fellow I.L.P. colleague and later bitter political foe J. Ramsay MacDonald. These four and a handful of others stood in uncompromising opposition to the feeling of the House, as each of them in turn admitted. Trevelyan especially showed himself to be well informed on Russian developments and their wider implications for Central and South-Eastern Europe. He cited the categoric statement of a few days before from Michael Skobolev, Chairman of the Soviet's International Relations Section, that "no conquest of the Straits, no partition of Austria will be tolerated by the representatives of the Soviet . . . either here or at the front."[27] This, and not Miliukov's fanciful remarks, represented the genuine war aims of democratic Russia. To urge the destruction of Austria-Hungary in the interest of its nationalities was, Trevelyan claimed, the exact opposite of the Provisional Government's intention. It was a Pan-Slav idea, now discredited in Russia along with Miliukov and likely only to solidify the Monarchy's alliance with Germany. To persist in the idea in the name of the limitless rights of nationality ran counter to the intentions of the Russian democracy, threatened to prolong the war unnecessarily and—a point made by other speakers—was hypocritical from British politicians. If the formula was good enough for Austria and the Balkans, why not for Ireland? But the *New Europe* contributors in the House, to say nothing of the Government, preferred not to embark on that perilous sea. The only Radical consolation was the sight of Irish Nationalist M.P.'s joining their ranks for the final vote on Snowden's motion. Their combined numbers were swamped by the massive majority in favor of war to total victory.[28]

Outside Parliament the latest events in Petrograd continued to agitate London Balkan circles. The main issue was a Bulgarian secession from the Central Powers. Could it be arranged and at what cost? On May 22 Buckler sent details to House of two recent meetings at Noel Buxton's residence where this subject came under scrutiny. On the first occasion those present included, besides Buckler and the host, several army officers from the

Salonika front, Brailsford, Edith Durham and F. W. Hirst.[29] All opposed the destruction of Austria-Hungary. Thanks to the absence of any "Iugo-Slav idealists" the group was quickly able to agree that Russia's current weakness "killed the ambitious plans for a greater Serbia (or Iugo-Slavia) . . . as well as similar plans for Tchecho-Slovakia." The meeting felt that the Serbs would consequently be "in a more yielding and modest mood [and] more disposed than hitherto" to make concessions to Bulgaria in Macedonia.[30]

This discussion continued at a subsequent session with Lloyd George. Buxton again urged that the United States government take the initiative in contacts with Bulgaria, "partly because the Bulgars are well-known to be pro-American and partly because you could discuss matters with [Bulgarian minister in Washington] Panaretov free from the prying of enemy diplomats," wrote Buckler to House. Lloyd George was openly pessimistic on the chances of anything happening in the Balkans to help the Entente. Buckler recorded the Prime Minister's warning, repeated three times, that in their plans for territorial redistribution the Balkan experts "must not count on Russia nor on the dismemberment of Austria," this last a piece of good news to his audience. If Russia's plight continued to worsen, the Premier could see no possibility of satisfying the *New Europe*'s program. "Serbia's land-hunger" could not, therefore, be appeased with "slices of Bosnia &c." Buckler attributed Lloyd George's gloom to his belief that Russian military impotence would oblige Britain to "make those Near Eastern concessions which no Entente belligerent except Russia ever had the power to avert."[31] Probably equally responsible was the Premier's inability, thanks to the Russian Revolution, to detect any Balkan exit from the military impasse in the West.

There were significant repercussions to the Soviet triumph in the one Entente Great Power with annexationist designs in South-East Europe. Adherents of the "patriotic" wing of Italian Socialism began to question the scope of the Government's war program in the Balkans and Anatolia. In the Chamber of Deputies a prominent member of the group, Arturo Labriola, took the lead in calling for some modification of Italian ambitions in Slavpopulated regions. Labriola had been independent of the main body of the Italian Socialist Party since 1908; his strong support since of the Libyan War and intervention put him alongside Plekhanov in the forefront of European Socialists championing their countries' war efforts. He had also been a strong supporter of the rabidly nationalist society *Pro Dalmazia Italiana*; now the strength of the Petrograd Soviet brought him to soften his stance. On April 25, at Labriola's instigation, the Parliamentary Socialist leadership and the Confederation of Labor issued a joint declaration hailing the Revolution and its momentous consequence: the end of "the imperialist longings of the Muscovite empire." For Russia the war had become one of simple defense against German aggression:

> The freedom of nationalities and classes [and] the liberty of all Balkan states—those cradles of European conflict—is proclaimed and guaranteed, [as is] the internationalization of the Bosporus. The treaties which have linked Allied forces with Tsarist Russian imperialism have fallen.[32]

The last sentence impelled the Government to forbid the statement's dissemination in the Italian press.

Official displeasure left Labriola unmoved. On April 27 an article appeared over his signature in the liberal Rome daily *Il Messaggero*, examining the meaning of the Russian Revolution to Italian war aims. Hitherto, he wrote, Italy's Adriatic claims had been justified by the threat of a reactionary Russian regime in control of the Dardanelles. Just as intolerable would have been a Tsarist Russia behind "a hypothetically Serbian Dalmatia."

> Now [the article went on] Russia is a democratic republic. Her renunciation of Constantinople makes it possible to consider more coolly the problem of Dalmatia. With the fall of Tsarism in Russia, Serbia can no longer count upon the natural protection of the Russian state. . . . [S]urely this Serbia, who might be tempted to make fresh approaches to Germanism, must be given full assurances as to Italian intentions and is not the first condition for this the recognition of the rights of Dalmatia's Serbo-Croat population?[33]

Interestingly, Labriola accepted that the March 27/April 9 Provisional Government declaration on war aims bound Russia to the renunciation of Constantinople, in spite of Miliukov's all too evident contrary opinion. Later, in Petrograd, Labriola would display some hesitation in his call for a reconsideration of Italian war aims, but the mere suggestion that these were not sacrosanct provoked a furious reaction from the right and center parties. But Labriola was not entirely friendless. In his weekly journal of opinion, *L'Unità*, the historian Gaetano Salvemini reminded readers of Mazzini's injunction in 1871 that it was always in Italy's interest to help Hapsburg Slavs in their struggle against the common foe.[34] The Chamber's leading Patriotic Socialist, Leonida Bissolati, conscripted into the Boselli Cabinet in October 1916, also concerned himself with the Slav populations of the Adriatic hinterlands and broke with Sonnino in 1918 on the minister's persistent refusal to modify his anti-Yugoslav irredentism.[35]

Criticisms and reservations from Labriola, Bissolati et al. found no echo in the Consultà. There, on the contrary, the main concern was to prevent the

Socialist formula from damaging Italian interests any further. While some case could be made in nationality terms for Italian ambitions along the North-East Adriatic coastline (Labriola was to make such an attempt before the Soviet), the designs on Turkey could have no such sanction. These became for Sonnino and his lieutenants the citadel to be defended at all costs, particularly in London where counter-propaganda to the Italian position was more vocal than in any Entente capital save Petrograd. The cables exchanged in May and June between Sonnino and Ambassador Imperiali mirrored their central pre-occupation, to protect the St Jean concessions in and around Smyrna without provoking a Russian veto that could spoil everything.[36] Italian diplomacy conducted a two front campaign to that end, firstly by strong pressure on London to water down the Russian condition—the second proviso of a more vigorous Italian military effort was swept aside as undeserving of notice—and, secondly, by assurances to Petrograd of Italy's complete solidarity with the principles of the April 9 Declaration.[37] This tactic cut little ice in the Russian capital but as long as the public amenities of the alliance were observed and Tereshchenko did not begin openly to denounce Italian appetites, Sonnino need not worry unduly about Miliukov's successor. The nationalist press agreed; who could fear the intentions of a man worth sixty millions? The semi-official *Giornale d'Italia* went so far as to see in Tereshchenko Miliukov's "best friend," a judgment the Cadet leader would have repudiated with some warmth.[38]

The *Giornale*'s clear implication that the fallen minister's "best friend" could be expected to continue his policies turned out to be justified in one respect of interest to Sonnino. Four days after Tereshchenko moved offices, Sir George Buchanan reported the minister's "strong views" about Italian aims in Turkey and, more importantly, Kerenskii's equal revulsion. Could not this be the occasion for a thorough airing of the secret treaties and the future conditions of peace, Buchanan queried the Foreign Office?[39] Evidently Tereshchenko was still moving cautiously, more so than the Soviet would have liked. His attention too, however, was beginning to focus more narrowly on the affairs of South-East Europe. For Tereshchenko, unlike Miliukov, circumstances rather than inclination forced the pace.

Balkan Challenges

Since Miliukov's resignation no minister of the Provisional Government knew much about or was especially interested in Balkan issues. This was ironical, as from mid-May on, these questions came increasingly to engage the attentions of all Entente governments. With the new Russian Cabinet barely settled in office, two chronic problems suddenly exploded. The first had to do with Albania, the second with Greece. The outcome of each had repercussions on the political situation in Petrograd and on the course of Russia's relations with her Allies.

The Treaty of London of May 1913, ending the First Balkan War, had acknowledged in principle the desirability of a new Albanian state, but had left precise details of frontier drawing to be worked out at some future date. That seemed a remote prospect in 1913. Three of the victorious Balkan powers presented their conflicting views on the subject and the task of the new state's ruler, Prince William of Wied, plucked from the inexhaustible reservoir of minor German royalty, became impossible. When the European War erupted, foreign ministries shifted their attention to weightier matters. Left to their own devices, pro-Greek Albanians battled pro-Turks, and Prince William was compelled to abandon his ungrateful charge for the more orderly life of the German officer corps. By December 1914 Albania was split into six geographical regions, each boasting its own ruler.[40]

From Rome, Baron Sonnino was following Albanian affairs with close interest; they had a not unimportant role in his wider Adriatic ambitions. Throughout the period of Italian neutrality, he relentlessly pressed both sides to recognize an Italian preponderance in Albania. Austria-Hungary was unreceptive; Entente scruples proved more easily surmountable.[41] In December 1914 the three Great Powers acquiesced in the Italian occupation of Valona; a few months later they accepted the rest of Sonnino's demands. By the terms of Article V of the London Treaty of 1915, Italy agreed "in the event of a small, autonomous and neutralized state being formed in Albania" not to oppose the "possible" desire of her Allies to distribute portions of Albanian territory to deserving neighbors, Montenegro, Serbia and Greece. Italy was to conduct the foreign relations of the rump state so created.[42] By this clause of the London Pact the Entente allowed Italy's claim to the status and consideration of a major Balkan Power.

The Italian soldiers stationed in Albania did not for long remain confined to Valona. Their expansion southward and into the interior developed as Entente relations deteriorated with the last of the Entente neutrals, Greece. Involvement in that country's affairs was for Russia a two-year tale of frustration and failure, and when the coalition ministry took office in May events in Greece quickly presented it with perhaps its most formidable diplomatic challenge while in office. The background of the issues involved merits some consideration.

From August 1914 to June 1917 two men dominated the Greek political scene: King Constantine and his sometime Prime Minister, Eleutherios Venizelos. In large measure the wartime history of Greece was determined by the fluctuating relationship of these two very different personalities. The King, brother-in-law of the German Emperor, was from the start resolved to keep his nation out of a war which, in his eyes, promised Greece no advantage. His insistence on Greek neutrality, combined with an understandable, tactless and not unshared sympathy for the Central Powers, gave his domestic foes and their Entente sponsors valuable ammunition in their struggle to push Greece into the war against Turkey and Bulgaria. This was the goal of Venizelos' ambitions. He himself best described his policy: "to tie Greece to the apron strings of the Sea Powers."[43] For Greece, no less than for Italy, it would be the height of folly to expose a virtually undefended coastline to the threat of British reprisal.

As the war spread into the Balkans, the dispute between the two men grew steadily more bitter. The Bulgarian threat brought matters to their first crisis. On September 21, 1915, Venizelos, freshly triumphant in national elections, requested the King to authorize mobilization preparatory to aiding Serbia against the imminent Bulgarian offensive. The Premier argued that Greece must honor the pledge given to Belgrade of joint action should Bulgaria resort to arms to avenge her 1913 defeats. Constantine reasoned that that arrangement did not envisage war against Great Power allies of Bulgaria and hence was no longer valid. Venizelos employed the same stratagem as Sonnino in such emergencies: he proffered his resignation. The King yielded to the extent of permitting an invitation to the Entente to furnish the troops due from Serbia in the event of war, a bitter concession on Constantine's part.[44] London and Paris hastened to comply. Early in October the first Anglo-French detachments began disembarking at Salonika. To satisfy international appearances, Venizelos lodged a public protest at the rupture of Greek neutrality, with the understanding that none of his new partners would pay any heed.[45] Further Greek progress into war halted at that point as Constantine dug his heels in at actual belligerence. Venizelos thereat made good his earlier threat of resignation with the first part of his work done. The Entente units began digging in around the kingdom's second city for a period of extended residence.

In the course of the next eighteen months the Entente thrust itself ever more deeply into the affairs of what remained in theory a neutral and independent state. France took the lead. She justified her interference on the grounds that the three senior Entente Great Powers, as the original guarantors of Greek independence, were obliged to defend the nation against internal subversion, meaning the Greek sovereign.[46] With the Salonika army under French command, the Briand Cabinet was able and eager to fulfill its legacy from the Bourbons in the hope that protection might knock Greece off her neutral perch. The naval and military commanders, Admiral Dartige du Fournet and General Maurice Sarrail, menaced local authorities with the direst consequences should they fail to obey Entente instructions. The French campaign received useful support in October 1916 when Venizelos arrived in Salonika under Allied protection to proclaim a provisional government pledged to lead Greece to her glorious destiny at the side of her protective powers.[47]

France's Allies endorsed her tactics with noticeable restraint. Ambassador Benckendorff cabled Sazonov and Stürmer in his impeccable French that the British Cabinet seemed unaware of Paris' ultimate intentions in Greece, but wished above all else to maintain diplomatic unity with France.[48] Sonnino profited from worsening Entente relations with the Royal Hellenic government by moving Italian troops into Southern Albania. His pretext that Russia's progressive enfeeblement in the Balkans required a stronger Italian presence in that part of the peninsula was an early illustration of the policy to be seen in greater scope some months later. Russian officials frequently complained at French high-handedness and the Imperial family itself set the tone.[49] Their objections, apart from the personal affronts to "poor Tino," stemmed from an apprehension that France and the Venizelist movement harbored anti-monarchical designs in Greece. A republican, French-dominated regime in Athens would not, in Tsarist opinions, be a suitable neighbor for a Russian-held Constantinople. But was the dynastic principle worth a breach with the Allies? Izvol'skii for one thought not:

> It appears to me [he wrote to Stürmer] much more to our advantage to renounce our protection of King Constantine, recognize France's leading role in the Greek question and demand that a similarly [dominant] role be recognized as our due in questions of greater importance to us.[50]

Petrograd thought otherwise. Through its representative in Athens, E. P. Demidov, the Tsarist Government continued to resist the open partiality of its two largest Allies for the spreading Venizelist movement.

French irritation finally forced the issue. In his report to Nicholas II on the Inter-Allied Conference in Petrograd of February 1917, Foreign Minister Pokrovskii alluded to the demand "of one of the conference members"—undoubtedly French—"for decisive measures in Greece to force the submission of the Royal Hellenic government to the will and interests of its Allies."[51] This meant the installation in power of Venizelos and its by now inevitable precondition, the expulsion of the King. With Lloyd George showing more favor than Asquith had done, Briand evidently felt less need to spare Russian sensibilities. Two weeks before the Tsar's abdication,

Paléologue received instructions to remind Pokrovskii of certain facts of international life. He was to state that, while the French Government fully admitted the need for a more closely co-ordinated Entente policy in Greece, it was nevertheless of the opinion

> that in this question a prior arrangement should be reached between the three Guarantor Powers and especially between England and France, since for her part Russia had expressed her readiness to associate herself in the memoranda [to the Royal Hellenic Government] of both these Powers who are making the greatest material sacrifices in Greece and have at their disposal the most effective means of influencing the Greek Government.[52]

In brief, Tsarist authorities should cease their useless agitation on behalf of a regime that France was able and willing to destroy.

The March Revolution did nothing to cause Paris to defer to Russian complaints. Quite the contrary, it now appeared as if the French Government was prepared to ignore Russia altogether. Two days after Nicholas vanished, Ambassador Giers telegrammed from Rome that a project sponsored by the Briand Cabinet proposed the division of key administrative functions in Greece among three of the four Entente Powers. France, it transpired, was to supervise all communications, Britain all food supplies and Italy the police. No responsibilities were to be entrusted to Russia, though it was conceded she might have representatives in each sphere at a subordinate level. Each of the three directors should have a French assistant and a French general should exercise supreme control.[53]

This was asserting French primacy with a vengeance and even the normally complaisant British objected. Sir Francis Elliot, the minister in Athens, took issue with the exaggerated preponderance assigned to France, while Sonnino, very much disliking the way Greek affairs were developing, drew the line at Russia's lack of representation.[54] At that point French domestic affairs intervened to impart a new urgency to the situation. On March 17 the Briand Cabinet fell, to be replaced two days later by a ministry under Alexandre Ribot. On the 21st the new Premier appeared before the Chamber to promise fresh efforts at improving the nation's overall military position. "Victory," he reminded the deputies, "depends on the energy with which we gather all our strength to be used in a united effort on all fronts with the same vigor."[55] Almost at once, as Izvol'skii was quick to note, the Prime Minister's attention was directed to the relevance of this statement to Greek affairs. The Foreign Affairs Committee of the Chamber demanded that the new Cabinet act more vigorously in Athens than its predecessor, a request the press was happy to second in view of the four-month-long failure of the Salonika forces to make military headway against the enemy.[56] *Le Temps* reminded readers that the Russian Revolution had deprived Constantine of his last support within the alliance.[57] Demidov himself confirmed that opinion. Elliot, agreeing, thought the only way to restore "normal relations" with Athens was to replace General Sarrail, now becoming an object of intense British dislike.[58] It hardly needed saying that such was not the intention of the French Government. Greek affairs were to be the area where Ribot would prove his resolution in prosecuting the war.

From April to mid-June French diplomacy worked to bring the Greek problem to a conclusion satisfactory to Paris: Venizelos in dependent power, the King in exile. First France had to swing other interested parties into line; she began with Italy. At St Jean, Sonnino accepted with bad grace that Constantine should go though, mindful of the instability of his own King's throne, he had sought and received assurances that the Greek monarchy itself would remain; there would be no constituent assembly nor encouragement of republican propaganda.[59] Ribot then turned to London to ask that Sarrail be authorized to occupy Thessaly in order to gather the harvest which could thereafter be doled out to deserving areas.[60] Lloyd George demurred at this suggestion but gave in at a follow-up Anglo-French session in Paris where it was also decided to provide for the co-ordination of Allied policy in Greece that Miliukov's immediate predecessor had once been promised.[61] Proposals from London of a British appointment that might underline the multi-national nature of Entente involvement were passed over in favor of Ribot's preference for a fellow countryman. His choice fell upon Senator Jonnart, a former Governor of Algeria, who prepared to assume office in Salonika as High Commissioner with a reputation confirmed in North Africa of possessing a talent for administration and "a fist of iron."[62] He was to have a free hand, "not excluding the possibility of deposing King Constantine."[63] The major players were moving into position for the last act of the Greek drama without anyone in Paris apparently feeling it necessary to ascertain the thoughts of the new regime in Petrograd.

P. N. Miliukov looked upon the Greek imbroglio with mixed feelings. While in opposition, he had expressed complete agreement with Anglo-French policy in Athens. In contrast to Tsarist judgments, he accepted the charge of Germanophilia levelled against the King whose "personal policy" in Miliukov's opinion justified the Entente's campaign against him. He also approved Venizelos' proclamation of the insurgent Salonika regime, believing that the Cretan must "save Greece and perhaps even the King against his [Constantine's] will."[64] Once in office he permitted a Venizelist agent to reside in Petrograd and, reportedly, welcomed him with an expression of his greatest esteem for Venizelos and his hope for the decisive triumph of the "national" movement.[65]

Yet he was bound to have certain reservations once he had moved into the Foreign Ministry. How would a Venizelist Greece affect Russia's, or rather his own, plans for South-East Europe and Asia Minor? Miliukov was quite familiar with Venizelos' ambitions for Greek expansion in Anatolia.[66] What was to be Greece's future role in the Eastern Mediterranean? Heavy dependence on the Western Powers suggested that the latter might soon enjoy an undesirably large influence near a Russian Constantinople. In the weeks ahead Miliukov would continue to remind Entente colleagues of these causes for Russian concern, even while agreeing with Izvol'skii that Greece was "of secondary importance to Russia."[67]

In Salonika Miliukov's greeting to Venizelos came in refreshing contrast to the months of Tsarist hostility. The press encouraged his goodwill. On March 22 a local correspondent of the conservative daily *Russkaia Volia* commented approvingly on "the distinct Russophile tendencies" of the Venizelist press. "The Salonika government," he wrote optimistically, "in order that it should be a national . . . government needs the official recognition of Russian and the appointment of a Russian diplomatic representative in Salonika." This had of course hitherto been denied the Venizelist movement. Then, writing as if the Russia of March 1917 were still that of July 1914, the correspondent went on to account for Venizelos' alleged partiality to the new Russia:

> Seeing that Constantinople is promised to [us], the Venizelist press realizes that it must not count on the conquest of the ancient capital of the Byzantine empire. In addition, the imminent collaboration [in the war] with Russia encourages Venizelist circles to settle Greek policy in relation to the [Provisional Government]. They realize that Russia, a great Orthodox Power, up to now has always been favorable in its attitude to Hellenism and it is possible that such a relationship might continue in the future.

Russia could no longer have anything to do with King Constantine; "the honor and dignity of Russian protection falls upon Venizelist Greece."[68]

This effusion was hardly realistic in Russia's circumstances at the time and became steadily less so. Nonetheless, Venizelist elements were by no means averse to taking the hint. The Salonika *Neologos*, a vociferous pro-Venizelos organ, acclaimed the prospect of a Russian owned Constantinople and a South Slav state on the Adriatic under Russian sponsorship. With emphasis on the Greek political scene, *Neologos* hoped that the Revolution would "put an end to all the shifts of Russian policy in the Balkans" and infuse new energy into Russia's diplomatic treatment of "that German puppet in Athens."[69] This faithfully reflected Venizelos' own view. Publicly he accepted the need to preserve the dynasty; privately his ideas tended to the republican solution feared by Sonnino. On April 19, as the Italian Foreign Minister was unfolding his opinions on the subject at St Jean, the Venizelist "Foreign Minister" Politis wrote to his agent in Paris that their leader intended, once in control, to proclaim the King's deposition and place the question of republic or monarchy before a constituent assembly to meet after the war.

> Of course [Politis went on] in the interval members of the Royal Family would be invited in the public interest to withdraw abroad. . . . Thus we would imitate the Russian example, avoid questions now dividing the Powers and reserve final decision to the verdict of the people.

Three days later, having heard something of the St Jean proceedings, Politis returned to his theme. With Britain firmly opposed to "a radical solution," i.e. a republic (Politis said nothing of Italy whose objections, via Sonnino, were much stronger), Venizelos now felt that the best answer would be a British prince on the Greek throne. Should this fail, as it certainly would,[70] Politis and Venizelos considered a republic the only possible alternative. And with Russia pointing the way, what was to be feared in that? In Politis' view, nothing whatever:

> I have even begun to think that if the republican regime is adopted in Russia, it could not be dangerous for Greece as well. . . . As long as the Entente Great Powers were, with one exception, monarchies, I had for international reasons to exclude a republic. But this objection has vanished before the democratic current.[71]

Politis obviously assumed as a matter of course that the new Russia would welcome any such change in Greece.

Venizelist agents were not alone in this belief. On April 24 Izvol'skii transmitted a message from Ribot that the French government would not be able to oppose Greek attempts to establish a republic and presumed that no objections to this need be expected from Petrograd. Ribot assured Miliukov that he had nothing to fear from any changes in the Greek constitution, nor did France have the slightest intention of supporting Venizelist aims to expand in Asiatic Turkey.[72] The first part of the Premier's message directly contradicted French promises to Sonnino at St Jean de Maurienne which Miliukov may have known nothing of. At any rate he was quick to protest that if the King were forced to abdicate, the question of a new constitution must be left for the Greek people to determine; there must be no French imposed republic in the Aegean. Neither was he swayed by Venizelist protestations of disinterest in territorial issues of concern to him. Izvol'skii must explain to Ribot that, while it was impossible for the Provisional Government to support the King or openly oppose Venizelos, Miliukov thought the latter's known fantasy of a "Greater Greece" raised dangers "contrary to Russia's interests and to the necessary pacification of the Balkans."[73] It was Miliukov's last official comment on Greek matters.

On May 3 a new Greek Cabinet took office with the intention, in the words of its head, Zaimis, of "wearying France with concessions."[74] Zaimis spoke too late, even though there had been concessions in plenty from his predecessors back to Venizelos. The continued Entente inability to pierce the German-Bulgarian lines in Macedonia convinced many, none more than Sarrail, that the source of all Allied misfortunes was to be found in the Athens Royal Palace. On May 28 Ribot and Jonnart arrived in London to dissipate Lloyd George's last scruples at the use of force should Constantine balk at abdication. It was in any event agreed that French troops should occupy the Isthmus of Corinth to prevent royalist troops in the Peleponnesus from going to their King's assistance. Once Greece was safely in the war for national self-determination, the British proposed to retire one division and two brigades from the unproductive Salonika front for service in Egypt.[75]

Through the next two weeks French diplomacy worked in Greece against a rising chorus of Allied discontent. On June 4 Tereshchenko protested to Paris and London at every aspect of the Greek affair. A political coup in Greece with its attendant risk of civil war was an inadmissible hazard. So also was the intention to withdraw British troops, a move that jeopardized Russia's planned offensive later that month in Rumania. For both reasons Tereshchenko recommended that the Anglo-French scheme, "which is not at present justified by any special circumstances nor corresponds to any general Allied interests," be indefinitely shelved.[76] From Athens, Demidov, much disliked by the French for his championing of Constantine and nicknamed by Sarrail for that reason as "that fierce royalist," remarked that France's course hardly seemed consistent with professed Allied goals of freedom for small nations and self-determination. Tereshchenko agreed. He had assumed office with the intention of defending those principles in Allied councils. Unlike Miliukov he had no inherited suspicion of Venizelist designs on Constantinople, nor of a republican Greece provided the Greek people achieved this status on their own. Yet he was bound by the facts of his accession to office to speak out more forcefully than Miliukov against Allied pressure to force political change in Greece. The overriding diplomatic fact remained, however, that Paris paid no attention to Russian appeals, whether couched in the name of national self-determination, Allied solidarity or the common obligations of Greece's guarantors. If any changes were to be brought about in French policy, Russia's other partners would have to do the work.[77]

Italy too objected strenuously to French actions and found Ribot deaf to complaints. More fortunate than Tereshchenko, though, Sonnino was able to compensate his wounded amour-propre elsewhere in the Balkans. Demidov's Italian colleague, Bosdari, remarked that Italy's "vital interests" did not permit her to remain indifferent to French interference in Greece, an observation Demidov guessed to be the forerunner of some new Balkan irruption.[78] His foresight was faultless. On June 3 the military command in Valona announced the independence of Albania under Italian protection and the return to that distracted land "of the civilization of the Romans and Venetians." Sonnino justified the violation of the 1915 agreement on grounds of military expediency but Giers had no doubt it came in response to French policies in Greece. Lloyd George preferred, in retrospect if not at the time, to believe that the latest Italian failure to break through on the Isonzo (the tenth) encouraged Rome to find an easier triumph somewhere else.[79]

With a relatively free hand at last won, the French decided the time had come to cut the Greek knot. Jonnart's open advocacy in Salonika of coercive measures against the King, coupled with a warning that Athens would be bombarded in the event of resistance, galvanized the faint-hearted British ministers into last minute counsels of moderation. Jonnart received the appropriate instructions but with them an expression of Ribot's confidence that the High Commissioner would take all decisions "which circumstances might require."[80] This was scarcely the restraint desired by the London War Cabinet which found itself reduced to the extremity of soliciting Russian diplomatic co-operation to achieve Sarrail's recall and his replacement at the head of the Salonika armies by someone less disposed to involve himself in non-military matters. When that produced no results, Cecil warned of the adverse effects in Russia and upon the exiled Serbian regime of French strong-arm methods. Jonnart's reaction to all this was a pointed reminder to all concerned that he was answerable only to Paris.[81]

The crisis was placing a severe strain on the fabric of Entente diplomatic unity. Whether a public rupture could be avoided depended on the speed and nature of the denouement. Ribot afterwards was to tell Jonnart that total success alone could have saved his sacrifice to the requirements of the alliance. The High Commissioner hardly needed any reminders; at the risk of exceeding his instructions he resolved to bring about the consummation so ardently desired in Paris and Salonika but nowhere else. On June 11, in the name of the three Guarantor Powers, he delivered an ultimatum to Zaimis demanding the King's abdication as a violator of the constitution and his immediate departure from Greece along with his eldest son, deemed to have been contaminated by the same political virus as his father. The King's second son, Alexander, destined to succumb to a monkey's bite, was to succeed. Entente units, including a Russian detachment, moved into position to enforce Jonnart's will and Greece, in Demidov's words, "[was] delivered into the hands of our present Allies." Tereshchenko's sole recourse was a protest at Jonnart's invocation of the three Powers. Since Russia had not consented to the expulsion of the old King, nor to the accession of the new, the High Commissioner should stop pretending he spoke on behalf of the Provisional Government. It scarcely mattered. A triumphant Venizelos rode back to power on June 27, first taking pains to assure "that fierce royalist" that if King Alexander did not do exactly as he was told, "we shall deal with him as you did in Russia."[82]

CHAPTER VII
REVOLUTIONARY DIPLOMACY

The Offensive

"All's well that ends well" was Cecil's epitaph on the Greek affair.[1] The Provisional Government profoundly disagreed. In its first diplomatic test on taking office, the Coalition Ministry failed completely to impress its Allies abroad with the relevance of the principles proclaimed so eloquently on May 1st. In Petrograd those principles had swept Miliukov from office; in London, Paris and Rome their impact was much less spectacular. The replies received from the three capitals to the Russian statement of May 1st professed to see nothing incongruous between their respective peace programs and the noble aims of the Russian democracy. On the question of treaty revision the British note expressed a readiness "if need be" to cooperate; the French smothered a refusal in skillful verbiage; Sonnino ignored it altogether.[2] The cumulative voice from the West seemed in fact to lend some substance to Miliukov's fears: Russia could give up whatever she chose in the regions set aside for her exploitation; her partners felt no urge to imitate her abnegation.

This situation could not pass unchallenged. Domestic pressures and revolutionary prestige required that Tereshchenko prove to Russia's Allies the seriousness of his nation's intention to infuse Entente diplomacy with a new just and democratic spirit. Under the impetus of recent Balkan events, Government and Soviet opened their compaign to win converts to their side.

Italy's Albanian annexation started matters off. Sonnino had consulted none of his Allies, large or small; two of the latter directed their first complaints to Tereshchenko as the legatee of Tsardom. The Royal Greek Government, understandably seeing no point in appealing to Britain, still less France, turned for comfort to Greece's third Protecting Power. Pašić spoke in similar terms from Corfu, relying on maternal Russia's traditional concern for her Slav brethren confronting yet another Great Power intrusion on their borders.[3] Tereshchenko went through the motions in responding. He was "surprised" at the Italian act, one that affected the entire peninsula and not just a small part of it—such was the gist of Russian indignation reported to Rome.[4] He apparently contemplated an identic note of protest from Italy's three largest Allies, a meaningless gesture discouraged by the British War Cabinet, itself "painfully impressed" by the news from Valona.[5] All these were moves in the traditional style, made mechanically and with little expectation that they would produce any changes in a matter that did not impinge directly upon long-standing or recognised Russian interests. Tereshchenko was more concerned with the act's side effects on domestic Petrograd politics, "provoking strong excitement in our press and political circles and again raising questions about annexations, publication of the secret treaties and their revision" he cabled lamentingly to his chargés in London and Paris.[6] Perhaps to his surprise, his fears proved groundless. Apart from an expected sneer from the Bolsheviks the Petrograd political scene digested Albania's annexation with less fuss than the Roman.[7]

Tereshchenko was, nevertheless, committed to action of some sort. On June 13, as events in Athens were moving to their climax, he proposed to the French Government, via Albert Thomas, that Allied representatives meet at an early date, "as soon as the circumstances become favorable . . . to revise the agreements concerning the basic aims of the war." He made this approach, he said, since the Allied Governments had shown themselves willing to meet the Provisional Government on the revision question.[8] This was a hopeful reading of the high-flown circumlocutions addressed to him in response to the May 1st note. Tereshchenko's vagueness, coupled with his insistence on Russia's continued loyalty to the common cause, allowed the other Entente members to put his invitation to one side for the time being. Allied reservations in turn further encouraged the suspicions of the Russian left and drove Tereshchenko publicly to admit on June 19 that "the most irritating factor in Russian foreign policy [was] undoubtedly the question of our attitude on Greece." The rest of his remarks made it plain that he had no desire to increase the discords between Russia and her Allies; he had indeed not yet lost hope that some French concessions might be salvaged out of the whole business.[9] On June 20 he instructed Nabokov and Sevastopulo to propose that King Alexander be recognized as "temporary regent" until a final solution of the Greek form of government after the war.[10] Nothing came of the suggestion and in its aftermath the minister was bombarded with advice from Athens and Paris as to how Russia should react to Greek events. Demidov sent in a dirge over Great Russia's Balkan position:

> "I am obliged to note with the greatest sorrow the temporary decline of Russia's traditional influence in the Balkan peninsula. . . . Insufficient attention to Greek affairs, meagre, badly handled military aid to the Serbs . . .

> finally our internal crises which have for some time paralyzed the military and diplomatic activity of Great Russia, have created a seriously unfavorable situation for us."[11]

Sevastopulo struck a more realistic and pessimistic note, arguing that French opinions on Balkan matters carried considerable weight and should be carefully heeded.[12] His implication seemed to be that Russian interests in South-East Europe must be abandoned whenever they conflicted with French or British priorities.

None in Petrograd was yet prepared to admit the point. The Albanian and Greek disputes had for the first time, apart from the Constantinople issue, focused the attention of the Russian left squarely upon Balkan concerns. *Izvestiia* sounded a more aggressive theme on June 17 by writing that the "favorable conditions" referred to in Tereshchenko's note four days previously on war aims revision "can arise only as a result of an international struggle of democracy against world imperialism." The Stockholm conference would play the decisive role here but, in preparing for that meeting, the Soviet itself must move more energetically in the war aims question.[13]

Among the first to feel the impact of this greater Soviet energy were the latest arrivals in the continuing procession of foreign Socialist delegations. On May 31 a four-man Italian team arrived in Petrograd headed by Arturo Labriola; two days later they were followed by Arthur Henderson, Minister without Portfolio and lone Socialist member of Lloyd George's War Cabinet. Henderson was of greater political consequence than his three British trailblazers Sanders, Thorne and O'Grady, but his mission was essentially the same. He was to encourage a more favorable attitude from Russian Socialists towards the war and serve as a British equivalent to Albert Thomas in replacing the courtly Buchanan as ambassador. Unlike Thomas, Henderson concluded that his Socialist loyalties did not automatically qualify him as a better representative to the Russian democracy; the Petrograd Soviet would probably have agreed, after the visit if not before.[14]

A week after his arrival Henderson appeared for the ritual session before the Ex. Com. He endorsed the Soviet's peace formula, doing so "as the representative of the British workers' and soldiers' movement." He spoke cautiously on the territorial issues then most contentious:

> Important re-organizations must . . . be effected in Turkey in the interest of the security of Armenians and Arabs. Constantinople, if possible, must be converted into a free port and the Dardanelles must be internationalized.
>
> Ways and means must be found for a more satisfactory and just solution to the

> Balkan problem. The British proletariat of course desires peace and will welcome peace, but it must be peace with honor, it must be an efficacious peace, it must be a peace that would preclude the possibility of the ascendancy of brute force in the future.[15]

It was all rather vague; moreover his emphasis on an "efficacious peace" was not unlike Miliukov's earlier enthusiasm for "guarantees and sanctions." In fact Henderson had a miserable time in Russia. The normal strains of foreign travel were compounded by the hazards of wartime, the discomforts of revolutionary Petrograd, including the theft of his top hat and dress suit, the appalling heat and the conviction, according to his loyal biographer, that nothing he said on the war had the slightest effect on "the vague, muddled, unbusiness-like" Socialists he met—these did not include Lenin.[16] Apart from his intervention in a tin plate workers' strike, winning them a thirty-seven and a half per cent raise in wages in a grand gesture of Socialist solidarity, his trip to Russia had no benefits for his audiences and none for himself.[17] He returned home deeply impressed by his experiences and, like Thomas and Cachin, a strong proponent of the Stockholm conference. An annoyed Lloyd George attributed this defection of a Cabinet colleague to "more than a touch of the revolutionary malaria" now unfortunately endemic in the Russian capital.[18]

The four Italians[19] encountered a stormier reception. Their job was more difficult than Henderson's for, in addition to the common goal of whipping up war fever, the visitors from Rome had to face hostile interrogation on their country's Balkan and Turkish war aims. They could not have arrived at a more awkward moment for the success of their mission. On May 31 *Pravda* published on its front page a short warning letter from the Russo-Italian Socialist Angelica Balabanova. Her credentials as a commentator on the four guests were impeccable as far as *Pravda* and its readers were concerned. A prominent member of the Italian Socialist Party, editor of its newspaper, she had stayed steadfast in her opposition to the war while others, notably those now purporting to speak in Russia on behalf of Italian workers, were strident in support of Italian belligerence. Balabanova had figured prominently in the Zimmerwald and Kienthal conferences; she was, with Lenin, sharp in her criticisms of European majority Socialists and in 1917 she capped her revolutionary worthiness in *Pravda*'s eyes by joining the Bolshevik Party.[20] Her pen now denounced the spurious comrades from Rome. Labriola was nothing more than "a fervent syndicalist turned democratic monarchist"; Lerda and Raimondo had gone over to "the party of Freemasonry"; Cappa had "always been a Republican and anti-Socialist."[21] None of the four could be regarded as opposed to the 1915 London Treaty, whose general outline was splashed across the pages of the Socialist press in the days preceding the delegation's arrival.

Before their departure for Russia delegation members had undertaken to keep their home press supplied with details and impressions of their Russian sojourn. Accordingly, in June, the major newspapers carried vivid accounts of Labriola's triumphs: interviews with personalities of importance, Kerenskii, Tsereteli, Tereshchenko and Mandić of the Yugoslav Committee. Carlotti supplied corroborative material; the visitors were producing "an excellent effect" in Russia, Sonnino was told. It is evident the ambassador was deriving his information from sources other than Labriola's Soviet audiences.[22] The Ex. Com. took advantage of their Italian comrades' presence to query them on the precise intent and scope of Italian ambitions in the Adriatic and Turkey. All in all it was an embarrassing ordeal for the visitors, who pleaded ignorance to any treaty promises affecting Asia Minor. They stressed to their skeptical hosts that the proclamation of June 3 in Valona had spoken of Albanian independence, hence should not be seen as an act of annexation. One questioner then asked Labriola for his views on Dalmatia, a predominantly Slav province. Since Labriola was on record as favoring some Italian recognition of that fact but was in Russia with his Government's blessing, any answer he gave was bound to annoy someone. He and his colleagues agreed that the Dalmatian problem was "very complicated," but they did not want Russian popular opinion to be misinformed on the status of the Dalmatian nationalities. According to Italian statistics, "a significant part of the population of Dalmatia" consisted of Italians and Catholic Croats "linked to Italy by ties of culture and religion."[23] This half-way reply earned for Labriola a reputation of a nationalist in foreign policy matters,[24] but he finally managed to steer discussion to the subject that interested him and his Government the most, the willingness of the Russian democracy to stay in the war. He asked whether the Soviet would support Russia's continued participation in the fighting if the remaining Entente governments were to adopt the no annexations pledge. According to *La Stampa*'s account Tsereteli and Chernov would admit only that the Socialist slogan "recognizes in principle the rights of France, Italy and Serbia."[25] There was not in any case the least chance that the delegation's own Government would go along with the formula. On June 20 Sonnino faced the Chamber of Deputies for the first time since Miliukov's fall and dismissed the formula "purely negative in meaning, much favored by a strong party in Petrograd: No Annexations or Indemnities." Italy's conscience was clear: "reasons of international justice" precluded the slogan's applicability to Italian war aims anywhere. "Loud and prolonged applause . . . ministers and deputies jump to their feet

[and] congratulate the honorable Minister of Foreign Affairs" was a reaction that told its own tale of the dominant Italian view on foreign expansion and the likelihood of any immediate change.[26]

The Coalition Ministry's difficulty in making its position on foreign policy heeded exposed it to some sharp rebukes from more radical leftists outside.[27] But inside the Cabinet too, serious misgivings were emerging over the course of recent Entente policy in South-East Europe. These fears did not all derive from Socialist resentment at persistent Allied flouting of Petrograd's peace formulas. The threat of a British troop withdrawal from the Salonika front spurred Tereshchenko to protest that not only was Russia's planned offensive thereby imperilled, her entire position in the Balkans also faced ruin. The British action, if emulated by other Allies, would permit a further advance of the Central Powers south and west, a prospect that "would have the most deplorable efforts on our Balkan policy and create innumerable difficulties for us."[28] The gist of Tereshchenko's messages to his foreign colleagues following the Greek coup lay in reiterated appeals for more consultation between the Allies on matters relating to South-East Europe.[29] Results were at length forthcoming. On July 6 the Government gazette announced the intention of the Entente Powers to meet shortly in Paris "to co-ordinate Allied views" in dealing with "the extraordinary complexity of the political and strategic situation in the Balkans." Citing the Greek affair in justification, the announcement promised that the Russian representatives at the conference would be instructed

> in the settlement of political questions arising in the Balkans to defend the viewpoint of the Provisional Government and with especial vigor to insist on the establishment of the general fundamentals of foreign policy as proclaimed by the Russian democracy.[30]

A major test lay ahead for Russian diplomacy if these ambitions were to be realized. In South-East Europe the omens were everywhere unfavorable.

Balkan Disillusionments

Miliukov's successors surveyed the affairs of the Balkan peninsula from a different vantage point than he. In part this came as the natural consequence of the new democratic theme in Russian foreign policy after May 1st. By July even more relevant was a rising tide of disenchantment with all three of Russia's Balkan Allies. The newest of that number, Venizelist Greece, inspired little enough enthusiasm from the Provisional Government, none at all from the Soviet. Both bodies saw the Cretan politician as the catspaw of Anglo-French diplomacy in the Eastern Mediterranean, and the Foreign Ministry continued throughout the summer to receive a spate of warnings from Demidov at Venizelos' hostile intentions in matters as disparate as the Russian monks on Mount Athos and plans for a Greater Greece in Anatolia.[31] The two senior partners in the peninsula incurred a still greater odium; it is difficult to judge which of the Rumanian or Serbian Premiers was the more disliked in Petrograd by the time of the July offensive.

Bratianu returned to Jassy from his Russian visit in mid-May publicly affirming his satisfaction with his discussions in Petrograd. Privately his feelings on the subject were less sanguine, the situation in the Russian Government "being so exceptionally uncertain that its good will [was] now paralyzed."[32] "Its" meant Miliukov, whose resignation on the day Bratianu left for home promised nothing but trouble for Rumania's cause, as the Prime Minister himself had tearfully recognized. His most desperate efforts went into a defence of the treaties by which Rumania had entered the war. Seeing that Italy too was a latecomer to the Entente, with territorial ambitions of her own and a Latin sister to boot, Bratianu selected Sonnino's minister in Jassy, Baron Fasciotti, as his favorite confidant amongst the diplomatic corps. Neither country, Bratianu emphasized, should count on the rising star of the Provisional Government, Alexander Kerenskii, for Miliukov's tenacity in their behalf. While in Petrograd Bratianu had turned all his considerable eloquence on the Justice Minister. Self-determination was unfair, the Premier reported himself as arguing, when it was a question of restoring lands once linked to the Motherland by race and separated since "by political and historical circumstances." In the Dobruja, Bulgaria had exterminated all pro-Rumanians; to admit self determination there would mean handing the province over permanently to the "Prussia of the Balkans." Bratianu then illustrated his point with a historical reference perhaps not entirely tactful when retelling it to the Italian minister. None had consulted the inhabitants of Nice in 1860 when they were handed over to Napoleon III, so why should people now worry about the inhabitants of the Dobruja? According to Fasciotti's report to Rome, Bratianu failed to get anything more than vague replies out of Kerenskii, whose links with the Soviet were not enough to get the Premier a hearing before that body.[33] The Ex. Com. declined absolutely to receive such an unabashed champion of annexations. Shortly after his departure, *Den'* revealed details of Bratianu's diplomatic dealings prior to Rumania's entry into the war. Drawing attention to his exorbitant and successful demands, *Den'* decided that Rumania's subsequent misfortunes came as a "guilt sacrifice to her own imperialism [and] frivolous greed."[34] For once *Pravda* endorsed a judgment from the moderate Socialist press. The Rumanian and Italian treaties showed how false was Russia's claim to be fighting for Slavdom. "Rumanian capitalists and landlords," wrote Gregory Zinoviev, "are to receive lands with Serbian, Ukrainian and Bulgarian populations. They will be treated in the same way as Rumanian Jews."[35]

To console himself for these slights and disappointments, Bratianu welcomed the peripatetic Albert Thomas to Jassy at the end of May. Thomas did not let him down. Holding the King by the arm the French visitor promised a parade of Rumanian soldiers the Greater Rumania of their Prime Minister's desire.[36] From the Rumanian end some preparatory work was also necessary, if only to improve Rumanian respectability in the eyes of a censorious Russian Ally. On May 17 King Ferdinand opened the sixth session of the current Parliament with a speech promising major steps on land reform and expansion of the electoral franchise. Parliament was requested to revise the constitution, Article XIX of which guaranteed the inviolability of private property, to authorize the liquidation of Crown landholdings and to limit estates to a maximum of five hundred hectares.[37] The program, modest though it was to Russian observers, set off prolonged howls from Rumanian Conservatives whose obstructionist tactics over the next several weeks probably confirmed the worst misgivings in Petrograd about the Rumanian political scene. A compromise measure passed both Houses of the Rumanian Parliament on June 29.[38]

The electoral issue was more explosive in the context of Russo-Rumanian relations because of the implications it raised for Rumanian Jews. In law this juxtaposition of nationalities was itself inadmissible. Jews were not and could not be Rumanian citizens and, in spite of fitful European intervention on their behalf since 1878, they remained subject to harassment, discrimination and, upon occasion, outright persecution. As several members of the infant Rumanian Socialist Party were Jews and were on both counts liable to repression, Russian army Soviets resolved to protect them "regardless of the fact that this is perhaps unacceptable from an international point of view."[39] Knowing Russian opinions, the King had promised Jews full citizenship rights in April, but the effect of his promise was negated by inherent Russian suspicions and subsequent events. On June 19 Rumanian army headquarters announced with much publicity the execution of thirty-two "Rumanians and Jews" for spying.[40] The Petrograd Soviet at once demanded information, brushing aside Tereshchenko's reminder that the matter was an internal affair of an allied state with the reply that Russian soldiers considered themselves Rumanian citizens by virtue of their blood shed for Rumania.[41] Left unsaid on this occasion was the admission made to the Soviet by a committee from the Rumanian front that "interference of the democracy in Rumanian affairs" had to be tolerated in order to pacify mutinous Russian troops in unoccupied Rumania.[42]

Bratianu thus found himself between two millstones. The upper was the High Command of the Rumanian Army, thoroughly reorganized since the 1916 disasters by a French military mission under General Berthelot, insisting on a vigorous campaign against German spies, a category into which as a matter of course were consigned all Jews and Socialists. The lower consisted of the Petrograd Soviet and its agents; it was their pressure that Bratianu chose to defy. He told the Soviet's commissar at the front, Tisenhausen, that since Rumanians did not interfere in Russia's affairs nor dictate to her the forms of her government, why should the reverse condition be any more acceptable? Warming to his theme (as reported to Fasciotti for onward transmission) the Premier remarked that when it came to the death penalty democratic Russia had nothing to teach Rumania. She had abolished its civil application long ago; it took a revolution to accomplish the same in Russia. Nor were Russian hands any cleaner than Rumanian on the Jewish issue; what of the pogroms of recent memory? His hectoring tone towards Tisenhausen permitted no doubt as to what Bratianu thought of the Russian democracy's principal organ that the commissar represented. Small wonder therefore that local Soviets grew more peremptory in their interference in Rumanian affairs: the evils seemed flagrant and polite exchanges got nowhere.[43]

Capital punishment also played a part in embittering relations between the Russian democracy and the exiled Pašić regime. The alienation was sudden. Until July Serbian prestige stood high in Petrograd and survived the change of foreign ministers in mid-May. When Tereshchenko assumed his new portfolio he assured the Serbian Premier of the warm sympathy of the Russian democracy.[44] Possibly exaggerated, his greeting was nonetheless distinctly warmer than the purely formal notification that went to Jassy. Friendly articles appeared from time to time in the Petrograd press, and in Geneva a much gratified *La Serbie* related minister Spalajković's emotional triumph before the assembled delegates of the Russian Black Sea fleet in Odessa. They must stay true to their small Slav brother; "if you betray us, if you abandon us to our fate, I could not bear it, I swear I would kill myself."[45] The sailors present reassured him this would not be necessary; all swore to fight for Serbia's liberty "and the territories to which she has a right."[45] From this crescendo there was an abrupt descent to the point where by the time of the July offensive the Russian left felt nothing but aggrieved contempt for Pašić and all his works. Wholly responsible for the change of mood was the execution at Salonika after a seven-month imprisonment and a highly dubious trial of the leaders of the Serbian secret society *Ujedinjenje ili Smrt* (Union or Death).[46]

The trial of Colonel Apis and his co-defendants opened at Salonika on April 2. For six weeks the Provisional Government withheld comment. Miliukov's resignation quickly saw a change in tactics. On May 30, as the trial drew to a close, Tereshchenko ordered his agent on Corfu, B. T. Pelekhin, to warn Pašić of unfavorable Russian reaction to the Serbian Government's handling of the investigation so far. Pelekhin, who seems to have adhered to the independent tradition of Russia's Balkan diplomats, was reluctant to press the issue and sent word on June 2 that there was no justification in his opinion for so open an intrusion in Serbian political affairs. Furthermore, any unfavorable repercussions in the Russian press to the Apis trial would be seen on Corfu as a sign of the Provisional Government's inability to control hostile elements; would Tereshchenko please send fresh instructions. On June 6 Tereshchenko did so, unaware that sentence of death had been passed the preceding day. With reiterated expressions of good will toward Russia, Pašić rejected all overtures on behalf of the condemned men. Despite a further appeal from Petrograd the prisoners were shot in a ditch outside Salonika on June 26. Their deaths were immediately followed by a political crisis on Corfu, as ministers who had fought to save Apis withdrew from the Pašić Cabinet.[47]

Ironically it was at that point that Tereshchenko's pressure became intense. On June 26 he renewed his demands in tones that recall Tsarist authorities confronted by Balkan willfullness. Pelekhin was directed to tell Pašić that the Russian government attached especially great significance to commutation of the sentences; "we count absolutely on Pašić's calming influence." Four days later, still without news, Tereshchenko fired off another warning to Corfu. Unless the sentences were commuted the Russian democracy would feel the most extreme resentment over the general question of Entente relations with Serbia. Pelekhin should insist in the most categoric manner on the importance of this question to the common war cause. French assistance was invited in making known the Russian objections. Finally, on July 1st, news of the executions got to Petrograd.[48]

Two motives underlay Tereshchenko's insistent pleadings. The first, one of strategy, concerned the effect on the Russian war effort of Pašić's dealings with the Black Hand leaders. The trial had a highly adverse impact on the Serbian volunteer unit stationed in Odessa.[49] The rank and file saw little reason anyway to care for Pašić or his lieutenants. Their local officers were for the most part Serbs from the Royal Army; the men themselves, despite the name of their unit, were Serbs, Croats and Slovenes from the Dual Monarchy. While true that nationality tensions existed in Odessa independently of political events outside, these latter, whether in Petrograd or on Corfu, inevitably sharpened relations all the more. Sir George Buchanan reported to his government on May 18 that the Serbian divisions were becoming "the object of attentions" from local Soviets claiming excessive brutality on the part of officers toward their men. The British consul on the spot was able to smooth matters over but none could pretend the matter was solved.[50] Socialist, republican propaganda made heavy inroads and no Serbian official, civilian or military, seemed able to do very much to stop it. Apis' misfortunes, culminating in his execution, stimulated a fresh burst of resentment against Pašić personally from younger officers susceptible to the prisoner's appeal. Their distaste communicated itself in turn to Russian troops en route to the Rumanian front and lessened their already waning desire to fight on in support of small Balkan nationalities.[51]

A more powerful factor still was revolutionary prestige. Russia had accepted war in defence of Serbia. Through its lone representative in the first Cabinet, the Russian democracy had lost no time after the March revolution in expressing sympathy for "fraternal Serbia."[52] If there were any place in Europe that democratic Russia might expect a hearing, surely Serbia and her government were there? Pašić speedily proved otherwise, progressively defying some of the revolution's most cherished ideals. Everything that was known in Russia of the most prominent of the accused, Dmitriević-Apis, suggested the falsity of the charges against him. Even had they been true, Russian Socialists were scarcely going to defend the cause of aggrieved Balkan royalty. Apis was a much worthier figure. He had dedicated his life to the cause of national self-determination and freedom for the South Slavs of the Hapsburg Empire. His career seemed to give ample evidence of personal courage and love of liberty. To condemn such a man on such charges was a parody of justice. To shoot him, after free Russia had herself abolished the death penalty and intervened on his behalf, was to deliver an unforgivable slap to the Russian democracy. The two main organs of Socialist opinion in Petrograd united in rage, so vast was the provocation. *Pravda* and *Izvestiia* considered the executions a challenge to revolutionary Russia, "an insult to her efforts to free the world from the scourges of imperialism and militarism." The Russian people should purge itself of an alliance with Serbian executioners against whom the Serbs themselves must be defended. Of course Pašić was quite unrepentant. He regretted to Pelekhin that he had not found it possible "fully to reconcile his obligations to the state with the generous suggestions of the Russian government." He then proceeded to draw an implicit comparison between the helplessness of the Provisional Government in the face of plots and his own vigor in dealing with "criminals and traitors to Serbia and the Entente," a judgment that had to await the Tito regime before reversal.[53] His tone told its own story: the fact that Pasic and Bratianu, once the most zealous Balkan suppliants for Russian favor, could speak in such terms to the successors of Ignat'ev and Hartwig indicated better than anything how far "Great Russia" had fallen in less than half a year.

Pašić might be unyielding before Russian pressure but that did not mean Russian events ceased to interest him or the Yugoslav Committee. Serbian and Yugoslav still remained largely synonymous in untrained, foreign ears including Russian ones. Ante Mandić, sorrowfully recognising that fact, wrote on June 18 to his headquarters in Paris that the Yugoslav cause had suffered a catastrophic blow in the death sentences passed at Salonika. The Italian ambassador was happy to confirm that opinion; "the Revolution has almost completely paralyzed the Pan-Slav current," Carlotti cabled, and relations between Miliukov's successors and the Serbs were "cold."[54] The Italian threat to Slav interests in the Adriatic kept the Committee very much concerned to mobilize Russian opinion. As late as July 26, in the midst of the Paris Balkan conference, an appeal went out to Petrograd for help in the two year old struggle against the substitution of one foreign regime for another in South Slav and Balkan lands.[55]

Midsummer found Serbian and Yugoslav leaders understandably nervous at the state of their diplomatic interests in the alliance. Italy's thrust into Albania at least demonstrated the consistency of Sonnino's land hunger, but General Sarrail's equally arbitrary and offensive conduct in Greece that went without any correction from Paris disabused Pašić of any notion that Ribot might be more attentive to small power complaints.[56] These unwelcome developments encouraged a degree of collaboration between the Serbian Premier and the Yugoslav Committee that their previous difficulties might not otherwise have allowed. Equally conducive to common action was Pašić's weakened political position on Corfu following the Salonika trials, the unending flow of bad news from Russia and the open talk of treaty revision on the basis of no annexations and national self-determination. Just how these last two ideas were to be reconciled in Serbia's favor was a matter of more than passing concern to Pašić and Trumbić; it made only sense for the two men to maintain a united front for the dangerous reefs ahead. It was also not inappropriate to keep the Provisional Government, as the one ally committed to the no annexations and self-determination formula, fully up to date with their views.

On June 13 the Prime Minister and the Committee's President met on Corfu to begin charting their course of action. In the ensuing weeks of discussion Pelekhin reported home on the participants' major preoccupations. Trumbić was pressing him strongly about treaty revision; without it a

Yugoslav state would remain an illusion given the official Italian program "and the distinct Austrophil tendencies" Trumbić anticipated in the British and French Cabinets. The Serbian side was, understandably, less keen on the revision aspect. Pašić and the Prince Regent took Pelekhin to one side during a break in the talks to express their regret that Russia had ever renounced her claim on Constantinople. This was more than a cant overture toward a diplomatic holdover from Tsarism. Russia's withdrawal from South-Eastern Europe, whatever others might think about it, promised no advantage to Pašić. He could foresee without difficulty her reassuring bulk being replaced by nefarious French, Greek and, worst of all, Italian schemes—the Roman press rarely let a day go by without touching on the opportunities opening for Italy in the wake of a retiring Russia. For that reason more than any other, Pašić was anxious that his country be represented in any conference on war aims revision and, since his other Allies showed no sign of any great interest in Serbian claims, he hoped democratic Russia would continue with Tsardom's traditional benevolence.[57] A few days later news of the Salonika executions put that benevolence in some doubt. In their immediate aftermath Tereshchenko would go no further, in referring privately to Serbia, than to support her re-establishment within her former limits. Yugoslav hopes on the other hand, "based on the principle of national self-determination and Russia's warm sympathy for the growing idea of South Slav federation," would deservedly obtain Russian support.[58] It was the exact reverse of the Miliukov formula in confronting as minister the future prospects of Russia's Balkan "younger brother."

The Balkan Conferences

The announcement of an Inter-Allied conference to discuss Balkan affairs came at a time of more than mere diplomatic trial for Russia. The long heralded summer offensive, on which so many Russian and foreign hopes rested, opened under Brusilov's command on July 1st against the background of bombastic speeches from the Minister of War. After a few days of skirmishes Russian momentum slowed, then stopped. Within two weeks units up to division strength were abandoning their positions. On July 18, when the Austro-German armies began their counter-offensive, Brusilov's front dissolved. Kerenskii had summoned his troops "not to a feast, but to death": most of those who survived preferred flight.[59]

Political confusion followed hard upon military disaster. On July 15 all Cadet ministers resigned from the Cabinet, accusing their Socialist colleagues of usurping the functions of the projected Constituent Assembly. The second ministry of the Provisional Government vanished into limbo on the issue of Ukrainian autonomy after a lifetime of approximately the same length as its predecessor. The next day mass demonstrations, eventually supported by the Bolsheviks, erupted in the capital; for the forty-eight hours of the "July Days" the ten bourgeois ministers were the focus of popular vituperation along with their policy. Tsereteli, not a member of the ten in political allegiance but fully their equal in his support for the hated war, narrowly escaped kidnapping: his would-be abductors settled instead for his automobile. The forces of order at length managed to re-impose some degree of control; the bogey of Bolshevik treachery served to keep all but the most refractory subdued for the time being. The "triumphant Mamelukes" then confronted as their most urgent piece of business the need to reconstruct the Cabinet whose head, Prince L'vov, long an anachronism, withdrew into private life on July 20.[60]

His successor as Prime Minister was the man who, to L'vov, stood out in the army as a recognized leader, in the country as a symbol of the Revolution, Alexander Kerenskii.[61] Since Miliukov's fall he had been the government's dominant figure and was seen by his erstwhile chief as the only man of action among Russian Socialists and alone capable of saving the nation at the hour of its maximum peril from "the extreme Socialist tendencies expressed in so-called Bolshevism." Other nicknames were less flattering to the first of history's anti-Bolshevik cavaliers; the one that best described his role in the crisis now at hand was "Persuader-in-Chief," a mocking variant of his military function bestowed by some fellow Socialists. His persuasive talents could not have asked for a greater challenge than that which existed in Petrograd by the third week in July. For seventeen days, using every tactic in his armory from histrionics to resignation, he wrestled with the problem of stitching together a Cabinet in a ministry of national unity where the Left would have a decisive role.[62] His efforts were not successful until after the Paris meeting had dispersed, so that it was against a background of political uncertainty at home and military chaos at the front that the Russian government announced its intention to struggle for the triumph of revolutionary ideals in the most delicate questions facing the Entente.

What lay behind the July 6 promise in the Russian press of a Balkan conference? In the first place, though this was of course unknown to most readers, it represented a concession to political and diplomatic realities that Tereshchenko would have preferred to ignore. When the French government made its initial approach on the matter, Tereshchenko expressed the wish that the meeting should limit its discussions to military issues affecting the Macedonian front. Thus, on June 29, he cabled Sevastopulo:

> Taking into consideration our present position at the front and inside Russia, we must recognize that it is more to our advantage to limit, if possible, the subjects under discussion at the proposed conference, confining them primarily to military and strategic questions.

To his surprise, however, he heard on the 30th from the French chargé, Doulcet, that unnamed "political questions" could also be included. The expression rang alarm bells in the foreign ministry. Tereshchenko had no wish to see the currently most pressing "political question," war aims, come up for analysis at the July session, no matter what he and other ministers might be proclaiming to the contrary. Not until mid-August, he told his ambassador in Washington, would the government be ready to address itself to that subject; that is, when Russian arms might have succeeded in raising the nation's stock to the point where Tereshchenko's opinions could command greater respect. He proceeded to throw up defensive positions. If political issues had to be raised at all, it should be on the basis of an exchange of views. If decisions were nonetheless required, they must be made subject to ratification by participating governments. Clearly the Provisional Government, through its responsible official, was approaching the Balkan conference in a spirit decidedly less challenging than the July 6 announcement had suggested.[63]

In sending out the invitations to Paris, the Ribot Cabinet stressed military affairs of the Salonika Army and various problems connected with the Allied occupation of Greece as reasons for the meeting.[64] It was evident also from the location of the conference and the tone of the invitations to it that the French primacy in the Macedonian war theater, displayed so forcefully during the Greek business, would be defended with especial zeal.[65] The other participants saw the Paris session through the prism of Russia's misfortunes. In London a memorandum prepared in the War Cabinet Secretariat on "The Russian Situation and Its Consequences" stated flatly that the outstanding result of the change in Russia's position was that the first of Germany's two main projects—the creation of a Middle Europe extending from Hamburg to the Red Sea and the Persian Gulf—was practically made good. Britain could still achieve something on the periphery of this land mass, such as the liberation of Belgium or the conquest of Palestine,

> but without Russia we are powerless to dispute the settlement of the Polish, Roumanian and Serbian problems according to the wishes of the Central

> Powers and within the orbit of their sphere of future economic and military control.[66]

This gloomy assessment found no denials in the War Cabinet whose feelings on the forthcoming talks tended as a result to coincide with Tereshchenko's. On July 6, when the news of the meeting was released in the Russian press, the American ambassador in London, Walter Hines Page, informed Secretary Lansing that Balfour felt further progress in the war was necessary before there could be any agreement "about Austria-Hungary and some of the Balkan states." The Foreign Secretary told Page that Italian claims were bound to provoke strong resistance, while Russia's attitude to the whole question "needs clearer definition." For these reasons the British government too wanted at this stage to confine the conference's scope to military matters. Balfour entertained no illusions on the practicality of any grander designs in the political-diplomatic arena. Russia's collapse closed the door for the time being on that possibility; the vindictiveness of the Balkan states toward each other locked and barred it.[67]

The Italian government was more openly nervous as to what the conference might entail. The language of the Russian announcement was not reassuring on the point with its talk of "insisting with especial vigor on the establishment in the Balkans of the fundamentals proclaimed by the Russian Revolution." The Russian statement was held up for one or two days while the military censorship debated whether the inflammatory words should be allowed through. They eventually passed intact.[68] Concern then shifted to the likely scope of the conference, a matter of greater importance to Sonnino than to his Entente colleagues. Whether the meeting took up Balkan issues only or whether it took up wider questions of war aims amounted, as far as he was concerned, to much the same thing. After all, his ambitions for Italy were, he hoped, to be satiated in the ruins of the Hapsburg and Ottoman Empires.

Sonnino left for Paris on July 24. Prior to his departure he told Rennell Rodd how important it was that the Allies hammer out a unified policy of some sort at Paris. Otherwise leftist forces would take advantage of their disagreements; "the poison of the Russian movement is spreading rapidly and encouraging Socialists everywhere," he confided over a lengthy dinner.[69] For all his pessimism, however, Sonnino was leaving with one potentially strong card in his pocket. An interesting article in the *Corriere della Sera* on the day of his departure spelled out the card's value and the use Sonnino should make of it in Paris. At stake, said the *Corriere*, was the Russian legacy in the Balkans:

> With Russia's withdrawal from her old moral and political positions in the East and in the Balkans there vanishes one of the pillars on which reposed the entire traditional concept of Balkan politics.

One country alone was in a position to replace her—Italy:

> The feeling that peace will be restored in the Adriatic only by Italy, that Italy is the chosen and necessary element of balance and control in the Adriatic is making itself felt even in the Slav world. There, now that Russia has once and for all renounced her old Pan-Slav policy and is leaving the Slav lands to themselves, [the local inhabitants] now tend to expect from Italy the support they once counted on receiving from Russia.[70]

Although the *Corriere* did not mirror Sonnino's opinions as faithfully as the *Giornale d'Italia* (practically a Consultà house organ), its hopeful prognosis of an Italo–South Slav rapprochement on the wreckage of Russia's Balkan power was no idle fancy of the paper's editor, Luigi Albertini, future historian of the war then raging. Sonnino himself had thrown off occasional hints of a softening, though when Pašić visited Rome at the end of June he found no substantial evidence of it.[71] A more powerful incentive came on July 24, as Sonnino left on his Parisian odyssey, with news of the Corfu Pact of four days previously between Pašić and the Yugoslav Committee. This, on top of Russia's feebleness, opened new Balkan perspectives. Even the hitherto most extreme defenders of the Italian war program, such as the *Giornale* and the *Popolo d'Italia*, realized that some more positive attitude from Rome was now in order: it would never do to have the new state begin life considering Italy an enemy. This was a real possibility. Carlo Sforza, beginning as minister on Corfu what was to be a distinguished diplomatic career, drew Sonnino's attention to the ostentatious omission of Italy's name in the Corfu Declaration's opening invocation to "the champions of democracy and self-determination, France, Great Britain, the United States and the new Russia."[72] Russian impotence increased Italy's weight in the alliance; mutually satisfactory relations between Sonnino and the architects of the new Slav country could increase it still further.

On the eve of the Paris meeting two questions, fundamental to any conference, had yet to be settled: who should attend and what subjects should be discussed? Squabbling broke out behind the scenes on both points. Russian diplomats pressed for the admission as equal partners of Serbia and Rumania; they were less anxious on behalf of Venizelist Greece. Later also the United States might be asked to join in. Italy urged the total exclusion of the Greeks, while Britain and France after some foot-dragging were ready to admit all Balkan representatives in a consultative capacity only. None of the smaller powers liked that idea very much; neither did Russia, whose government may have anticipated its own relegation to that category if a distinction was allowed between consultative and participating members. Frantic lobbying ensued of the Great Powers. Bratianu concentrated on Rome, Pašić on Petrograd and Paris, Venizelos on Paris and London. They were all promised the right to take an active part in the proceedings, except the Montenegrin delegate, suspected of being in Austrian pay.[73]

The question of an agenda was more complicated. Everyone agreed that the military situation in Greece should be the main focus of attention. But Russia's Allies had by now abandoned any belief that discussions of strategy could or should entirely avoid political topics. Russian weakness and American strength were instrumental in bringing about the change in emphasis.

As had been foreseen in Jassy with dread, Russian chaos had a swift, disastrous impact on the one ally at the mercy of Russian armies, or what was left of them. The Rumanian offensive was fixed for July 19; last minute nerves on Bratianu's part postponed it a few days. In the interval Fasciotti reported the Premier's latest confidences. Once again through tears he bemoaned his country's cruel lot in being dependent on Russia. If the Kerenskii-Brusilov offensive failed, as now seemed not improbable, Rumania would go down with it.[74] As usual that summer, Bratianu's worst fears about Russia were amply justified. The Rumanian army went over to the offensive in the same way as it had done eleven months before, at the precise moment when the Russian juggernaut ran out of steam and was falling back before an enemy counterthrust. The Entente statesmen made for Paris as Rumania's Calvary began in earnest; they deliberated against the background of rising lamentation from Rumanian leaders literally not knowing where next to turn. But to save something out of the Rumanian mess something would first have to be done for Russia, since there was no other Entente route between Jassy and Western Europe. The question of what, how and by whom Russia was to be aided to her feet again was for the Great Power delegates at Paris to ponder, if not settle.

The American role was more direct and won from the Quai d'Orsay elucidation of those non-military concerns that Tereshchenko wished to avoid. In its anxiety at Russia's failing strength, the French government was eager to associate the United States in Entente planning for South-Eastern Europe. President Wilson was not so willing. On July 20 Acting Secretary of State Frank Polk cabled Page that the President was against American representation at the Balkan conference as the United States was not at war with Bulgaria, Austria-Hungary or Turkey and he did not wish to give the impression that he was interested in discussing peace terms for Germany's Allies. This decision was duly conveyed to Paris but Ribot stuck to his guns. On July 23 he asked William Sharp, the American ambassador, to discover the views of his government on the three subjects likely to be discussed, "exclusive of those relative to the Balkans, which are the stated object of the conference." These three were the Russian proposal for an Entente meeting on war aims revision, the possibility of a separate Austro-Hungarian peace and the future of the treaties affecting Asia Minor. Yet Wilson continued to refuse the bait. Politically America would have nothing to do with "this so-called Balkan conference."[75]

Where the diplomats failed, the soldiers succeeded. On the strict understanding that American participation would be limited to military matters only, the United States military commander in France, General John J. Pershing, declared his willingness to join his Entente military colleagues in Paris.[76] The American concession on this point—there were no American troops at Salonika and no prospect of there ever being any—widened the context of the discussions and led to a significant change in organization. Instead of the delegates meeting together to thresh out all questions before them, it was arranged for Pershing's benefit that the military chiefs should confer in separate session. Political affairs, which concerned only the European members of the alliance, would be discussed elsewhere. On this note, ominous for Tereshchenko, the meeting finally opened under the gilded chandeliers of the Salon de l'Horloge at the Quai in the morning of Wednesday July 25.

Throughout the two days of discussion events in Russia dominated the thoughts of all present. Ribot struck the appropriate note in his welcoming address. Delegates had as their responsibility to determine if the recent developments of the previous few months in Russia and Greece did not require the Entente to change their plan of operations in the East.[77] The British party, led by Lloyd George and Balfour, arrived in Paris with its collective mind very much made up on that score. A "specially secret" conclusion of the War Cabinet had decided on July 20 that nothing more was to be counted on from Russia in the way of offensive action in Rumania. Instead therefore of keeping large numbers of troops pinned down in wasteful inactivity at Salonika where they could not effectively tip the scales against the enemy, some British units would be siphoned off to Palestine to increase pressure on the Turks. Other delegates fought this decision tooth and nail and, like Lloyd George, fell back on Russian weakness to bolster their arguments. General Zankevich, Russian military attaché in Paris, pointed out that the Balkan theater served the interests of all the Allies, the Palestine front (by implication) only the British. Thinning out the Macedonian front would mean undermining the Russo-Rumanian and South-West Russian fronts, thus exposing Odessa and the Ukraine to the foe. Lahovary, the Rumanian minister, eagerly agreed. He too, like every Rumanian of note that summer, was obsessed with the specter of German troops forcing the Pruth and the Dniester, swarming into the Southern Russian steppes and finishing off en route the Jassy regime. Sevastopulo interjected one line of support to the effect that Serbia and Greece would also be endangered by any precipitate action; it is unlikely that anyone saw his intervention as significant. On the stenographic record of the first day's proceedings the name of the Russian envoy appears twice, the first time misspelled as Sevastopulos, probably under the impression he was attached to the Greek delegation. Lloyd George was deaf to all appeals: "I must insist on the difficulties which the temporary eclipse of Russian power have placed us in." The Balkans were lost; it was time for fresh initiatives elsewhere.[78]

The purely military sessions reluctantly concurred in this evaluation. The British and French delegates, Generals Robertson and Foch, arrived at the Quai d'Orsay with some hopes that Russia's military strength might still be restored and her armies galvanized into another offensive against Austria-Hungary at least: the latest news from the front dispelled these illusions.[79] On July 26 Foch and Robertson, with Pershing and the Italian Supreme Commander General Cadorna, assessed the likely results in Eastern Europe "when the Russian defection takes place." After some debate they drew up their conclusions:

> Political. It would modify the political aims of the Entente. It is therefore suggested that the Governments should at once consider what would be the new political aims to be pursued.
>
> Economic. It would place at the disposal of the Central Powers the vast resources of Russia, especially grain, and thereby greatly minimize the efficiency of the blockade.
>
> Morale. It might result, especially in the case of the smaller Allies in the Balkans, in a profound depression which might cause them to seek a separate peace. It is practically certain that Roumania would be compelled to share the fate of Russia . . . .[80]

In the political part of the conference Russia's role was minor and, in effect, scarcely even the consultative one she had resisted for the smaller participants. Her insignificance reflected the enervation of her diplomacy, deprived by domestic turmoil of effective guidance and control. Of the seven countries taking part in the non-military sessions, Greece and

Rumania were represented by their ministers in Paris; Britain, France, Italy and Serbia by their Premiers, Foreign Ministers, ambassadors or all three. Russian interests were defended by the chargé, Sevastopulo, and an embassy counsellor.[81] Neither was well prepared for the task. It was, for example, known long in advance that Greek military matters would occupy a large part of the meeting's attention. Yet when conflict arose on the presence and purpose of Italian troops in Albania, on Greece's northern frontier, Sevastopulo had to confess himself without instructions.[82] He was not invited to the talks on Greek affairs, nor were his views solicited in the exchanges between the other Great Power spokesmen on the question of a separate Austrian peace. Privately Ribot, Lloyd George and Sonnino agreed that final decision on that, on the Asia Minor accords and on the British troops withdrawals could await a second, follow-up meeting in London. With a few kind words from Ribot recognizing the Provisional Government's efforts to restore order, gratefully acknowledged by Sevastopulo, the Paris conference adjourned with nothing beyond Russia's impotence definitely established.

On August 7 the three statesmen and their teams gathered in the British capital, this time without the Balkan members of the alliance. The interval had seen some stabilization of Russia's political situation but her diplomatic position was weaker than ever. On July 28 Tereshchenko admitted as much in a telegram to Washington in which he "deem[ed] it necessary to postpone somewhat the proposed conference [on war aims revision] . . . in order to concentrate all our attentions on continuance of the war."[83] The Paris meeting had exhibited no taste for treaty revision and the Provisional Government, by Tereshchenko's own admission in the same cable to the Washington embassy, had not yet got around to inviting anyone to take part. Anyway, with the Entente turning over plans for the re-organization of Russian military and industrial power, there hardly seemed to be an opportunity for a Russian initiative in so fundamental an area of war strategy.

In London Russian diplomats obtained a painfully realistic impression of their country's diminished stature in the alliance. The very fact that a conference was meeting at all came as a surprise to the chargé, Nabokov. His complaints at this slighting of a loyal ally produced a belated invitation to attend which he did without stopping to change into the requisite morning coat. Once in 10 Downing Street he may have wished he had been a little less importunate. Lloyd George opened the proceedings with the motion that a stern protest be sent to Kerenskii at continued anarchy in Russia. Just how a protest note was going to help the Russian Premier bring anarchy to an end was not clear. At any rate, thanks to the invaluable

Thomas, the final draft of the message turned out to be nothing more than a string of congratulatory regrets. No Russian was invited to any of the subsequent sessions. Nabokov, resigned to the inevitable, countered objections inside his embassy with the reminder that their absence from the meeting spared Russian representatives the humiliation of hearing adverse comment on their country's military prowess.[84]

Though Russia's diplomats were ignored, her domestic griefs still overhung the talks. Each delegation again resorted to Russian frailty to advance solutions with Lloyd George and Sonnino opposing Ribot. This was a change from the usual Anglo-French line-up against Italian cajolements: Sonnino himself must take the credit. He wasted no time in following up the recommendations of the *Corriere della Sera*. The Paris session had given a good example of British *sacro egoismo* in Balkan matters; now it was Sonnino's turn. He hurried over to London ahead of Ribot to urge upon the Foreign Office Italy's Asia Minor claims free of the vexing Russian veto sanctioned at St Jean de Maurienne. After a mutual rejection of each other's opening gambits, he and Lord Robert Cecil got down to business. An elaborately prolix formula finally worked out between the two men took care of every conceivable combination of circumstances.[85] It cost Cecil nothing more than a few hours of his time; it kept Sonnino happy, and that was more useful than it might otherwise have been in the days of Russia's power; best of all it would be distasteful to the French and Ribot would have to bear the onus for its rejection, as he rather sourly recognized in his journal. He played his part nonetheless. Sonnino invoked the threat of resignation if he did not get his way but "this usual procedure" now alarmed nobody.[86] The three Allies settled on a memorandum restating the St Jean terms for the dismemberment of Anatolia. It would be submitted to Petrograd for an expression of Russian views, though the ministers agreed, at Sonnino's urging, that the current political situation in Petrograd precluded any approaches at that moment. Finishing off a piece of unfinished business, the two Europeans "authorized" the British troops withdrawals from Salonika. To put the best possible face on a disagreeable affair, Ribot and Sonnino claimed a similar right for their own forces in the theater. The remaining contributors to Entente strength on the Macedonian front would be informed in due course.[87]

The last item on the agenda was the question of detaching Germany's Allies. Here too the prospect of a Russian collapse was in every mind. Foch once more expressed his conviction that Russia was on the way out, though she might still recover "if the [Provisional] Government strengthens itself and accepts our advice and assistance." This should take the form of a complete re-organization of Russia "by any means in the power of the

Allied nations"—here already is a germ of future intervention. Only in that case might the Entente work for the defection of Bulgaria, Austria-Hungary and Turkey, an eventuality that Foch, a relentless Westerner, doubted would greatly harm the principal foe.[88] The two Premiers were more pessimistic. Contrary to his most recent public utterance on the war at the Queen's Hall on August 4, when he had held out the possibility of an improvement in the Russian situation, Lloyd George argued throughout on the fundamental assumption of a total Russian breakdown. "What do we do then?"—his repeated question rang like a refrain through the hours of argument and debate. If he was expecting an answer he got none. Those present had no solution other than to wait upon events, consider means of keeping Russia in the fight, send admonitory messages to Petrograd and keep in touch on all political issues arising out of the war and Russia's decomposition.[89] With agreement to meet again in six weeks the delegations dispersed on the evening of August 8. In effect they had just sung a diplomatic requiem over "Great Russia": not until 1922 would diplomats from Moscow again sit opposite Anglo-French statesmen as the recognized representatives of a very different Russian regime.

CHAPTER VIII
SALVAGE EFFORTS

Bruce Lockhart, acting British Consul-General in Moscow through the summer of 1917, described in his memoirs the impact of a Kerenskii speech shortly after Miliukov's fall. Like many others that frenzied season the address was delivered before an audience of thousands keyed to fever pitch either by the speaker or the events around them. The scene was the Bolshoi Theatre; from its vast stage the newly appointed War Minister expounded his gospel of suffering. The troops at the front, he proclaimed, were enduring unimaginable horrors; he himself—or so it seemed to Lockhart—was in his final agonies. But his audience, rich, comfortable, lazy, behind the lines, why were they grumbling? "Were they to bring Russia down in ruins, to be guilty of the most shameful betrayal in history?" For two hours the minister screamed out his reproaches to respectable Russia and then fell fainting into the arms of an aide. Lockhart observed the denouement:

> "The man who only had one kidney, the man who had only six weeks to live would save Russia yet. A millionaire's wife threw her pearl necklace on the stage. Every woman present followed her example and a hail of jewelry descended from every tier. . . . [The speech] was an epic performance. . . . Its effect on Moscow and the rest of Russia lasted exactly two days."[1]

To this man Russia's Allies, great and small, now looked for Russia's salvation. It would be for this hero and object of domestic, middle class adoration (even if his admirers were nothing more to the perceptive Sukhanov than "Philistines and nondescripts")[2] to confront the unprecedented confusions of Russia's diplomatic and domestic situation. As far as the first was concerned, the lesson of the two Balkan conferences was inescapable. There could no longer be any doubt that in the eyes of its European Allies, the Provisional Government had forfeited any serious voice in the settlement of diplomatic questions, including those of greatest traditional interest to Russia. Notice had been served that there would be no increase in Allied respect until a major improvement occurred in Russia's military performance. This in turn depended on the restoration at home of political order. Only then might the Government consider new initiatives abroad.

The London meeting coincided with the formation of a new Cabinet in Petrograd, the third since March. The seventeen day long crisis had subjected the fabric of national cohesion to almost unbearable strain. Rivalries between political factions, bourgeois and Soviet, were so fierce that Kerenskii abandoned his efforts at cabinet making and retired in offended dignity across the conveniently nearby Finnish frontier. For the moment he was the indispensable man of Russian politics and he knew it; his departure shocked the squabbling cliques of Cadets and Soviet defensists into an appeal to the absent Premier to return with a free hand to his duties.[3] He acceded to the request, to him "a command from the country to form in the shortest time and in spite of all obstacles a strong revolutionary government."[4] The result of his labors was announced on August 7 with the personnel of the new ministry. Socialists were now in the majority (by one), but the Cadets figured prominently enough to have one of their number, N. V. Nekrasov, named Kerenskii's deputy. Tereshchenko, who had briefly followed his mentor into retirement, resumed his old portfolio. It was a government based on the *union sacrée* of revolutionary defense; remaining outside were, in *Rabochaia Gazeta*'s comforting words, "only irresponsible groups of Bolsheviks . . . and both covert and avowed counter-revolutionaries of the right."[5] Yet for all Kerenskii's flamboyance, "revolutionary defense" meant one thing only, political survival. Foreign concerns, though far from ignored, necessarily became a secondary issue.

Russia's Allies now prepared to take a hand in her affairs. Their attitude after the London conference was characterized by the Russian charge as "diffidence mingled with irritation."[6] The second emotion was well to the fore. Events in Russia, an American observer commented, had caused "keen disappointment" among delegates to the Balkan session in Paris and a general realization "that no helpful co-operation could be expected for some time" from those now governing Russia.[7] Until that moment there was slight hope of wresting control of Eastern Europe from the Central Powers. From the distance of Whitehall and the Quai d'Orsay it seemed that the speediest way to reverse that unfortunate fact was to remove the obstacles in the path of Russia's fuller participation in the war. Lloyd George may indeed have argued during the two conferences that Russia was militarily finished but his Allies were not prepared to endorse his conclusion with complete finality. His generals, his Cabinet, possibly even he himself, wavered on the question, if only because the logical deductions from Russia's powerlessness were as yet too painful to accept. As late as August 10 a high powered War Cabinet committee decided that Russia's value as an ally was "difficult to estimate," despite what was termed "the remarkable successes" of the July offensive.[8] There was always the distasteful possibility, recognized by the committee, that Russia might refuse to fight another winter campaign. In that case the talk a few days previously of massive aid to re-organize Russia internally would have to be followed up, or else recognition must result of Germany's unconquerable hegemony for the foreseeable future over the eastern half of the continent.[9] But was there any way Russia's partners might hasten the day of her regeneration? For a few weeks in August-September it looked as if the right moment and the right man had arrived together.

The tragi-comic revolt of the Cossack General L. G. Kornilov marked the final disenchantment of the Entente governments in the competence of the Kerenskii regime. Their embassies, backed by vociferous elements of their domestic press, scarcely bothered to hide their partiality for the energetic Supreme Commander and for his prescription of an iron fist against anarchy at front and rear.[10] The strong, silent man of action appealed more than "the chatterbox" (the epithet is Lloyd George's) currently heading the Russian Government; even the American embassy made no audible protest on being told by some Kornilov lieutenants that the Prime Minister would be hanged within forty-eight hours, the executions to begin "tomorrow at 3 o'c-lock."[11] As Kerenskii rushed about, the left closed ranks against the threat of counter revolution. By September 14 the revolt was over and Kornilov a not too closely guarded prisoner. The fiasco of his march on Petrograd did greatest harm to those forces the Allies were most anxious to support. The right was irretrievably compromised, while the army's disintegration proceeded unchecked. The Premier ranted in the face of crisis; only the far left emerged with enhanced stature. British and French credit in Socialist circles disappeared utterly. So too did the remnants of its Russian counter-part in London and Paris, to say nothing of their embassies in Petrograd where much was being made of a popular song doing the rounds to the effect that Kerenskii slept in the former Imperial bedroom, had the male version of the Empress' name and appeared as prone as she to hysterical fits.[12] In short, what Konstantin Nabokov termed the period of "disillusion and resent-ment" now set in.[13] It would long outlast the Provisional Government.

* * *

In spite of domestic convulsions Tereshchenko did not lose sight of longstanding Russian interests abroad. The points at issue in September were unchanged from July: the future of the secret treaties, the fate of the Ottoman Empire and the chances of a separate peace with Germany's partners. His main task also remained the same: to convince his Entente colleagues of the relevance to their common efforts of Russia's new foreign policy principles.

The Kerenskii Government defined its position on the war in its inaugural statement of July 21, subsequently confirmed by Premier and Soviet on August 4 and 6 respectively.[14] That statement promised loyalty to Russia's Allies and the determination not to shed a drop of Russian blood "for foreign ends." The Government's ultimate aim remained the conclusion of peace on the basis of no annexations or indemnities and national self-determination. To this end it would summon its partners to meet "during August" (the date was dropped a week later)

> in order to determine the general course of the Allies' foreign policy and to co-ordinate their actions in carrying out the principles proclaimed by the Russian Revolution. Russia will be represented in this conference by members of the diplomatic corps as well as by representatives of the Russian democracy.[15]

The last sentence of course was the clearest sign to date of the Soviet's enhanced foreign policy role: if the Government's representatives could not bury Miliukov's ideas of diplomatic continuity, the Soviet's agents would. At least, for Kerenskii, revolutionary defensism remained the official order of the day. A Soviet voice on war aims revision was his recognition of a fact of Russian political life, infinitely preferable to the breach with the Allies that a separate peace or unilateral publication of the secret treaties would bring.

It was on this latter point that the first dispute arose between the reconstituted Cabinet and a foreign ally. Although the clash centered on an issue not directly concerning the Balkans, it provoked a vigorous expression of official Russian opinion on the nature of Entente aims in the Eastern theater of the war.

The stage was set by the Imperial German chancellor. In the course of a press conference on July 28, Michaelis referred to "written proofs" in his Government's possession of the Entente's aggressive, expansionist plans. He "publicly challenged" the Ribot Cabinet to deny that its predecessor had signed, shortly before the Tsar's downfall, an agreement with Russia allowing France full liberty of action in determining her post-war Eastern frontier. In such a case, Michaelis suggested, French and Entente claims to be fighting on behalf of nationality and self-determination rights were the purest hypocrisy.[16] The Chancellor was referring to the pact of February 1917 between Foreign Minister Pokrovskii and Gaston Doumergue.[17] Its provisions for France's borders were indeed difficult to reconcile to the ideals for which the Entente proclaimed itself to be fighting, though this would have been an easier task than defending on the same basis the parallel concessions to Russia with respect to her Western border. The Chancellor's provocative question probed the most sensitive aspect of French politics and, in doing so, showed the security of Parliamentary procedures in Paris was open to some challenge. The whole business of the secret treaties and of the Doumergue-Pokrovskii pact in particular had sparked a stormy three-day secret session of the Chamber of Deputies from June 1 to 3; Michaelis drew upon details of this debate in making his comments.[18] Ribot had managed to beat back the onslaught, led by Cachin and Moutet, but the German thrust threatened to exacerbate the problem in public, nowhere more than in Petrograd as the Premier at once saw. In a fighting reply to the Chancellor, delivered before a tense Chamber on July 31, Ribot clarified to his own satisfaction the democratic nature of French war aims and hopefully stigmatized Michaelis' remarks as too clumsy a maneuver to deceive anyone, "especially the democratic Russian masses whom he is vainly seeking to detach from their Allies." As long as the Russians consented he had no objection to publishing the Doumergue-Pokrovskii notes.[19] Tereshchenko also had no objection. Unfortunately, as he admitted in a private telegram to Sevastopulo, the pact in question was "not deprived of a certain imperialistic tinge" and if Ribot were to insist that all its terms still remained in effect an unfavorable impression would be made upon Russian democratic circles, as upon Russian public opinion toward France. If Ribot were now to decide against publication—and Tereshchenko's hope that he would is evident in every line of his cable—he should make the appropriate comment in Paris. This would at least take the pressure off Tereshchenko to make some spectacular gesture of disassociation from the bad old ways of Russian diplomacy. Sevastopulo wired back his impression that the Quai wanted to bury the whole contentious business and that Ribot would take it as a real favor not to be pressed for a further public statement on the question. Tereshchenko was in no position to refuse the recommended service, even though Ribot's sudden taciturnity could leave the impression that the Russian government stood between an obscure imperialist deal and its exposure to democracy's clear light. Tereshchenko had feared as much but lacked both means and will to bring force to bear on Paris for a thoroughgoing clarification.[20]

For the next few weeks, as the Kornilov affair sputtered on, nothing was heard on the publication problem. A Cabinet reshuffle in Paris conferred the

Premiership on Paul Painlevé but Ribot stayed on at the Quai. On September 19 a Socialist deputy's query why, in spite of his earlier promise, the Foreign Minister had so far done nothing to publicize the Doumergue-Pokrovskii texts elicited the response that Ribot would be delighted to comply were it not for "Allied objections." Since only one ally could be involved, Sevastopulo hurried off to the ministry to complain. There the Permanent Secretary, Jules Cambon, offered sympathy without explanation: "nobody could understand how Ribot could have fallen into such an error."[21]

Hitherto the Franco-Russian wrangle concerned a specific wartime agreement of marginal relevance to Russian concerns elsewhere. On September 20 the area of dispute widened suddenly to include more sensitive issues. On that date Sevastopulo sent off a cable with his thoughts as to how the Provisional Government might extricate itself from its current difficulties with Paris. He suggested that Russia could regain the initiative by offering to publish all pre-war agreements between the two countries, plus the Doumergue-Pokrovskii notes along with a rider that the latter had since lost all validity. The Asia Minor accords of 1916 could not be included in this number proposed for publication as in Ribot's opinion they were not yet "complete" and could not therefore be published or annulled. A follow-up telegram gave Tereshchenko more food for thought. On the 21st Sevastopulo reported that Paléologue's successor in Petrograd, Noulens, had informed his government of Tereshchenko's belief that the publication of the Doumergue-Pokrovskii pact would oblige the Provisional Government to declare its position on the future of the Turkish Straits. This, Tereshchenko was quoted as saying, was "not desirable under present circumstances." Since he knew nothing of the purported statement which threatened to raise once again the volatile subject of Russia's discarded war aims at "Tsargrad," Sevastopulo was unable to comment on Noulens' information.

Tereshchenko hastened to remedy the lack. In a long, two-part cable of September 24 and 25 he detailed his objections to the several points raised by his chargé. He denied flatly he had ever suggested a connection existed between the Straits agreement and the Doumergue-Pokrovskii settlement. He had merely reminded Noulens that publication of the pre-war treaties would encourage Russian public opinion to demand similar treatment for wartime commitments as well. Russia would place no obstacles here, if her partners did likewise. But since Italy and Rumania would certainly reject the idea of untoward publicity it was for Ribot to approach them. Russia had no interest in defending on her own the principle of wartime secrecy.

The future of Asia Minor was something else. It was to that issue, Tereshchenko wrote, rather than to the future of Franco-German or Russo-

German frontiers, that the Straits question was inseparably linked. Citing the relevant passage from the 1916 convention he declared:

> From the viewpoint of Russian interests the Asia Minor agreements cannot be regarded as standing apart. Their fulfillment depends on the fulfillment of the Straits accord . . . . Any changes in the latter invariably reflect in one way or another upon the former. Therefore even if, according to Ribot, the Asia Minor agreement is to be considered still incomplete, it nevertheless has binding force.

Sevastopulo replied to these broadsides with excuses for Ribot, distinguished though he was in Parliamentary circles for his slyness and insincerity. Apparently Tereshchenko suspected duplicity where none was intended; at any rate no serious challenge was made to his views as relayed by Sevastopulo. The French government may of course have concluded by the time these exchanges petered out that soothing noises or silence were more appropriate than argument for a regime in the condition of Kerenskii's Cabinet.[22]

The final stages of the controversy revealed some ambiguities in Tereshchenko's position. His statement that changes in the Straits agreement must inevitably reflect upon the Asia Minor treaties raises the question whether Russia's renunciation of her war aims at the Bosporus and the Dardanelles constituted such a change? All appearances and logic suggested an affirmatory answer; if so, was Tereshchenko suggesting that, since Russia had abandoned her prospective gains in Turkey her Allies were obliged to do so too? That they should renounce their Turkish (and every other) aspirations was, of course, the Soviet position and one to which the government had committed itself in its search for a war aims revision conference. Yet the last sentence of the telegram of September 25 insisted that the Asia Minor accords remained fully operative, if incomplete. Did this, then, imply that in spite of every indication to the contrary the Provisional Government, or at least Tereshchenko, regarded the Straits agreement too as still valid?

In a strictly legal sense the minister was correct in asserting, and Ribot in agreeing, that the two sets of obligations were interdependent. A Russian note of March 4/17, 1916, had laid down "as a matter of course" that Russian consent to Anglo-French claims in Asia Minor remained conditional upon the dispositions made the previous year regarding Constantinople and the Straits.[23] Neither Britain nor France had protested at this reservation at the time or since; consequently it was still in force eighteen months later. It went without saying, however, that since the Declaration of March 27/April 9 majority opinion in Petrograd and Russia saw acquisition of the

Straits region and "Tsargrad" a dead issue for Russia. No member of the government could reverse that situation and Miliukov's political fate was instructive to those who might like to try. Yet the Declaration was a unilateral act. Russia's Allies had not been consulted prior to its publication either to the people of Russia or themselves, even though it "inevitably reflected upon another Allied agreement," to quote Tereshchenko. Naturally her partners were not going to force Constantinople upon an unwilling Russia but neither were they going to feel any compulsion, moral or legal, to follow her lead. Indeed, as has been seen, Italy tried at the Paris and London Balkan conferences to use Russian renunciation as a lever for wider gains in Anatolia.

It was this eventuality that prompted Tereshchenko's concluding sentence in his cable. Yet in writing it he demonstrated the basic flaw in his position. How could he simultaneously speak for a revolutionary government that demanded an end to all acquisitive war aims and for a weakening European Power insistent that all plans made for the division of Turkish loot remain inviolate? His justification could only be the desire to prevent a new settlement still more injurious to traditional Russian interests. The stratagem was one dictated by Russian feebleness, military and diplomatic, but it did show that the renunciation of Constantinople was not synonymous with a Russian abandonment of interest in the fate of that part of the world. Neither did it imply that the Provisional Government, through its minister, had washed its hands of Turkey-in-Asia. To the contrary, Tereshchenko was adamant that no diplomatic distinction was possible between the two wings of the Ottoman state. His stand in the face of burgeoning Allied encroachments in Asia Minor was thus an integral part of his defense of Russian concerns in South-East Europe. The indivisibility of the two regions for diplomatic purposes accounted in large measure for his strenuous opposition to Italian inroads in both.

The dispersal of the Allied conference in London had left the future of the Asia Minor treaties in some doubt. On the one hand the Italian program elaborated at St Jean de Maurienne still commanded formal Anglo-French acquiescence, albeit grudging. On the other hand the irritating Russian veto, though watered down since April, also remained a potential source of trouble. Sonnino's fear on this score was not so much that Russian resistance itself would prevent the realization of Italian goals, but more that Britain and France might later capitalize on Russian unwillingness to qualify their own consent to Rome's designs on Anatolia.[24] As long as the two Western Powers insisted, for whatever reason, on dragging Russia into the matter, Italian diplomacy had two courses open to it. It could attempt to stampede Paris and London into solidarity with Rome by parading the Russian bogey in the most lurid and alarming colors. This was the method preferred in particular by Ambassador Imperiali who made use of it during the Kornilov uprising.[25] But this tactic was not producing, at least not so far, results that Sonnino could profitably use. That left the option of a direct overture to Petrograd. On August 10, just back from England, Sonnino asked Carlotti to advise him how and when the text of the London protocol might be most expeditiously transmitted to the Provisional Government. Great care was needed. It was extremely important, Carlottie was told, that he avoid an unfavorable Russian reply: "it is much more to our advantage to receive no Russian answer at all than one which is opposed to our territorial claims in Asia Minor."[26]

Sonnino's cable at once caused Carlotti to redouble his visits to the Foreign Ministry. He was a wealthy aristocrat, like all Italian representatives abroad, marginally more agile than Paléologue in responding to the new regime. Noulens, Paléologue's sharp-eyed successor, observed how his Italian colleague limited his revolutionary fervor to a change of hairstyle and the substitution of a wide-brimmed hat in place of a top hat for his public appearances.[27] In spite of such boldness there was no sign he shared to the full his government's devotion to the territorial imperatives of *sacro egoismo*. All he got out of Tereshchenko, however, was a point blank refusal to discuss the question "under present political circumstances, no matter from what quarter the initiative came."[28] Obviously Russia alone was powerless to stem Sonnino's offensive. Britain and France seemed improbable candidates as allies, given their recent exclusion of Russia from the decisions of the two Balkan conferences. That left one potential ally, from Tereshchenko's viewpoint the most hopeful partner in the struggle against predatory war aims, the United States. On August 18 he extended his first diplomatic feelers on the subject to Washington. He told his ambassador there, Boris Bakhmetev, of Carlotti's pressure and of his own refusal to succumb to it. To anticipate efforts by Italy or any other ally to gain American support for their designs in Turkey, Bakhmetev was to enlist Secretary Lansing in the Russian campaign against annexations. He should also solicit the opinion of the United States government on Turkish questions generally with an eye to the possible co-ordination of Russian and American actions at the end of the war.[29]

In spite of Tereshchenko's optimism, often excessive according to Sir George Buchanan, Russo-American relations had been far from intimate since the advent of Russian democracy. In part this was the result of sheer distance and ignorance of each other's condition; in greater part perhaps it was the consequence of inept or weak representation in each other's capital. The Russian envoy at the time of the Tsar's abdication, Yurii Bakhmetev, suffered an emotional shock at the change of regime and refused to represent Nicholas' upstart successor. He lasted nonetheless until mid-April; two months later a namesake, Boris Bakhmetev, took over, no relation to his predecessor. Bakhmetev II, as he was sometimes referred to in Washington, owed his appointment to his work on the Russian Supply Committee in the United States and his friendship with A. I. Guchkov. His expertise in problems of military and economic organization was obviously helpful in promoting Russia's welfare in the capital of the newest and wealthiest of Germany's foes, but it did not open the doors of the White House any more widely to him. His opposite number in Petrograd, David Francis, had even less influence over the government to which he had been accredited shortly before the March revolution. Lockhart has left a faintly malicious portrait of the elderly American ambassador, sublimely ignorant of the Russian language (at one here with Lockhart's own chief), of Russian culture (identifying Alexander Pushkin as a current opera idol) and of the maelstrom through which he lived that summer. Lockhart's comment on this latter deficiency is familiar but irresistible: "Old Francis doesn't know a Left Social Revolutionary from a potato."[30]

More discouraging than these flaws, to Miliukov at any rate, was Wilson's stubborn refusal to become enmeshed in the toils of Entente diplomacy. This disappointment first made itself noticed in a lead editorial in *Rech'* at a time when the Anglo-French missions were settling down to their American tour. Whether or not actually written by Miliukov, the article certainly reflected the then minister's views, as Francis pointed out to Lansing. It was a matter of regret to the writer that Wilson refused to endorse Russia's legitimate ambitions at the Straits and in Turkey. Furthermore, the President's readiness to discuss Russia's vital interests in the absence of Russian representatives struck the author as "indiscreet." Clearly he did not care for the Washington meetings and echoed all Miliukov's fears as to their potential harm on diplomatic issues of the day.[31]

Russian Socialists too found Wilson unresponsive to appeals for solidarity with the new Russia. On May 25 Konstantin Onu, chargé between the two Bakhmetevs, cabled Petrograd that he had detected some embarrassment in the American capital over the interpretation to be given the Soviet's formula of peace on the basis of no annexations or indemnities. The State Department apparently felt that this might impede the return of Alsace-Lorraine to France "and the liberation of the Serbian regions of Bosnia-Herzogovina." At any rate Onu was confident the President himself would clarify the whole area of Russo-American relations with an indirect reply to the Coalition Ministry's inaugural statement of May 5/18 on its basic principles.[32] That reply followed two weeks later when the Russian press published the text of a Presidential message to Russia's new rulers. It greatly disappointed those who had looked to Wilson to furnish something different in tone and spirit to the other Allied commentaries on democratic Russian war aims. Tereshchenko even held up publication in a vain effort to get some softening of Wilson's uncompromising anti-German language. The President had no comfort for the champions of the Socialist formula which, so he hinted, really served German interests: "practical questions can be settled only by practical means. Phrases will not accomplish the [desired] result." Cautious endorsement of the formula's approach was followed immediately by qualifications:

> No territory must change hands except for the purpose of securing those who inhabit it a fair chance of life and liberty. No indemnities must be insisted on except those that constitute payment for manifest wrongs done. No readjustments of power must be made except such as will tend to secure the future peace of the world and the future welfare and happiness of its peoples.[33]

The "excepts" destroyed the note's value to the non-Bolshevik Left; they were enough to put Wilson alongside Lloyd George, Ribot and Sonnino, if not Pašić and Bratianu, as defenders of the old order. *Izvestiia* commented, turning Wilson's strictures on phrase-making against him:

> President Wilson is mistaken if he thinks that such thoughts can find acceptance in the hearts of the revolutionary people of Russia . . . . It cannot be led astray by any vague, high flown phrases. And it is easy to understand the kind of feelings which will be aroused by the strange pretense that the growing revival of the spirit of brotherhood and peace in international Socialism . . . is the result of German intrigue. This is not the language that the Russian democracy speaks.[34]

Socialist disenchantment with the President, his language and his policies was not lessened by the presence in Petrograd through June of an American mission under former Secretary of State Elihu Root. His function, according to a preliminary message to Francis, was to testify to American sympathies for the new-born Russian democracy "in the confident hope that the Russian Government and people will realize how sincerely the United States hopes for their welfare and desires to share with them in their future endeavors to bring victory to the cause of democracy and human liberty."[35] Like Francis, Root knew nothing of Russian political complexities. He met all the accessible notables, including "Tereschenki" [sic] who referred to the storm brewing up over the various Asia Minor claims. Understandably, Root had nothing to say on the subject. He had himself photographed at the desk of Catherine II ("whose morals," he reminded his wife, "differed from Queen Victoria's"), and took innocent pleasure from the fact that the fallen Russian autocrat's private train had been placed at his disposal. His trip had no beneficial effects on Russo-American relations and Wilson put off hearing his report when Root got back to Washington. When he finally penetrated the President's study it became obvious that Wilson had no great interest in his Russian observations.[36]

Four days before Root sailed from Vladivostok, Bakhmetev sent off a long telegram analyzing the course of Russo-American relations in the light of the July offensive and Root's messages home. The ambassador felt it was now time for some serious rethinking in Petrograd on how the powerful transatlantic partner should be handled. By encouraging American initiatives the Provisional Government might convince Wilson that close collaboration with Russia in political and diplomatic questions was a sure way for America to win what Bakhmetev called "a significant position in the European concert." The alternatives were all unpleasant, particularly when it came to disputes with the three other Entente Great Powers. Bakhmetev thought that America's involvement in foreign policy issues, up to then "reserved and passive," could definitely endanger Russian interests. It left the field open to England to advance her claims on American financial and diplomatic generosity, whereas co-operation between Russia and the United States would greatly assist the former to carry out her democratic foreign policy tasks.[37]

It does not appear to have occurred to Bakhmetev that the United States government might feel it was already sufficiently intimate with its foreign associates and did not need Russian help to become more so if it chose. The ambassador seized upon Tereshchenko's request to sound out American officials on Turkish and related issues, seeing Lansing on August 24. He found the Secretary sympathetic. Lansing said the United States had received no communication from Rome regarding Italian ambitions in Asia Minor; if one were received it would not meet American approval. Bakhmetev then turned to the second, more delicate aspect of his commission, the testing of official United States sentiment on the future of the treaties that divided the Ottoman Empire. The vague nature of his instructions obliged him, he reported to Tereshchenko, to proceed with extreme caution:

> Since I fear the awkward consequences which might ensue were these conversations to be given a certain official character, I have considered it necessary to raise the subject in purely private discussion with the influential

> [Secretary of the Treasury William G.] McAdoo, as well as with the Secretary of State.

His talks convinced Bakhmetev that the thinking of "local statesmen" came very close to the views of the Provisional Government, as expressed by Tereshchenko:

> American statesmen appear to be convinced that because of America's participation in the war and her financial assistance [to the Allies], it would be desirable to clarify fully the actual aims of the war and [Entente] opinions on the bases of the future peace.

Best of all was the belief in Washington, as relayed by Bakhmetev,

> of the possibility of a certain pressure on the Allies to bring them to renounce their annexationist intentions in Turkey, thus promoting [her] elimination from the war . . . . A similar idea seems to be emerging regarding the situation in the Balkans, especially Bulgaria.

Bakhmetev thought something might come of these ideas and requested instructions if Tereshchenko agreed. Candor obliged the envoy to advise his chief that Russia's "present position" made it expedient to allow the Americans the major role in any negotiations: "we should content ourselves with supporting their approaches."[38]

It will be seen from his report that Bakhmetev considered his earlier recommendation now well justified and himself successful in getting what seemed a positive response from Petrograd and Washington to his thought of a more vigorous American role in questions of interest to Russia. Yet his remarks on Turkey and Bulgaria present something of a puzzle. Whoever else may have given him his information as to American pressure for the elimination of Turkey and Bulgaria from the war, it was certainly not Lansing. Possibly McAdoo, the President's son-in-law with political ambitions of his own, speculated a little too freely with Bakhmetev. The two men knew each other as a result of McAdoo's supervision of American disbursements to the Allies. But in questions of Entente diplomacy, especially on the super-sensitive issue of peace planning, the only American opinions that could materially help foreign states at this stage were those of Wilson and, lower down, of House and Lansing. While true that the Secretary of State was now moving slowly toward an endorsement of the nationality principle in Balkan affairs, on the practical questions of wartime diplomacy the President had made his position clear prior to the Balkan conferences that he would not be a party to negotiations with Germany's Allies. There was no reason for him to have changed his mind in the intervening month.[39]

This fatal liability aside, Bakhmetev's recommendation presumed affirmatory answers to two implicit questions. Were there, by the late summer of 1917, reasons to believe that Bulgaria, Turkey and Austria-Hungary wished and were able to abandon Germany? If so, was Russo-American co-operation necessary and, from Washington's viewpoint, desirable to bring it about? In retrospect, the head of the Provisional Government had no doubts on either score, though he provides his readers with some. Ten years after the revolution A. F. Kerenskii wrote:

> The Austro-Hungarian Government, having realized that the situation of Austria-Hungary was untenable, addressed to the Provisional Government a request for a separate peace. The move was made without the knowledge of Berlin. It was particularly significant because Foreign Minister Tereshchenko had long been preparing, with the co-operation of the diplomatic representatives of the United States in Bulgaria and Turkey, a plan for negotiations which would have meant the exit of Bulgaria and Turkey from the war . . . . Russia was on the verge of her greatest victory . . . . The news of Austria's separate peace proposal reached Petrograd on November fifth.[40]

Five years later his emphasis shifted:

> The new war diplomacy of the Provisional Government . . . made it possible to prepare the exit from the war of Bulgaria and Turkey . . . . It is not surprising that the result of the ardent work of our Foreign Minister, M. I. Tereshchenko, together with the diplomatic representatives of the United States . . . was that both [Bulgaria and Turkey] were quite ready to go out of the war even without the agreement of Berlin and Vienna. They were planning to go out about November 1917 . . . . Austria-Hungary too had definitely decided to conclude peace, even a separate peace, at whatever cost.[41]

Hard on the heels of this account came a third version which left out all reference to the overture from Austria-Hungary:

> When the Provisional Government renounced Constantinople the result was quite like winning a great battle on the Turkish front. After the Russian Revolution the feeling in the ruling spheres of Stamboul began to change rapidly and drastically: in the autumn Turkey was quite ripe for dropping out of the war. The ground for this move was fully prepared by Tereshchenko and

> the American diplomatic representatives in Constantinople. . . . Bulgaria was also preparing to drop out of the war. Free Russia had at one stroke succeeded in morally disarming the Bulgarians.[42]

In 1965 a fourth and final statement appeared in terms more definite than anything hitherto:

> By November 15 Turkey and Bulgaria were to have concluded a separate peace with Russia. Suddenly, on about October 20 we received a secret communication from Count Czernin . . . through Sweden that Austria-Hungary was ready to make peace unbeknown to Germany. Lenin's plan was to seize power before the Government could play this trump card.[43]

These selections from fifty years of brooding upon the events of 1917 contain the essence of Kerenskii's defense of his regime and of his indictment of its successor; he maintained the same arguments in private discussion.[44] Each claim is open to searching challenge, even if the last sentence of his concluding history is ignored. His assertion that Austria-Hungary requested a separate peace with Russia on October 20 or November 5 is, to say the least, mysterious. The first question that must come to mind in seeing the statement is why the Dual Monarchy should have turned to Russia as an avenue for its own exit from the war? Vienna's desire for peace was undeniable enough. The new, young Emperor made it an early piece of business to tell William II of the growing unrest among his Slav subjects over the continued fighting with Russia. For that reason he urged the two Central Empires work jointly on Petrograd for peace.[45] But it was a separate Russian, not Austrian peace that Czernin and his Emperor had in mind. Quite apart from the fact that the Hapsburg regime, for all its evident difficulties, was still in better condition than its Russian enemy, the Socialist self-determination formula ruled out any chance of Austro-Hungarian acceptance of Russian terms. By October, it is true, certain inconsistencies would be discernible in Russian Socialist attitudes towards Austria-Hungary's future, but in Vienna's eyes, or rather Budapest's, the Soviet's basic position on war aims was and remained incompatible with the Monarchy's continued existence in the form Czernin and his Magyar colleagues preferred. On October 20, far from proposing his country's surrender to Russia, Czernin was in Germany preparing to bind Austria-Hungary more tightly than ever to her partner.[46] Such soundings as Czernin was and would be making were directed west, not east, and even they served in their fruitlessness to underline Austria-Hungary's subjection to the

German military machine.[47] Assuming that an Austrian approach of some kind was made to Petrograd in late October, it is far likelier to have been an exploration of the Russian scene, rather than a suing for Russian terms. An analogous feeler in July from the Austro-Hungarian legation in Stockholm provoked no Russian reaction, and Tereshchenko thought the incident not worth mentioning in a later speech on the state of affairs in the enemy camp.[48]

The mirage of a separate Bulgarian peace was more energetically pursued in London than in Petrograd in conformity with Lloyd George's well known penchant for "knocking the props" out from under Germany. Balfour was always more skeptical.[49] Unsubstantiated rumors of deals to be made with various shadowy oppositional groups flowed from neutral capitals into the Foreign Office which treated them with some circumspection. August saw diplomatic speculation rise to fever pitch. Mysterious figures, "a man named Oustabashieff and a monk called Stephan," flitted through the cables from Berne, Stockholm and The Hague, and if Oustabashieff was eventually dismissed from British consideration as "a lunatic of an advanced type" there were others to take his place. The whole "plot" (with which the Russian government was supposedly au courant) originated from the same talkative, overheated and ineffectual exiles in Switzerland who had once engaged Miliukov's attention. The Foreign Office at length admitted as much when Nabokov queried the reports he was getting from his friends on the London dinner circuit.[50]

The "new war diplomacy of the Provisional Government," that is, the foreign policy statement of the Coalition Cabinet on May 18, undoubtedly made, as Kerenskii was to claim, a favorable impression in Sofia and Constantinople. Ottoman officials regarded it with renewed hope that the first serious step toward peace had now been taken. It should, they believed, provide a basis for rapid negotiations now that Russia had finally abandoned her hopeless longing for the Straits.[51] In the Bulgarian capital the traditionally pro-Russian *Narod* wrote of "this opening of a new era. The Russian democracy is the only people with its hands free . . . . Humanity has reasons to expect from it a clear and precise language which all nations will well understand."[52] It still went without saying that, as with Vienna, both capitals envisaged a separate Russian peace, rather than one between themselves and the Entente. This conviction spanned the Bulgarian political spectrum, probably even including the "Narrows." A German agent in Stockholm tutored the "Broad" emissaries in whom Philip Snowden had such hopes on the proper attitude they should adopt towards the Russian revolution and Bulgarian war aims. Their King and Premier were still obdurate, though there had been no improvement on the Dobruja problem.

Radoslavov noted on a telegram reporting British readiness to do business with Bulgaria and Turkey that the smaller ally would in no case agree to conclude a separate peace apart from her partners.[53]

If, as Kerenskii later maintained, Russia's renunciation of Constantinople was comparable to a great military victory, her resumption of offensive warfare on July 1st heralded an even greater defeat. *Voenni Izvestiia* in Sofia saw in the attack proof that Russia had capitulated finally and completely before her Western Allies. From now on there could be no question of her exemption from the counter-blows of the Central Powers. To the South-East, *Ikdam* reflected an apparent inclination of the Young Turk leadership to downgrade Russia among Turkey's foes. Her greatest enemy, *Ikdam* explained, was no longer Russia, helpless and chaotic, but Italy.[54] Thereafter the Turkish metropolitan press paid decreasing attention to Russia. Comment, when forthcoming, was bitter and derisive at the ruin engulfing the hereditary foe.[55]

Bulgarian interest in Russia remained high, as even the official press was forced to acknowledge by the prominent attention it continued to pay to Russian developments. The Balkan conferences attracted much press comment, mostly to the not inaccurate effect that Russia's paralysis deprived them of any real significance.[56] Kerenskii's difficulties at cabinet-making evoked a condescending sympathy; a more approving tone was taken towards the Soviet's efforts in October to define a position on European territorial questions. The press regretted that Russian Socialists, beginning with the Prime Minister, seemed unaware of the facts in the matter of Bulgarian frontiers. With perhaps not totally unconscious irony *Mir* observed that if only the Soviet had questioned that excellent authority on Macedonia, Mr Miliukov, it could not have made any reservations on the future of that province.[57] The far Left took heart at the growing power of its Russian brothers. In mid-September the "Narrows" held their first party conference since Bulgaria's entry into the war to take stock of the political position at home and abroad. Speakers, headed by Blagoev, found cause for satisfaction. Party membership had almost tripled in the two war years from 1,800 to 5,000, while circulation of the party's newspaper enjoyed an even more impressive leap in the same period from 2,000 to 11,500. Interestingly, there was no great stress on Lenin or on Russian Bolshevism during the two-day session. This stance mirrored the usually diffident "Narrow" line on the divisions within Russian Socialist ranks in 1917: after November this reluctance was abandoned and, still later, much deplored. It in fact says something for the Bulgarian political scene that the meeting seems to have gone off without governmental impediment. A profusion of red flags and provocative slogans hailing the Russian revolution was removed by police only after some weeks of display.[58] It is improbable that official inaction resulted from fear of proletarian anger were the government to resort to repressive tactics. Throughout all the diatribes, the war weariness and the occasional strike, the ministry retained a firm grip on power and on the Bulgarian political process. All hinged on a victory that might still be won.[59]

Kerenskii to the contrary, the United States did not chase after the vision of a separate peace with Germany's Allies. Overtures to Bulgaria via Washington were vetoed; in the case of Turkey it is difficult to see how "American diplomatic representatives in Constantinople" could have been negotiating with the Ottoman government in the autumn of 1917. Turkey broke relations with the United States on April 20; by June 1st all American embassy personnel had left the country.[60] Save on one occasion, the Wilson Administration did not thereafter display an even sporadic interest in a negotiated Turkish withdrawal from the war.[61] In November the President's position on the future of European Turkey was what it had been the preceding January when he had agreed with House that Turkey-in-Europe should cease to exist.[62] On November 28 he instructed Lansing to tell Ambassador Page that unofficial British suggestions of the utility of a separate Turkish peace were "chimerical and of questionable advantage." An undefeated Turkey would never accept what Wilson saw as "the radical changes of control over Constantinople and the [S]traits" necessary for any durable peace with that Empire.[63]

The situation differed only slightly with Germany's two other Allies. One quixotic incident, recorded by the methodical Lansing in his diary, does resemble Kerenskii's version, though the timing is badly off. On April 3 a certain Sosnowski, a Polish born agent in Washington of the Russian General Staff, submitted on his own initiative a memorandum to the Secretary giving details of a conversation between himself and a fellow Pole, the Austro-Hungarian ambassador Count Tarnowski. It was apparently the ambassador's idea that peace negotiations be instituted under American good offices between Bulgaria and Russia. If successful, it would serve to bring pressure on Vienna to break with Berlin. The Bulgarian minister, Panaretov, would make a convenient intermediary, for, though a patriot, he was married to an American lady and was therefore deemed likely to be receptive to American views. Lansing made non-committal noises but the rupture of relations with Austria-Hungary a few days later spared him the need to pursue Sosnowski's will-o'-the-wisp any further.[64]

Even had Wilson been more enthusiastic about a separate, negotiated peace with Germany's Allies, there was no compelling reason by October for him to look to Russia for aid and co-operation. Good reasons existed why he should not. Russian chaos was one; more to the point, Russian leftists now controlled the formulation of policy, whatever diplomats in the field might advise, and very few members of the Petrograd Soviet, Bolshevik-dominated since mid-September, bothered to hide their scorn for every ideal Wilson defended and stood for. This he found not unnaturally exasperating; he was already confused enough by the bewildering speed and intricacy of Russian events. Neither he nor any other Entente leader could distinguish among the many voices claiming to speak for democratic Russia. By the eve of the Bolshevik uprising he was ready to write off Russian Socialists from Kerenskii leftwards as incapable of coming to terms with reality. Four days after Lenin's coup he castigated "the fatuous dreamers in Russia" who hoped to negotiate peace with the enemy. He too wanted peace, "but I know how to get it and they do not."[65] The first essential was the defeat of Imperial Germany: on that priority, unseen by most Russians, Wilson concentrated his energies.

CHAPTER IX
THE CURTAIN GOES DOWN

The Rumanian Debacle

A Russian diplomatic triumph at this stage was not to be won over Balkan enemies with or without American support. Still less were Balkan allies able to furnish Kerenskii with badly needed foreign laurels. The Serbian and Rumanian Premiers were now struggling to save what they could from Russia's anarchy. Pašić's efforts went into extricating Serbian–South Slav military units from the Odessa region before the Rumanian front collapsed in the south, Archangel froze in the north or the units themselves succumbed to revolutionary infection.[1] Otherwise he was not dependent save in his memories on a traditionally benevolent Russia now almost out of sight. His government's other partners were of obviously greater practical value, especially the United States where Pašić was trying to dispatch a mission similar to the earlier Great Power delegations.[2] All the same, he did not entirely turn his back on Petrograd. Right to the end he looked, or said he did, to democratic Russia for protection of Serbian interests in the alliance.[3]

Bratianu was not disposed to such generosity: his past experiences and present apprehensions left no room for faith in Russia. The picture was as gloomy when viewed from the other side. For the Kerenskii regime Rumania had become by October a microcosm of Russia's worst afflictions: military disaster, political and diplomatic impotence, provincial separatism.

The first ingredient in the tragedy came, as Bratianu had helplessly anticipated, with the derailment of Brusilov's July offensive. Rumanian troops opened their own attack in supposed co-ordination with the Russian armies only a few days before local front Soviets ordered Russian soldiers to stop fighting.[4] For one month, between the battle of Maraşti on July 22 and the week long engagement at Mărăşeşti (August 12-19), Rumanian conscripts proved that General Berthelot's mission had not been without benefit to Rumanian fighting capabilities. Unfortunately it was only a question of time before "Russia's second betrayal of Rumania," to quote the official Rumanian view, worked its effect at the front.[5] The operative word in Jassy for King, politicians and diplomats alike became "evacuation" and much ink and worry was devoted to deciding who should go where, when and how. Of these, "where" presented the fewest difficulties, if only because the options were so limited. Russia was the only possible refuge. Once more Baron Fasciotti lent a willing ear to Bratianu's torrent of recriminations. The Provisional Government offered a sanctuary to the Royal Family at Kherson, near Odessa, but far from a railway line and unhealthy according to all accounts.[6] The King decided to risk all by staying at the front with the Crown Prince, while his wife and younger children prepared for the dubious safety Russia afforded. Perhaps it was just as well that neither local Soviets nor the far-away government could persuade some Russian deserters to vacate the house in Kherson that had been assigned to the Queen. She steeled herself in consequence for the known trials of Jassy.[7] Excited warnings went out almost daily from Bratianu's office to the diplomatic corps to hold itself in readiness for an immediate departure which never materialized. In the long run the only substantive Rumanian asset transferred to Russian hands was the state gold reserve, shipped off in palmier days of Russo-Rumanian cordiality. Like the Spanish Republican treasure twenty years later, it was destined to remain in Moscow "in trust for the people" beyond the reach of local oligarchies.[8]

With nothing to expect from Russia except news of fresh calamities, Bratianu flung himself at the representatives of his country's remaining allies. Collective notes, demarches, proposals and counter proposals kept communications links busy between Jassy and the outside world. However, sooner or later, officials had to admit that nothing could make up for vanished Russian strength, not even the Saint George cross which the King received from Kerenskii on the first anniversary of Rumania's entry into the war.[9] Fear for the treaty which had brought about that entry reigned equally in Bratianu's mind with alarm for his country; the two causes were in fact inseparable. No issue was too trivial if it might advance the welfare of either. In the midst of the evacuation panic the Premier warned Andrews, the American chargé, that he could not expect the same accommodation as the ministers of the signatory powers to Rumania's alliance and he would therefore have to depart in a third class train when the others would go first class. Of course if Andrews would commit his country in writing to the Rumanian treaty, he could travel on an equal footing with the others. The chargé declined, taking refuge in the American constitution and his professed indifference to the quality of Rumanian trains.[10]

An ordeal of a different sort, also rooted in Russia, was the continued activity of a handful of Rumanian leftists led by the irrepressible Rakovsky and aided and abetted by local army Soviets. In late June Rakovsky and a few cronies, including one Mihai Bujor, had organized in Odessa a "Rumanian

Social Democratic Action Committee" whose self-appointed task was ceaselessly to denounce the Rumanian governing class "[responsible for] the pellagra, tuberculosis, illiteracy, corruption and moral decay" currently afflicting the nation.[11] Although it was of slight comfort to Bratianu, Rakovsky still remained faithful to revolutionary defensism, as did *Rumcherod.* Defeat by Germany would only help the forces of counter-revolution, he told his readers in *Golos Revoliutsii*, exactly Kerenskii's position. His comrade Bujor was much more fiery. For him, Russian revolutionary armies were, or should be, the natural vehicle of socio-political change: "we appeal to you for aid, citizens of revolutionary Russia." It was now their turn to imitate the example once given Europe by the armies of revolutionary France "and carry . . . to the unhappy Rumanian people the great ideas bound up in the red flags."[12]

This rhetoric won for Bujor Bolshevik esteem as a genuine Rumanian proletarian-internationalist, but it was ineffectual in significantly raising Rumania's social temperature. Illiteracy and the other evils listed by Rakovsky restricted the number of Rumanian workers capable of appreciating the Socialist slogans. The various soldiers' committees in and around Jassy were a more immediate source of vexation, one Bratianu never tired of denouncing to anyone who would listen.[13] But radicals of the Rakovsky-Bujor stripe, because of their Rumanian nationality or associations, became objects of particular concern to the Premier and his police who pursued them with every force at their command. These were not many; as usual the weapon Bratianu fell back on most readily was a desperate appeal to Petrograd that for once met a sympathetic response. Orders went out for Rakovsky's and Bujor's arrest and their surrender to the Jassy civil authorities. Tereshchenko's willingness to act in this instance undoubtedly reflected Kerenskii's wish to move against troublemakers partially, if not in his eyes wholly, responsible for the deplorable state of things at the front. Moreover, as foreigners, the two men might be more vulnerable to Petrograd's sanctions and their seizure might reduce the stridency of Bratianu's complaints against Russia.[14] As matters turned out the question proved an academic one, since the High Command was unable to carry out its instructions. *Rumcherod* intervened to protect its own and the Prime Ministers had to settle for an undertaking from Army Headquarters that the two meddlesome Socialists would be kept at a safe distance from the frontier. Even this proved impossible of attainment. One of the many notes out of Jassy that summer recounted indignantly how Rakovsky, in the uniform of a Russian colonel "and accompanied by a Rumanian Jew [probably Bujor] in Russian military uniform" had addressed a *Rumcherod* session in October. The Rumanian social and political scene came in for their customary lambasting in spite of Tisenhausen's promise to Bratianu that this would not occur. Simultaneously from Petrograd Kerenskii was storming that "measures" had to be taken at once against Rakovsky's inadmissible behavior at the front.[15] Commissar and "Persuader-in-Chief" agitated in vain. The only way Rakovsky was going to leave the site of his triumphs was if he found a more promising audience elsewhere. Later in October it was reported he had done so among fellow Socialists in Stockholm.[16]

So far Bratianu could justifiably claim, as he monotonously did, that his was the aggrieved nation in relations with revolutionary Russia. On one score, however, the roles were exchanged. At issue was the threat of Bessarabia's secession from Russia and union with Rumania.

Early in its existence the Provisional Government began to concern itself with the province's loyalty to the new Russian order. The proximity of the front and distrust of Rumanian irredentism across the Pruth induced the regime to send agitators to explain the promise of the revolution and to discourage outbreaks of pogroms, an endemic regional feature.[17] Among the emissaries was Catherine Breshko-Breshkovskaia, "little grandmother of the Russian Revolution." She and her team found that, while strong sentiment existed in the middle class population of Kishinev for wider cultural autonomy, including the use of Rumanian in schools and administration, very few of those encountered advocated actual separation from Russia. The rural temperature was much hotter. Peasant expropriations of the landed estates mounted sharply during the summer, as in the rest of Russia, though in Bessarabia's case the turmoil across the Pruth kept fires on the land well stoked. Nevertheless, all was not yet lost by Russia in the Bessarabian town and countryside. A National Moldavian Party emerged in April, analogous to national parties in other parts of the former Empire but one which made a point of denying a wish to unite with Rumania. On this occasion at least Rumanian backwardness worked to Russia's advantage. There was no point in joining a nation whose structures were so much less progressive than those held out to Russia by the revolution.[18] In addition, Bratianu did not inject himself into the issue as long as Miliukov remained at his post. The loudest voices for incorporation of the province into Rumania came from occupied Bucharest and could be dismissed as hostile to Russia and Rumania alike.[19]

These factors began to shift with the political and military fortunes of each country. Bratianu hinted at the Bessarabian issue in winning Parliamentary support for his reform program, a measure bound to attract Rumanians "everywhere." During the later stages of debate Tereshchenko anxiously demanded information on reports reaching him that the Premier was encouraging separatist elements across the Dniester.[20] A further complicating factor by July was the growing fear in Kishinev that Ukrainian "autonomists" in the Rada might insist in their dealings with the Provisional Government that Bessarabia formed part of the Ukraine. V. K. Vinnichenko, head of the Rada's delegation to Petrograd, evidently thought so, and when Kerenskii was dissuaded by an envoy from Kishinev from himself admitting the point, Vinnichenko lamented he would be leaving the capital with nine Ukrainian provinces when he had arrived with ten.[21]

As the bonds of unity slipped the regional loyalties grew stronger at the expense of the national. The process was perceptible in Bessarabia as in other non-Russian parts of European Russia. In April, protestations of loyalty from the National Moldavian Party; in September a representative of that same party told a Congress of Russian Nationalities in Kiev that his province was friendly to the Russian democracy and still looked to a life within a federated Russia. "But should we be confronted in our political aspirations with disillusion we would follow the dictates of our needs which know no limit and become separatists."[22] In effect, if not perhaps in language, the speaker was following the lead given to the nationalities by the Rada, which by the end of September stood on the very brink of se ession from Russia.[23] A month later, with the Bolshevik uprising around the corner, a Congress of Moldavian Soldiers in Kishinev heard demands for Bessarabia's political and territorial autonomy, her own army and regional assembly, though still within the wider Russian federation. The army already existed de facto; the assembly followed hard upon Lenin's triumph in Petrograd. Autonomy in a Russian federation lost both appeal and likelihood in the aftermath of that triumph: the single alternative of incorporation into Rumania came in due course after some help from the Rumanian army and not without some heart searching from the Bessarabian representatives involved.[24]

The result of the wartime partnership between Russia and Rumania was thus the elimination for the foreseeable future, not of Russia's power in South-East Europe—that vanished with Brusilov's offensive—but of her very presence as a participating political force in the peninsula. Rumania was the graveyard of pre-Bolshevik Russia as a Balkan Power. The progressive annexation of a Russian province unmistakably pointed up the magnitude of the change in the facts of Balkan politics and in a personal sense, no doubt very satisfying to himself, symbolised Bratianu's revenge over the Russian revolution. His government bears in return the distinction of being the first to receive a Bolshevik declaration of war. As matters turned out, it was a price Bratianu could well afford to pay. Rumania emerged from war, defeat and foreign revolution even "greater" than her Prime Minister had once contemplated.

The Socialist Alternatives

The Cabinet which Kerenskii had constructed with so much difficulty proved incapable of withstanding the shock of the Kornilov uprising. The Premier, conscious perhaps of the precedent marking the end of the French Revolution, appointed a Directorate of Five, including himself and Tereshchenko, to go through the motions of governing while the non-Bolshevik Left collectively made up its mind whether to continue the coalition experiment. The question came to a head during the so-called "Democratic Conference," convened to consider the position of all Socialist factions on the issue of further co-operation with the non-Socialist parties. In Sukhanov's view, opinionated but not unshared, they might just as well have spared themselves the trouble. The delegates sat through interminable speeches, beginning with an emotional and much interrupted *éloge* of the Prime Minister by himself. Nothing new was said; "everything had been heard or read already."[25] By a majority of seventy-eight the Conference decided in favor of maintaining the coalition and then voted by a majority of over a hundred against admitting the Cadets, compromised by Kornilov but without whom no Socialist-bourgeois union was possible.[26] It was then resolved to sound out the government on changes in official policy in a number of areas. The first subject to be raised was foreign affairs.

The Left now forced the pace. The delegation sent to confer with the Cabinet insisted that "an active struggle for peace" must form the basis of Russian policy. In practical terms this meant the summoning in the shortest possible time of the deferred Inter-Allied conference on war aims revision. A Soviet delegate was to be present on the Russian team. The conference itself had by now been rather shakily fixed for November. The Democratic Conference agreed next to expand its members to include non-Socialist representatives and that this body, to be known as the Pre-Parliament or Provisional Council of the Republic, should have the right to interpellate ministers. Tsereteli assured his colleagues that although the government would not be formally responsible to the new assembly, "it stands to reason that no Provisional Government will be able to exist without receiving a vote of confidence from it."[27] The Democratic Conference accepted this arrangement by a vote of 109 in favor, 84 opposed. Representatives of the Petrograd Soviet, where the Bolsheviks won a majority on September 22, stood in opposition to every one of the approved motions. The Soviet itself, to lend substance to its agents' conduct, greeted the last coalition Cabinet on October 10 with total hostility. No prominent Menshevik or Right SR sat in the ministry whose effective leadership, for what that was worth, remained in the Directorate's hands.[28]

After a brief search for appropriate quarters, the Pre-Parliament settled for the familiar Mariinskii Palace, opening to the inevitable speech from Kerenskii on October 20 at 5 in the afternoon. "Powerless, sickly, alien and repugnant to every revolutionary principle," wrote Sukhanov, "it was a de facto power compared to the comic opera government."[29] Allowing for revolutionary fervor, Sukhanov had accurately assessed the political realities of the day. Kerenskii's hand was played out; it was for the Socialist ranks themselves to speak up on the questions of the day, even though those ranks no longer included the Bolsheviks who marched out of the hall after a contemptuous address from Trotskii.[30] As Tsereteli had announced, foreign affairs ranked first in importance on the Socialist agenda: two Socialist pronouncements on the subject appeared side by side in *Izvestiia* on the day the Pre-Parliament began its work. One of these, drawn up by the Central Executive Committee of the combined All Russian Soviets of Workers' and Soldiers' Deputies, purported to define the Soviets' position on questions which would presumably confront delegates to the projected war aims revision conference in Paris. The second document appeared over the signatures of the Dutch-Scandinavian committee that had been trying to organize the Stockholm reunion of European Socialists.

The Instructions, or *Nakaz*, worked out for the designated Soviet representative at the war aims conference, M. I. Skobolev, contained the first official statement of the Russian Left on specific territorial problems of the war. Five of the ten clauses on border disputes had to do with South-East Europe.

5. Serbia and Montenegro to be restored and to have material aid from an international fund. Serbia to have access to the Adriatic. Bosnia and Herzogovina to be autonomous.

6. Disputed areas in the Balkans to have temporary autonomy to be followed by plebiscites.

7. Rumania to have back her old frontiers with the obligation to give Dobruja temporary autonomy at once and the right of self-determination later. Rumania to bind herself to put into force the clauses of the Berlin Treaty of 1878 about the Jews and to give them equal rights with citizens of Rumania.

8. To have autonomy in the Italian parts of Austria, to be followed by plebiscites to determine to what state they should belong.

10. To re-establish Greece . . . .

The next section, governing freedom of the seas, called for the neutralization of all straits giving access to inland seas. That disposed of the Bosporus and the Dardanelles.[31]

The second document, giving the Stockholm program, saw the light of day long after it had become evident that the conference itself would never get off the ground. The refusal of the major Entente governments, including the United States, to allow their Socialists to attend spelled the end of any hopes to re-unite the sundered portions of the Second International in war on the war.[32] Moreover, by frustrating the desire of moderate Russian Socialists to meet their Entente and German comrades on neutral ground, Messrs. Lloyd George, Ribot, Sonnino and Wilson strengthened the domestic appeal of the Bolsheviks who had come down hard against the Stockholm meeting as useless in its very conception. The Central Powers put no such obstacles in the way of their several Socialist factions, perhaps out of a deeper conviction than the Entente of Socialist powerlessness to impede their governments' intentions.

The Bulgarian team to Stockholm played an interesting role illustrating this German confidence. Four of its members, "King Ferdinand's well drilled Socialists" to quote a British observer, were from the "Broad" faction under its leader Sakyzov.[33] They could be relied on to support the official line on war aims and Russian affairs. The two remaining delegates, both "Narrows," were not so dependable. They went along as window dressing to assure the Soviet of Bulgarian (and German) sincerity in desiring a just settlement with Russia.[34] Once in Sweden they published a rousing message from their chief Blagoev, encouraging the revolutionary Russian proletariat in its further activity.[35] They were unimportant all the same. The Dutch-Scandinavian committee, chaired by the Swedish Socialist Hjalmar Branting, got Bulgarian views on desired territorial changes solely from "Broads," who first co-ordinated their strategy with a representative of the German Foreign Office. This gentleman, using the alias "Bam," reported to Berlin with evident satisfaction that the Bulgarians would clarify Balkan problems to the committee from the standpoint of Bulgarian national interests. As for Russia, Sakyzov assured "Bam" of his familiarity with that nation's affairs and of his influence over the Menshevik delegates present in Stockholm that summer. He exuded optimism over the outcome of the Revolution: peace or anarchy, either one advantageous to the common cause.[36]

Sakyzov held forth for three and a half hours in German before Branting's committee. He himself spoke optimistically to "Bam" on the impression he felt he had made, especially on the chairman whom "Bam" regarded as "Ententiste." Unfortunately for the "Broads," their presentation came before anyone else's; four months later when the committee was ready to deliver its by now pointless report, other influences had been brought to bear including, as the last delegation to be heard, two Serbs.[37] Unlike the Skobolev statement, the Stockholm manifesto committed itself on two important Balkan issues: the future of Macedonia and of the Hapsburg South Slavs. Serbia, united with Montenegro, should divide Macedonia with Bulgaria along the Vardar River line. Both countries would share with Greece in free access to the Aegean and in joint administration of the port and region of Salonika. Czechs and Yugoslavs should enjoy complete national autonomy in a federation of Hapsburg nationalities. The report handled other contentious issues even more gingerly. "A multitude of questions" existed that the committee chose not to come to grips with. Among these were several "of an economic character, the Dardanelles, Baghdad and the interests of the Powers in Asia Minor." All were deemed in essence to be linked in their solution to the eventual founding of a "Society of Nations" that could bring relief much more competently than anyone else.[38]

The Central Executive Committee published its Instructions to Skobolev with the defiant preface that it called upon all peoples to judge its foreign policy for what it was.[39] The invitation was accepted with general alacrity. Balkan reactions to the *Nakaz* and the Stockholm program ranged from guarded approval to outrage, with attentions focused on those aspects of each document most distasteful to individual governments. Bulgarian sources expressed partial satisfaction with Skobolev's mandate which returned the Dobruja and said nothing directly of Macedonia, but would have nothing to do with Branting's idea of Macedonian partition.[40] Conversely, *La Serbie* lamented the grievous inadequacies of the Soviet plan which, apart from its silence on Macedonia, never mentioned Yugoslav aspirations. If the *Nakaz* were to become the determining impulse of Russian foreign policy, "Serbs with their Croat and Slovene brothers must despair for their future," the paper wailed.[41] The Greek minister in Petrograd told a reporter from the right-wing *Birzhevie Vedomosti* that the Dutch-Scandinavian proposals must have been written by Bulgarians, while the beleagured Rumanian authorities sent off frantic appeals to their Western friends to prevent Skobolev's participation in the Paris conference. Bratianu was probably encouraged to move fast by the enthusiasm with which *Rumcherod* endorsed the instructions given the Soviets' agent in Paris.[42] Finally, from Kiev, Thomas Masaryk dispatched his careful analysis of the

Nakaz omissions. Most glaring of these was its almost complete silence on the future of Austria-Hungary. Echoing Miliukov, Masaryk insisted in his commentary, sent to all Petrograd papers, that the Dual Monarchy's division into its national components remained still the basic aim of the war as far as he was concerned.[43]

Reaction in Petrograd itself was not much calmer. Right and far Left sneered at Skobolev's mission and had little scorn left over for the Dutch-Scandinavian recommendations.[44] One after the other, Allied ambassadors descended on Tereshchenko to underline the utter inadmissibility of Skobolev and his mandate to the Paris talks. Allied disapproval of their agent led Skobolev's sponsors to urge the Entente embassies to soften their hostility: the *Nakaz* reflected "wishes," not "demands." Even so, Russia's partners were adamant. Tereshchenko would be welcome, Skobolev would not.[45]

On October 25 Tereshchenko appeared before a closed session of the Pre-Parliament's foreign affairs committee. He came with two stated purposes in mind. First he wished to analyze the contemporary diplomatic situation, then to express the government's opinion on the war in the light of the two Socialist pronouncements. The sessions, public and private, where he spoke on these points lasted with interruptions for four days and turned out to be the regime's inquest on its foreign policy record. Two days before, after stormy debate, the Bolshevik Party's Central Committee had voted to prepare for an armed seizure of power.

The Foreign Minister began his observations with a brief survey of conditions in the camp of Russia's enemies. Turkey, he said, was weary of the war. Her troops were disintegrating and voices were even being heard for a reorientation of policy toward the Entente. But regrettably, "at the insistence of party leaders," Turkey stayed loyal to the Central Powers. Austria-Hungary too was in difficult straits, particularly over nationality problems. In Bulgaria, on the other hand, in spite of what Kerenskii would later claim, Tereshchenko could see no evidence "of a direct anti-government movement or of any real change in our favor."[46]

He turned next to the question which had excited so much passion and invective over the preceding seven months: "what must Russia try and achieve from the standpoint of her national interests?" What were the minimum, most essential conditions without which Russia could not make peace? Tereshchenko proceeded to supply the answers. First came the Baltic; second, just as vital, "the need to secure our access to the southern seas." What precisely did that mean? His language at that point became reminiscent of his predecessor in office, present in his audience. Access to the southern seas, Tereshchenko argued, might be gained in several ways "apart from the so-called imperialistic plan associated with the acquisition of Constantinople and the Straits." These several ways did not include neutralization, unless accompanied by guarantees of universal disarmament. Third and lastly, the minister laid down the need for an assurance of Russian economic independence in collaboration with the Western Powers. After some inconclusive remarks on the treaties Tereshchenko sat down and the meeting was open to questions from the floor.[47]

Miliukov rose first. His question was simple and predictable. Had there been any revision of the treaties left in Tereshchenko's charge? If not, it must be assumed they have remained in force. His successor replied that there had been no revision; he refrained from comment on Miliukov's conclusion from that fact. Martov, leader of the Menshevik Internationalist wing to which Sukhanov had attached himself, offered some comment of his own: what about the Rumanian and Italian treaties? Tereshchenko conceded both countries in question placed great value on their agreements, "which guarantee them certain advantages in return for their actions"—an overly discreet description to an audience generally familiar with the advantages referred to. In Italy's case, however, her war aims were so vast and disproportionate to her efforts that agreements with her could not be considered firm. Her occupation of Albania was a case in point, as also were her ambitions in the Adriatic at the expense of an independent Yugoslav state "which has encountered wide support in Russia." A second Miliukov query on the touchy issue of the Asia Minor accords drew the revealing admission that the distribution of these territories among the four Powers promised serious problems for Russia "especially in the case of an incomplete solution of the Straits question."[48] His words assuredly afforded his predecessor a deep sense of satisfaction and vindicated honor.

Four days later, on the twenty-ninth, Tereshchenko addressed an open session of the Pre-Parliament in much the same terms. He set out to examine the government's foreign policy in conjunction with the Skobolev program, speaking plainly, "without reference to national honor and dignity, only in terms of national expediency." That reason, if no other, required that Russia stay in the war while striving for a peace that humiliated neither Russia nor any other country. No annexations, no indemnities and self-determination were worthwhile goals that Russia wanted and the Central Powers rejected. Poles, Czechoslovaks and Yugoslavs must have their freedom. These were matters that the Paris conference could profitably do something about. The same could not be said for Skobolev. Quite apart from his personal role in Paris, his program contained details that were in some respects worse than the Stockholm manifesto. The *Nakaz* conceded the possibility of self-determination for the Baltic Provinces, a step that would return Russia to pre-Petrine times and did nothing comparably sweeping to Austria-Hungary. Rumania was to lose the Dobruja and neutralization of the Straits without disarmament threatened a return to a position infinitely worse than the status quo ante bellum.[49]

With these sentiments Tereshchenko uttered his swan song. Miliukov rose again to deliver his, and with it close the chapter on traditional themes of Russian foreign policy. The root of all Russia's present evils, he held, stemmed from "the original, purely Russian view on the problems of our foreign policy which . . . pretends to be the internationalist view." It was the old Slavophile dream, now under new colors and with a new prophet in "the nobleman Lenin." As for the *Nakaz*, the Germans could hardly have put it better. It penalized a Russian ally, Rumania; it failed to provide for the South Slavs and was wholly unrealistic in its proposals for the Turkish Straits. Moving his fire on to Tereshchenko, Miliukov then demanded whether or not the minister wished Russia to have the Straits herself. And what of the various nationalities oppressed by Kaiserdom? Citing Asquith's remarks in the House of Commons debate of May 16, Miliukov declared that "only when the legitimate demands of Italy, Rumania and the Slavic countries" were satisfied could a world policy be created uniting the peoples in alliance "with justice as its base and liberty as its cornerstone."[50] Socialist members greeted his words with mocking incredulity and an ovation to the revolution; the Right simultaneously applauded "our gallant Allies." The two gestures symbolized the unbridgeable split in the rival concepts of Russia's relationship to the rest of Europe.

In the few days that remained of the Provisional Government's existence, no settlement was or could be reached between two hopelessly antithetical bodies. Socialist unity itself was weakened by dissension inside the non-Bolshevik Left on the nature of Skobolev's Instructions. On November 2 a second revolutionary organization, the All-Russian Executive Committee of the Soviets of Peasants' Deputies, objected to the unqualified application of the self-determination formula to Russia and, so it seemed, nowhere else of mixed nationality. There were also complaints that the *Nakaz* did not specify Germany's obligation to pay for her depredations in occupied territories. The Executive Committee of the Peasants' Soviets corrected these omissions and also dealt with some of the other inadequacies noted by Tereshchenko, Miliukov and Masaryk. Rumania's duty to grant autonomy to the Dobruja was ignored (though not her obligations to her Jews) and an extra clause established that

> all national and territorial questions arising as a consequence of the present war or in connection with it, such as the Yugoslav, Transylvanian, Czech and

Italian questions in Austria shall be settled by means of a plebiscite with an effective guarantee for free elections.

Other clauses remained as in the original, although there was no mention made in the amended version of the need to neutralize the Turkish Straits. The Peasants' Soviets in fact ignored the subject altogether. The changed Instructions were submitted to the Executive Committee of the Workers' and Soldiers' Soviets for an expression of opinion, even as other disfranchised groups tried to climb aboard the bandwagon to Paris.[51]

In reality the exact terms of Skobolev's mandate now mattered not a whit. Russia's Great Power Allies had not the slightest intention of admitting him or any other Soviet spokesman to their Paris deliberations. More than this, at the moment when Tereshchenko was defending the utility of the Paris meeting before the Pre-Parliament, the British Chancellor of the Exchequer was informing his Parliamentary colleagues that the conference would consider only the more efficient conduct of the war, not the aims for which that war was being waged.[52] He was fully supported in his stand by the Balkan members of the alliance. Bratianu and Pašić eagerly looked to the new appearance in the Balkans that *Izvestiia* held up as a desirable result of four years bloodletting.[53] Only they saw that achievement in quite different terms and brought about by quite different means than did Skobolev's defenders. The triumph of the Entente, not of the *Nakaz*, would bring the longed-for rewards. On the opposing side, Bulgaria, Turkey and Austria-Hungary regarded Russian anarchy with much optimism and with the expectation that peace was at last in sight. On November 7 it seemed at hand. On the following morning Petrograd awoke to find Lenin's cohorts in full control and Tereshchenko en route to prison rather than Paris. Twelve hours later the Bolshevik chief appeared before the Second All-Russian Congress of Soviets to announce the immediate publication of the secret treaties and the inauguration of a new era in Russian and world history.

A Summary

The Tsarist government left its successor onerous burdens in South-East Europe. By circumstance, if not by choice, Russia's rank as a European Great Power had come in the half-century that preceded the downfall of the monarchy to depend primarily on her position and strength in the Balkan peninsula. That fact and not Pan-Slav ideology or the dream of Constantinople dictated the Russian response in the supreme crisis of July 1914.

War with Austria-Hungary and, still more, with Turkey enabled the

Empire to address itself to the task of securing South-East European objectives. Constantinople and the Straits, "the keys to Russia's doors," came first. Next in importance stood the government's desire to reassert the nation's role in countries it considered were Tsardom's special preserve: in the first place Serbia and Bulgaria; in the second, after 1913, Rumania. Here the gains were slight. In war nothing can be more conducive to diplomatic success than victory; Russia had too few. Her military failures and Balkan rivalries determined the wartime history of South-East Europe to 1917. By March of that year all that was left of Russian preponderance in the peninsula were the conditional promise of future prizes and a million near-mutinous troops on the Rumanian border. Judged by these standards Russia had ceased to be a Great Power.

The first Foreign Minister of the Provisional Government entered office with the resolve to restore Russia to her rightful place among her fellows. As a politician, P. N. Miliukov could reluctantly concede that the Tsar's enforced abdication implied "a new structure" in the government of Russia. As Foreign Minister he continued to insist that nothing whatever had changed in the nation's external priorities. All Tsarist goals became his goals; even his former sympathy for the Yugoslav cause receded before the older predilection for Serbia. At no time in office or out did he admit that such a program was an anomaly for Russia after March 15. Russia must have Constantinople and the Straits because her economic and strategic future depended on their possession. Turkey had proved herself an unfit guardian and was a German puppet to boot. Other aims, too, were entirely in accord, in his judgment, with the basic principles of the new Russian regime.

Foreign reactions to the revolution depended above all else on the state of affairs at the front. Russia's enemies in South-East Europe took heart. The Tsar's overthrow increased the desire for peace in each country, especially Austria-Hungary whose own Emperor saw in Russia's possible withdrawal from the war "the key to the situation" whereby his own Empire might be saved.[54] The Bulgarian and Turkish regimes were not above using the events in Russia to secure greater attention in Berlin to their own points of view. Fundamentally, however, all three remained loyal to their German alliance. Entente war aims, if not their own, left them no alternative. The picture was not vastly different on the popular level. For the Turks, culture, religion and history combined to exclude anything other than indifference or, at best, satisfaction over Russian developments. Bulgarians reacted to these, as could be expected, more sympathetically. Parliament and Press reflected that interest, as did sporadic labor unrest and defiant proclamations from the far Left. But none of this managed to fragment either the facade or substance of royal control which survived 1917 and the initial months of Bolshevik rule in Petrograd unimpaired.

Though the revolution appalled Russia's Balkan Allies, her larger partners, under Miliukov's guidance, welcomed it as the removal of barriers in the way of Russia's more effective participation in the war. But wrangling in Petrograd led to second and third thoughts in the West. No Russian charter, no matter how eloquent, was going to reverse the fact that Russia's decline left Germany the unchallenged master of Eastern Europe. Until Russia could regain her strength, her wishes were not going to command much respect from Allied governments on sensitive issues of war policy. Unofficially, on the other hand, the revolution directed much attention toward nationality questions in Central and South-Eastern Europe. In England in particular Radical critics subjected government policy on nationality issues to ever sharper attacks as the revolution swung further to the left. Their censure forced those at the other end of the spectrum into some verbal gymnastics. Thus, on May 16, the former Premier, H. H. Asquith, distinguished four types of annexation of which only the last, "conquest for the sake of expansion of territory and of political and economic aggrandizement" was, he claimed, objectionable to the Provisional Government.[55] This attempt to rechristen now obnoxious expressions so that they would, in William Buckler's words, "smell sweet" to the Russian democracy unsurprisingly failed, with one exception, to impress anyone of importance in Petrograd.[56] That the exception was Miliukov only underlined the futility of Asquith's subtleties.

Because he was the most prominent of Russian liberals, with excellent connections abroad and well versed in contemporary diplomatic conundrums, it was perhaps inevitable that Miliukov should have inherited the foreign affairs portfolio. His intellectual abilities were beyond challenge and his appointment unquestionably encouraged Russia's Allies. Yet it closed the door to the possibility of a fresh start for the new regime in foreign affairs. Miliukov assumed his duties committed by choice and conviction to wildly inappropriate goals, given the spirit prevalent in Petrograd and all Russia that spring. Even his endorsement of the self-determination formula for Austria-Hungary, which far exceeded the Stockholm or Skobolev programs, could only have originated in his wish to eliminate Russia's great traditional rival in South-East Europe. That at any rate would have been the result and Miliukov sedulously refrained from applying the same formula to other racially mixed areas such as Turkey or, for that matter, his own country. His refusal to compromise and occasional arrogance speak well for his integrity and self-esteem but they reveal in full clarity his limitations as a member of a revolutionary Cabinet. By May he was beyond a doubt the government's heaviest domestic liability. It was impossible, as Talaat had insisted, to maintain that Russia had really changed and still retain Miliukov at his post. A closer and more eloquent critic than the Grand Vizier put matters most simply:

> The Russia that had to declaim daily about the Dardanelles, the cross on Saint Sophia and to whom it was necessary to speak of war to a victorious conclusion—that Russia ceased to exist on March 12, 1917 . . . . [Diplomacy] must speak in a language corresponding to the attitude and sentiments of the country at war.[57]

This was the task of the regime's second occupant of the building at the Singer's Bridge. Where Miliukov had represented traditional continuities and, as a result, had been driven from office, M. I. Tereshchenko took over his duties as the representative of the revolution and the executant of its foreign policy principles. That a man of his social and political background should have been selected for so sensitive a post at so sensitive a time showed how hard the moderate Russian Left still found it to break completely with longstanding Russian continuities. Greece and Albania provided Tereshchenko with his first tests; he failed them. Yet his failure was not, as the press suggested, the consequence of his own lack of vigor, but of his country's. Her principal Allies made that brutally clear by the short shrift they gave to Russian views at the conferences of July and August on Balkan affairs. The main preoccupation by then of Britain and France was not to reshape their priorities on a Russian model, but to prevent the Russian and Italian disasters from dragging down the entire Entente. By late October the Balkans appeared beyond redemption. The combination of Russia's collapse and Caporetto rendered "chimerical" all Entente plans for the future of South-East Europe, so Buckler was informed by a senior member of the War Cabinet.[58]

It was at this point that both the Soviets and Tereshchenko raised Balkan issues once more. The Skobolev mandate gave the first detailed statement of Russian Socialism on specific issues of European peacemaking. In its own way, however, the *Nakaz* revealed itself as unrealistic as Miliukov's ideas. As Tereshchenko and Masaryk lost no time in pointing out, it made little sense to proclaim the gospel of national self-determination and then refuse to apply it in Austria-Hungary where European nationality tensions were currently most acute. The Soviet framers of the *Nakaz* may have concluded, along with the Dutch-Scandinavian committee and the U.D.C., that some kind of multi-national federation was desirable for post-war stability in South-Central and South-Eastern Europe. They certainly gave no encouragement to individual national aspirations in the area; the cautious phrases of the *Nakaz* with their talk of "restoration," "old frontiers," "autonomy for disputed regions," could not have sounded a more muted clarion call to submerged, oppressed or avaricious nationalities. *Izvestiia* defended this reticence. An article taking up the whole of the paper's front page one week before the Bolshevik rising re-examined the provisions of the *Nakaz* in the context of Tereshchenko's criticisms. *Izvestiia* came to the conclusion that the proposals were realistic and, in Russia's circumstances, honorable. Self-determination was not, as Tereshchenko thought, a penalty to be exacted but rather was a benefit to be enjoyed. It was certainly not something that could be rammed down foreign throats. If the Slav nationalities of Austria-Hungary were to win their freedom, the Russian democracy would applaud and support their efforts. But nothing more than that: "to continue the war until all the peoples of Austria-Hungary are satisfied and not to agree to peace until then would mean dragging out the war indefinitely. We cannot carry such a responsibility before our own people."[59] There was in *Izvestiia*'s words more than a suggestion of impatience with foreigners; the editorial presumed a clear wish to put the Russian house in order on the basis of principles which others should be encouraged to adopt but for which Russians could not be expected to exhaust themselves spreading abroad. It was as if *Izvestiia*'s last comment on pre-Bolshevik foreign policy were unconsciously anticipating and paraphrasing a later appeal in demanding "self-determination in one country" before involvements outside.

Tereshchenko could not opt out quite so easily. His duty to advance the interests of revolutionary Russia paralleled his desire to protect the interests of Entente Russia. His efforts to do both imparted a certain ambivalence to his public pronouncements that became most discernible in his address of October 29 to the Pre-Parliament. *Izvestiia* judged his remarks on that occasion to have been "nationalist but not national" and his predecessor sarcastically greeted him as a natural spokesman in an age of official hypocrisy.[60] From each source the reproach was a severe, though not inaccurate summary of the government's predicament.

Early in that speech of October 29 Tereshchenko threw off a statement to the effect that the principal reason for Russia's difficult position lay "not in material conditions but in the change in the psychology of the people to which we bear witness."[61] Although his reference was to the wider questions of Russian political life, it was most pointed when applied to the national attitude toward the outside world. Before the war, questions of Russia's relations abroad and external priorities interested few and involved fewer. The constituency which Russian Foreign Ministers had to bear in mind was the Emperor's study, Prince Gorchakov's "one chamber" as opposed to the several Parliamentary Chambers his foreign colleagues were obliged to confront and convince. Not so in Russia. On the few occasions between 1906 and 1914 when the Duma managed to discuss foreign affairs there were sometimes heated criticisms but nothing Nicholas and his ministers could not ignore if they wanted to. The war and its disasters widened that constituency. But neither Sazonov nor Stürmer lost their portfolios because of popular resentment at their diplomatic programs. To the end the Empire's foreign concerns continued to be determined and defended in accordance with "vital interests" defined by an irresponsible handful and, as Trepov discovered, ridiculed by most of articulate society. The Doumergue-Pokrovskii pact came as a dying gasp of this spirit.

The revolution of course provided the greatest impulse to the Russian people's "psychological change" as noted by Tereshchenko. It was not merely the Kerenskiis, Tseretelis and Sukhanovs who now thrust themselves into delicate questions with demands for new approaches. Behind them, for the first time, stood the anonymous man in the crowd whose interjections stud every transcript of the revolutionary year's proceedings. The voice that shouted to Miliukov on October 29 as he demanded respect for the treaties, for Italy, for Rumania—"but you cannot believe all this yourself!"—spoke for the thousands to whom the Izvol'skii-Sazonov-Miliukov traditions were utterly abhorrent, fit only for some historical limbo. That voice and many like it now counted for something and wanted to put their own rude stamp on matters reserved hitherto for an initiated elite. Hence the Skobolev *Nakaz*, the Peasants' Soviets' program and, on a humbler level, the intervention to protect Rumanian Jews and Socialists, "regardless of the fact that this is perhaps inadmissible from an international point of view."

By the end of October all non-Bolshevik initiatives in foreign policy, as everything else, had run their course. In Balkan matters which had provoked so much effort in past years, Russia, far from being nearer to the solution of historic tasks, was further off from them than ever. Dreams of territorial expansion were over, if they had ever begun, for all but a corporal's guard under Miliukov. Balkan dominance had also gone a-glimmering and foreign politicians, with the possible exception of Premier Pašić, succeeded in reconciling themselves to Russia's loss. Its replacement, as far as Balkan statesmen were concerned, was a lively anticipation, fearful or otherwise, of far-reaching changes possible in the peninsula. And for the Entente Great Powers there would perhaps be the consolation, expressed privately at the moment of victory by a French diplomat in Petrograd, that his country and Britain could now regulate once and for all "that wasps' nest in the Balkans" without Russia being present to mess everything up.[62]

Miliukov and Tereshchenko held in turn a portfolio that demanded more than any other with the least hope of success in a Cabinet that saw itself as both Russian and revolutionary. Miliukov had emphasized the first to the exclusion of the second; he fell from power with no regrets or doubts as to the correctness of his choice. It was not as easy for his successor. A multimillionaire, politically inexperienced, with no backing other than Kerenskii's prestige, he entered upon his responsibilities committed to goals far more in tune with popular sentiment than those pursued before him. He could hardly act in the grand manner even if he would; in any case the lack of attention paid to Russian wishes by erstwhile clients was not utterly new in the annals of Russian diplomacy. Russian apron strings, such as they were, had been badly frayed in 1912 and surely snapped in the four years thereafter. The effect of the revolution was to bring new hopes and fears throughout the peninsula and put an end for the time being to ambitions of reversing recent trends in Russia's Balkan involvement. Yet whatever the ambitions and whoever their interpreter, two choices alone were open to Russia by late October. Her leaders had either to acquiesce in a situation over which they obviously had no control and save what they could by bargaining and pleading, or else they could strike out on their own in the hope that complete independence would bring its own rewards. With his warnings of October 25 and 29 on the Straits, Yugoslavia and Turkish partition, Tereshchenko took the first course. Skobolev and the peasant deputies plumped for something in between. On November 8 Lenin chose the second.

NOTES TO PREFACE

1. E. C. Thaden, *Russia and the Balkan Alliance of 1912* (University Park, 1965), p. 136.

2. Rex Wade, *The Russian Search For Peace, February-October 1917* (Stanford, 1969).

3. V. S. Vasiukov, *Vneshniaia Politika Vremennogo Pravitel'stva* (Moscow, 1966); A. V. Ignat'ev, *Russko-angliiskie Otnosheniia nakanune Oktiabr'skoi Revoliutsii* (Moscow, 1966); K. E. Kirova, *Russkaia Revoliutsiia i Italiia* (Moscow, 1968); V. N. Vinogradov, *Rumyniia v gody Pervoi Mirovoi Voiny* (Moscow, 1969). These are cited *passim* below.

NOTES TO CHAPTER 1

1. B. H. Sumner, *Russia and the Balkans, 1870-1880*, (Hamden, 1962), pp. 78–79, 554–556.

2. G. Papadopoulos, *England and the Near East, 1896-1898* (Salonika, 1969), p. 246, Appendix II, Sir P. Currie to the Maquess of Salisbury, June 2, 1897.

3. V. M. Khvostov, ed., *Istoriia Diplomatii* (3 vols., Moscow, 1959-65), 2, 350.

4. In 1893 Rumanian Prime Minister Sturdza warned King Carol that public opinion held the Magyars to be "far worse enemies than the Russians [and that] this feeling is undermining Rumania's attitude to the Triple Alliance." C. A. Macartney, *The Hapsburg Empire, 1790-1918* (London, 1968), p. 733. This was recognized in Berlin and Vienna despite Carol's renewal in 1901 of Rumania's adherence to the alliance. *GP*, 18:2, nos. 5803, 5804.

5. Papadopoulos, pp. 53–54; J. S. Corbett, *History of the Great War Based on Official Documents: Naval Operations* (5 vols., London, 1920–31), 2, 204.

6. *Krasnyi Arkhiv* (Moscow), 69–70 (1935), 5ff.

7. O. Hauser, *Deutschland und der englisch-russische Gegensatz, 1900-1914* (Göttingen, 1958), pp. 85, 86.

8. *Khvostov*, 2, 647.

9. *Ö-UA*, 1, no. 40; H. Uebersberger, *Österreich zwischen Russland und Serbien* (Cologne, 1958), pp. 21-29.

10. *Ö-UA*, 1, no. 87.

11. Duma: *Ochety*, Third Session, First Sitting, April 4/17, 1908, cols. 1763–66.

12. *Ibid*, Third Session, Second Sitting, Dec. 12/25, 1908, col. 2629.

13. *Ibid*, cols. 2677–2704.

14. E. de Schelking, *Recollections of a Russian Diplomat, The Suicide of Monarchies* (New York, 1918), p. 229.

15. P. E. Mosely, "Russian Policy in 1911-1912," *Journal of Modern History*, 12 (1940), 73.

16. N. V. Charykov, *Glimpses of High Politics, Through War and Peace 1855-1929* (New York, 1931), p. 274.

17. *Ibid*, pp. 276–77.

18. *MOEI*, Series II, 18:2, no. 806; *Hauser*, p. 265.

19. S. D. Sazonov, *Vospominaniia* (Paris, 1927), pp. 94–95, 96.

20. *de Schelking*, p. 242.

21. For the Russian role see T. A. Meininger, *Ignatiev and the Establishment of the Bulgarian Exarchate* (Madison, 1970), pp. 193-97.

22. S. Radeff, *La Macédoine et la Renaissance Bulgare au XIX Siècle* (Sofia, 1918), p. 252; Carnegie Endowment, *Report of the International Commission to Inquire into the Causes and Conduct of the Balkan Wars* (Washington, 1914), p. 27.

23. H. R. Wilkinson, *Maps and Politics, A Review of the Ethnographic Cartography of Macedonia* (Liverpool, 1951), pp. 35-68.

24. *Ö-UA*, 2, no. 2045.

25. A. V. Nekliudoff, *Diplomatic Reminiscences Before and During the World War* (London, 1920), p. 45.

26. F. Stieve, ed., *Der Diplomatische Schriftwechsel Iswolskis, 1911-1914* (4 vols., Berlin, 1924), 2, no. 243.

27. E. C. Helmreich, *The Diplomacy of the Balkan Wars, 1912-1913* (Cambridge, Mass., 1938), p. 153.

28. *Nekliudoff*, pp. 96-97; *Mosely*, p. 78.

29. For the military conduct of the wars see *Helmreich*, chs. VII, X & XVIII, for the Macedonian issue ch. XIII.

30. *Sazonov*, pp. 87, 281; *Nekliudoff*, p. 120; *Stieve*, 2, no. 547.

31. *Stieve*, 3, no. 1116 where Izvol'skii reported details in this sense of a conversation with former Bulgarian Premier Danev.

32. *Krasnyi Arkhiv*, 6, (1924), 75.

33. M. Boghitschewitsch, ed., *Die Auswärtige Politik Serbiens, 1903-1914* (3 vols., Berlin, 1928), 3, no. 399; *Sazonov*, p. 129.

34. *Mosely*, p. 50.

35. *Sazonov*, p. 87. Text of the Durnovo Memorandum in F. Golder, ed., *Documents of Russian History, 1914-1917* (Gloucester, Mass., 1964), p. 7ff.

36. J. F. Hutchinson, "The Octobrists and the Future of Imperial Russia as a Great Power," *The Slavonic and East European Review*, L, no. 119 (April 1972), pp. 223-225.

37. R. R. Rosen, *Forty Years of Diplomacy* (London, 1922), pp. 95, 102. Rosen had been Russian minister in Belgrade before Hartwig but did not share the latter's enthusiasms.

38. *Boghitschewitsch*, 3, no. 31.

39. *Ibid*, no. 411.

40. B. Pares, *My Russian Memoirs* (London, 1931), p. 269.

41. *Ö-UA*, 8, no. 10617.

42. *Sazonov*, pp. 248ff.

43. F. Stieve, ed., *Iswolski im Weltkriege, Der Diplomatische Schriftwechsel Iswolskis aus den Jahren 1914-1917* (Berlin, 1925), no. 102.

44. C. Jay Smith Jr., *The Russian Struggle For Power, 1914-1917* (New York, 1956), p. 81.

45. *KiP*, 1, nos. 18, 21.

46. *Ibid*, pp. 156-199.

47. *Sazonov*, pp. 307-310.

48. Duma: *Ochety*, IV Session, 3rd Sitting, Jan. 27/Feb. 9, 1915, cols. 1-11; V. S. Diakin, *Russkaia Burzhuaziia i Tsarizm v Gody Pervoi Mirovoi Voiny, 1914-1917* (Leningrad, 1967), pp. 53, 54.

49. *KiP*, 1, nos. 38, 41.

50. *Ibid*, nos. 43, 49.

51. *Ibid*, nos. 76, 77, 99.

52. Adamov: *Aufteilung*, nos. 80, 104.

53. *KiP*, 1, nos. 289, 297. The agreement was formally promulgated in an exchange of notes between Russian Foreign Minister Pokrovskii and the head of the visiting French mission Gaston Doumergue. The British were not consulted during the discussion.

54. *Ibid*, no. 100.

55. The course of Russian wartime diplomacy in South-Eastern Europe is more fully discussed in Chapters III and IV.

56. C. E. Vulliamy, ed., *The Letters of the Tsar to the Tsaritsa and the Tsaritsa to the Tsar* (Hattiesburg, Miss., 1970), pp. 190, 200, 201, 203.

57. G. Buchanan, *My Mission to Russia and Other Diplomatic Memories* (2 vols., London, 1923), 2, 34; M. Paléologue, *An Ambassador's Memoirs* (3 vols., London, 1924-25), 3, 110.

58. *Krasnyi Arkhiv*, 17 (1926), 24.

59. *MOEI*, 9, nos. 44, 45.

60. *Paléologue*, 3, 196; *Buchanan*, 2, 57.

61. *Sazonov*, p. 151.

NOTES TO CHAPTER II

1. P. N. Miliukov, *Istoriia Vtoroi Russkoi Revoliutsii* (3 vols., Sofia, 1921-23), 1, 45.

2. V. Nabokov, "Vremennoe Pravitel'stvo," *Arkhiv Russkoi Revoliutsii*, 1, (1922), 52.

3. N. N. Sukhanov [Himmer], *Zapiski o Revoliutsii* (7 vols., Berlin, 1922-23), Eng. trans. & abridg. Joel Carmichael, *The Russian Revolution 1917* (London, 1955), p. 53. English edition hereafter cited as *Sukhanov/Carmichael.*

4. V. Chernov, *The Great Russian Revolution* (New Haven, 1936), pp. 172-73.

5. V. I. Lenin, "Letters From Afar," *Collected Works* (4th ed.), 23 (1964), 297-98, 303.

6. P. N. Miliukov, *Vospominaniia* (2 vols., New York, 1955), 2, 27.

7. D. N. Shipov, *Vospominaniia i Dumy o Perezhitom* (Moscow, 1918), pp. 525-26.

8. Miliukov, *Vospominaniia*, 1, 169, 175.

9. *Ibid*, p. 174.

10. *Ibid*, pp. 177, 178, 180.

11. *Ibid*, pp. 225, 232, 233-34.

12. P. N. Miliukov, *God Bor'by* (St Petersburg, 1907), pp. 97-142.

13. Miliukov, *Vospominaniia*, 1, 327.

14. T. Riha, *A Russian European, Paul Miliukov in Russian Politics* (Notre Dame, 1969), p. 97.

15. Miliukov, *Vospominaniia*, 1, 381; V. N. Kokovtsov, *Out of My Past* (Stanford, 1935), p. 147.

16. *Shipov*, pp. 456-57.

17. In April 1906 Georges Clemenceau, shortly to become Premier for the first time, told Kokovtsov that Miliukov's appointment as Premier would be "a good move" to satisfy public opinion. *Kokovtsov*, p. 117.

18. Miliukov, *Vospominaniia*, 2, 34-37.

19. Duma: *Ochety*, III Session, 2nd Sitting, Dec. 12/25, 1908, cols. 2677-2704.

20. P. N. Miliukov, *Balkanskii Krizis i Politika A. P. Izvol'skogo* (St Petersburg, 1910), pp. 133, 157.

21. Miliukov, *Vospominaniia*, 2, 110.

22. Duma: *Ochety*, III Session, 5th Sitting, April 13/26, 1912, cols. 2183,

2188-95.

23. Miliukov, *Vospominaniia*, 2, 110; P. E. Shchegolev, ed., *Padenie Tsarskogo Rezhima* (7 vols., Moscow, 1924-27), 6, "Pokazaniia P. N. Miliukova," 365, 366.

24. Miliukov, *Vospominaniia*, 2, 126-27.

25. Duma: *Ochety*, IV Session, 1st Sitting, June 6/19, 1913, col. 1027, 1029.

26. "Pis'mo v redaktsiiu," *Russkie Vedomosti*, No. 356, 1900 cited *Riha*, p. 36.

27. Carnegie Endowment, *Report on the Causes*, p. 10 & fn. 1; Miliukov, *Vospominaniia*, 2, 137-38.

28. *Ibid*, p. 140.

29. *Ibid*, p. 174.

30. *Ibid*; *Shchegolev*, 6, 367; Nabokov, "Vremennoe Pravitel'stvo," p. 54.

31. Golder, *Documents*, pp. 35-36.

32. Duma: *Ochety*, IV Session, 3rd Sitting, Jan. 27/Feb. 9, 1915, col. 50.

33. P. N. Miliukov, "Territorial'nye Priobreteniia Rossii," *Chego Zhdet Rossiia Ot Voiny?* (Petrograd, 1915), p. 57.

34. Miliukov, Vospominaniia, 2, 243-51; *Krasnyi Arkhiv*, *58* (1933), 3-23; *Riha*, p. 251.

35. For example A. Iashchenko, *Russkie Interesy v Maloi Azii* (Moscow, 1916); N. M. Zakharov, *Nashe Stremlenie k Bosforu i Protivodeistvie emu Zapadoevropeiskikh Derzhav* (Petrograd, 1916); R. W. Seton-Watson, *The War and Democracy* (London, 1914).

36. P. N. Miliukov, "Konstantinopol' i Prolivy," *Vestnik Evropy* (Petrograd), January 1917, p. 355.

37. *Ibid*, February 1917, pp. 233, 259.

38. P. N. Miliukov, "Tseli Voiny: Sud'ba Germanii, Avstro-Vengrii, Turtsii," *Ezhegodnik Rech'* 1916, p. 58, 108.

39. Miliukov, *Istoriia*, 1, 51.

40. *Paléologue*, 3, 244.

41. *Rech'*, March 10/23, p. 2.

42. *Izvestiia*, March 11/24, p. 3; March 18/31, p. 2.

43. Nabokov, "Vremennoe Pravitel'stvo," p. 58.

44. *Browder/Kerensky*, 3, no. 1043.

45. *Sukhanov/Carmichael*, p. 191.

46. *Ibid*, pp. 206, 241-43.

47. *Ibid*, p. 203; Text of the Appeal in *Izvestiia*, March 15/28, p. 1 as trans. in *Browder/Kerensky*, 2, no. 942.

48. *Ibid*, 3, no. 1048. Chairman of the Section was the Menshevik Michael I. Skobolev.

49. *Rech'*, March 23/April 5, p. 2.

50. *Paléologue*, 3, 293-94.

51. Miliukov, *Istoriia*, 1, 45-46; *Vospominaniia*, 2, 299-302 where his subsequent disenchantment with L'vov is evident.

52. *Ibid*, pp. 327, 329; *Sukhanov/Carmichael*, p. 230; Nabokov, "Vremennoe Pravitel'stvo," p. 62; *Chernov*, p. 184.

53. *Chernov*, p. 176; Miliukov, *Istoriia*, 1, 87; *Vospominaniia*, 2, 329.

54. *Sukhanov/Carmichael*, pp. 247-49.

55. *Ibid*, p. 250.

56. Text of the Declaration in *Rech'*, March 28/April 10, p. 1 trans. *Browder/Kerensky*, 2, no. 909.

57. *Sukhanov/Carmichael*, p. 253.

58. Miliukov, *Istoriia*, 1, 87.

59. *Rech'*, March 28/April 10, p. 2; *Novoe Vremia*, March 28/April 10, p. 6 trans. *Browder/Kerensky*, 2, nos. 910, 911.

60. *Delo Naroda* & *Rabochaia Gazeta*, March 28/April 10, p. 1 trans. *Browder/Kerensky*, 2, nos. 912, 913; *Izvestiia*, March 31/APril 13, p. 1; *Den'* and *Pravda*, March 28/April 10, p. 1.

61. Nabokov, "Vremennoe Pravitel'stvo," p. 60.

62. Foreign Ministry circular to Russian representatives abroad, March 4/17 trans. *Browder/Kerensky*, 2, no. 905.

63. Buchanan, *My Mission to Russia*, 2, 108.

64. *Vestnik N[arodnogo] K[ommissariata] I[nostrannykh] D[el]*, no. 4-5 (1920), pp. 90, 97. Nabokov had been acting head of mission since the death the previous January of Ambassador Benckendorff. Sazonov was named to the embassy but domestic political events kept him in Russia.

65. A. Knox, *With the Russian Army, 1914-1917* (London, 1921), pp. 269, 270. "It is now impossible to form any opinion as to the future course of events in view of such contradictory opinions held by members of the same government." Minute on Buchanan's cable of Knox's interview, F.O. 371 (Public Record Office), "Russia," no. 58780, March 20.

66. *Daily Chronicle*, March 21, p. 1; *KiP*, 2, no. 315.

67. *Manchester Guardian*, April 11, p. 4; *Daily News*, April 11, p. 2; *Daily Mail*, April 11, p. 2.

68. War Cabinet Papers (Public Record Office), "Peace Conference and Other Conferences," (Cab. 29), "P" (Peace) Series, P-16, P-17. Principal members of the Committee, set up at the Imperial War Cabinet's direction, were the Chairman, Lord Curzon, then Lord President of the Council, Lord Robert Cecil, Under-Secretary for Foreign Affairs and Minister of Blockade, the South African Defense Minister General Smuts and Leopold Amery who acted as Secretary.

69. *Le Temps*, March 22, p. 1; March 27, p. 1; April 6, p. 1; April 11, p. 2;

K. E. Kirova, *Russkaia Revoliutsiia i Italiia, mart-oktiabr' 1917 goda* (Moscow, 1968), p. 60 & *passim.*

70. *KiP*, 1, 468-69; *Paléologue*, 3, 269; V. S. Vasiukov, *Vneshniaia Politika Vremennogo Pravitel'stva* (Moscow, 1966), p. 54.

71. *KiP*, 1, no. 320.

72. *Ibid*, no. 321. Izvol'skii remained in formal charge until the end of April.

73. *Ibid*, no. 322.

74. N. N. Sukhanov, *Zapiski*, 2, 305.

NOTES TO CHAPTER III

1. *KiP*, 2, no. 348.

2. *Ibid.*

3. *Ibid*, no. 349.

4. A. I. Denikin, *Ocherki Russkoi Smuty* (Paris, 1921), p. 182. Denikin served from March-May as Assistant Chief of Staff to the Supreme Commander, General Alexeev, from May to July as C. in C. Western Front and from July-August as C. in C. South-Western front.

5. *KiP*, 2, no. 350.

6. *Ibid*, no. 352.

7. *Denikin*, p. 183.

8. *KiP*, 2, no. 352.

9. *Ibid.*

10. Riha, *A Russian European*, p. 309.

11. *KiP*, 2, no. 324.

12. For a further discussion of Allied views of Russian foreign policy at this time see below, Chapter V.

13. *KiP*, 1, no. 30 and fn. 2, 237-38.

14. Duma: *Ochety*, IV Session, 3rd Sitting, Jan. 27/Feb. 9, 1915, col. 50.

15. *KiP*, 2, no. 264.

16. *Ibid*, no. 265.

17. *Ibid*, no. 268.

18. In August 1915 Sazonov heard that the French minister in Greece was publicly expressing his government's belief in an imminent Turkish peace. *Ibid*, no. 269.

19. Briand became Prime Minister on October 29, 1915, on the fall of the Viviani Cabinet. He simultaneously assumed the foreign affairs portfolio. He lasted as Premier until two days after the March Revolution.

20. *KiP*, 2, no. 271.

21. *Ibid*, no. 275 and fn. 1.

22. *Ibid*, no. 277.

23. Quoted in B. Lewis, *The Emergence of Modern Turkey* (London, 1968), p. 226.

24. Turkish language press summaries in *Osmanischer Lloyd* (Constantinople), March 20, p. 3.

25. *Ibid*, April 6, p. 3.

26. *HAA*, "Akten betreffend die Turkei," no. 150, April 6.

27. State Department Records relating to World War I and Its Termination, 1914–1929, (U.S. National Archives), no. 763. 72119/543, April 5.

28. *KiP*, 2, no. 278 and fn. 1, 322.

29. Text of the Entente reply to President Wilson in the *Times* (London), January 12, 1917, p. 7.

30. *Osmanischer Lloyd*, April 25, p. 3; April 27, p. 3.

31. *Ibid*, April 27, p. 3.

32. *HAA*, "Akten betreffend die Türkei," no. 159, part 2, April 17.

33. *Ibid*, no. 204, Bethmann-Hollweg (Berne) to Foreign Office, May 10.

34. *Ibid*, no. 150, Kühlmann to Foreign Office, April 17.

35. *KiP*, 2, no. 280.

36. A. Savinsky, *Recollections of a Russian Diplomat* (London, 1927), p. 315.

37. *Ibid*, p. 200.

38. *Ibid*, pp. 207, 209. The details which follow are intended only as an outline of the complex negotiations between Bulgaria and the several belligerents prior to the former's entry into the war. For a sound and detailed analysis, see James M. Potts, "The Loss of Bulgaria" in *Russian Diplomacy and Eastern Europe, 1914-1917* (Russian Institute Occasional Papers, Columbia University, New York, 1963), pp. 194-243.

39. *Diplomaticheski Dokumenti Po Uchastieto Na Bulgariia v Evropeiskata Voina, 1915-1918* (Sofia, 1921), no. 351. Hereafter cited as Bulgaria: *Documents*; *MOEI*, 5, no. 484.

40. *MOEI*, 6:1, no. 205.

41. Bulgaria: *Documents*, nos. 516, 533.

42. *Potts*, p. 217.

43. Bulgaria: *Documents*, no. 894.

44. *MOEI*, 8:2, nos. 831, 855.

45. M. Erzberger, *Erlebnisse im Weltkriege* (Berlin, 1920), p. 93.

46. Cited V. Kuhne, ed., *Les Bulgares Peints Par Eux-Mêmes* (Paris, 1917), pp. 150–51.

47. *Ibid*, p. 151; M. Mileff, *La Bulgarie et les Détroits* (Paris, 1927), pp. 138-139.

48. *Kuhne*, p. 152.

49. War Cabinet Papers, *Memoranda* (Cab. 24), "G. T. Series," no. 1502, July 24 I[ntelligence] B[ureau] D[epartment of] I[nformation], Report on Bulgaria.

50. With the exception of that portion around Salonika taken by Greece in 1913 and occupied since October 1915 by the Entente units underGeneral Maurice Sarrail.

51. V. P. Semennikov, ed., *Monarkhiia Pered Krusheniem: Bumagi Nikolaia II i*

Drugie Dokumenty (Moscow, 1927), "Iz Oblasti Russkoi Politiki na Balkanakh: Rossiia i Bolgariia," p. 55.

52. N. A. Nekliudov, "Predskazanie Russkoi Revoliutsii," *Arkhiv Russkoi Revoliutsii*, 1, 257; V. Radoslawoff, *Bulgarien und die Weltkrise* (Berlin, 1923), p. 262; *KiP*, 2, no. 344; A. V. Ignat'ev, *Russko-angliiskie Otnosheniia nakanune Oktiabr'skoi Revoliutsii* (Moscow, 1966), pp. 87-88.

53. *Bor'ba Klassov* (Moscow), no. 5 (1931), p. 85; *KiP*, 2, 483 & fn. 1.

54. The Royal Greek government in Athens was still officially neutral but the movement under Venizelos proclaimed its adherence to the Entente in December 1916. See below, Chapter VI.

55. *Bor'ba Klassov*, no. 5, pp. 85-86.

56. N. Rubinshtein, "Vneshniaia Politika Kerenshchiny," *Ocherki Po Istorii Oktiabr'skoi Revoliutsii*, ed. M. N. Pokrovskii (2 vols., Moscow, 1927), 2, 369.

57. War Cabinet Papers, *Memoranda* (Cab. 24), "G. T. Series," no. 2954, "Some Notes on Peace Arrangements," u.d.; *Ibid*, no. 703, May 12 for Lord Curzon's own pessimistic evaluation.

58. FO 371, "Russia," no. 62232, March 23.

59. *Rubinshtein*, p. 380; War Cabinet Papers, *Minutes* (Cab. 23), WC-124, April 23.

60. *Kuhne*, p. 164.

61. *Rabotnicheski Vestnik*, April 21, 1916, cited *ibid*, p. 165.

62. June 15, 1916, cited *ibid*.

63. March 16 & 17, cited *ibid*, pp. 168-69, 171. *L'Echo de Bulgarie* (Sofia), March 24, p. 2; *Berliner Tageblatt*, April 4, p. 1.

64. J. Ancel, *L'Unité de la Politique Bulgare, 1870-1919* (Paris, 1919), p. 48; *Dnevnitsi (Stenografski) Na XVII-to Obiknovenno Narodno Subranie* (2 vols., Sofia, 1930), pp. 1217, 1229, 1243. Hereafter referred to as *Dnevnitsi*.

65. FO 371, "Balkans," no. 131780, P[olitical] I[ntelligence] D[epartment] Report on the Bulgarian Political Scene, July 30, 1918.

66. Quoted in *Deutscher Geschichtskalender für 1917* (Leipzig), 6:2, 859.

67. Bulgarian language press summaries in *L'Echo de Bulgarie*, April 14, p. 1.

68. *Ibid*, April 24, p. 1.

69. *HAA*, "Bulgarien (Beziehungen zu Russland)," no. 10, April 10.

70. April 23, cited *Kuhne*, p. 173.

71. May 12, 1916, cited *ibid*, p. 233; War Cabinet Papers, *Memoranda* (Cab. 24), "G. T. Series," no. 907, IBDI Report on Bulgaria, June 1.

72. April 25, cited *Kuhne*, pp. 173-74.

73. *L'Echo de Bulgarie*, May 8, p. 2.

74. Bulgaria: *Documents*, nos. 1096, 1097; Wolfgang Steglich, *Die*

Friedenspolitik der Mittelmächte 1917/18 (Wiesbaden, 1964), pp. 62-63.

75. *HAA*, "Bulgarien: Bulgarische Staatsmänner," no. 21, March 24.

76. Bulgaria: *Documents*, no. 1105; *HAA*, "Akten betreffend die Turkei," no. 150, March 30.

77. Bulgaria: *Documents*, no. 1134; War Cabinet Papers, *Memoranda* (Cab. 24), "G. T. Series," no. 827, May 21, IBDI Report on Bulgaria where the possibility is envisaged of Germany's allowing a separate Bulgarian peace to induce Russia also to stop fighting.

78. *Rech'*, May 19/June 1, p. 2. English text in *Browder/Kerensky*, 2, no. 939.

79. Bulgaria: *Documents*, nos. 1077, 1096, 1104, 1184, 1189.

80. *Ibid*, no. 1116.

81. *Steglich*, pp. 32, 70-74; Fritz Fischer, *Griff nach der Weltmacht: Die Kriegszielpolitik des kaiserlichen Deutschland 1914/1918* (Düsseldorf, 1962), pp. 447-53.

82. *HAA*, "Der Weltkrieg," no. 20h, April 21, Oberndorff to AA.

83. C. Mühlmann, *Oberste Heeresleitung und Balkan im Weltkrieg 1914/1918* (Berlin, 1942), p. 201.

84. *HAA*, "Der Weltkrieg (Die Zukunft Rumäniens)," no. 14g, "Sitzungsprotokolle des Ausschusses fur den Reichshaushalt," 148 Sitzung. He also dismissed the intrigues of Russian agents in Switzerland sent to make contact with Bulgarian oppositional figures.

85. *Ibid*, "Der Weltkrieg," no. 20h, Kühlmann to AA, May 14.

86. "Nur verwilderte Russen," *Ibid*, Memorandum on the Dobruja Question, ud. The author may have been Beldiman, Rumanian minister in Berlin before the breach with Germany.

NOTES TO CHAPTER IV

1. *MOEI*, 6:1, nos. 351, 352.
2. Milada Paulová, *Jugoslavenski Odbor* (Zagreb, 1924), pp. 16-17.
3. *MOEI*, 7:1, no. 202.
4. *Ibid.*
5. *MOEI*, 7:2, no. 434.
6. *Paulová*, p. 54.
7. *MOEI*, 7:2, no. 423.
8. *MOEI*, 7:2, no. 571; *ZRW*, "Russland und Italien," no. 92.
9. Miliukov, *Vospominaniia*, 2, 244.
10. *The Times*, April 3, p. 7.
11. In his strongly pro-Pašić study *Srbija i Jugosloveni za vreme Rata, 1914-1918* (Belgrade, 1922) M. P. Djordjević discusses this Petrograd statement attributed to Pašić and asserts that the Prime Minister did not in fact speak in these terms. He ascribed the story, widely reproduced in the Italian press, to a plot concocted by the Petrograd correspondent of the Milan *Corriere della Sera*, designed to provoke a breach between the Premier and the Committee, pp. 82ff. Pašić did, however, make a similar statement three weeks earlier in London and it is not improbable that he repeated it.
12. *Paulová*, p. 290; Ante Mandić, *Fragmenti za Historiju Ujedinjenja* (Zagreb, 1956), pp. 43-44.
13. *Paulová*, pp. 297-99.
14. *Ibid*, p. 299.
15. *Ibid*, p. 377.
16. *Djordjević*, p. 33.
17. P-H. Michel, ed., *La Question de l'Adriatique: Recueil de Documents* (Paris, 1938), no. 117.
18. *Ibid*, no. 119.
19. *MOEI*, 6:1, no. 256; 6:2, no. 546; *Paléologue*, 1, 96, 236.
20. *Paléologue*, 1, 122.
21. Priklonskii, head of the Foreign Ministry's Statistical Division, drew up a report in the autumn of 1916 on Russian alternatives in dealing with the defeated Central Empires. He was a strong opponent of Yugoslav federative views but his recommendations went unread by Stürmer and Pokrovskii. Merrit Abrash, "War Aims Toward Austria-Hungary," *Russian Diplomacy and Eastern Europe, 1914-1917*, pp. 104-117; *Paulová*, p. 153.

22. *Krasnyi Arkhiv, 54-55* (1932), 44.

23. E. Benes, *Souvenirs de Guerre et de Révolution, 1914-1918* (2 vols., Paris, 1928), 1, 213-214.

24. I. Jovanović et al., eds., *Jugoslovenski Dobrovolachki Korpus u Rusiji, 1914-1918* (Belgrade, 1954), p. 135.

25. *Mandić*, pp. 45, 46.

26. *Ibid*, p. 49.

27. *Ibid*, pp. 53, 54.

28. Pares, *My Russian Memoirs*, p. 367.

29. *Mandić*, pp. 52-54.

30. *Pares*, p. 367.

31. *Paulová*, pp. 178-81.

32. Duma: *Ochety*, IV Session, 4th Sitting, March 11/24, 1916, col. 3256.

33. See pp. 25-26.

34. *Mandić*, p. 54. In his book *Prolivy* (Petrograd, 1917) Petriaev is less rigid than Miliukov, being willing to admit the desirability of a negotiated settlement to the question of Russian access to the Mediterranean. From July to October he was Assistant Minister of Foreign Affairs.

35. *Paulová*, p. 313. For Priklonskii see above, fn. 21.

36. *Michel*, no. 199.

37. *Rech'*, March 28/April 10, p. 7.

38. *Mandić*, pp. 237-38.

39. Copy of the Committee's appeal to Miliukov in this sense sent to the Foreign Office in London, FO 371, "Balkans," no. 87660, April 22.

40. *Rech'*, March 28/April 10, p. 7.

41. See p. 75.

42. *Paulová*, p. 377.

43. *Mandić*, p. 55.

44. Rubinshtein, "Vneshniaia Politika Kerenshchiny," p. 369.

45. *Paléologue*, 3, 269.

46. Quoted in *La Serbie* (Geneva), April 29, p. 1.

47. *Zhurnaly Zasedanii Vremennogo Pravitel'stva*, April 7/20, p. 4.

48. So reported by the British minister on Corfu, FO 371, "Balkans," no. 82313, April 11; *Mandić*, p. 56.

49. *Paulová*, p. 316.

50. *La Serbie*, April 29, p. 1.

51. *HAA*, "Russland," no. 82, part 2, Bethmann-Hollweg (Berne) to AA, April 3.

52. Jovan Tomić, ed., *Jugoslavija u Emigratsii: Pisma i Beleshke iz 1917* (Belgrade, 1921), pp. 98-101.

53. *Jovanović*, p. 166; M. Sarrail, *Mon Commandement en Orient, 1916-1918*

(Paris, 1920), p. 247. On April 27 *Birzhevie Vedomosti*, a conservative Petrograd daily, carried a report to the effect that "a vast majority of the volunteers considers the question of a Yugoslav republican federation superfluous since [Serbian] King Peter enjoys limitless respect and confidence." April 14/27, Evening ed. p. 2. This was certainly not the case among non-Serbian officers, according to Mandic who regularly visited the Corps. *Mandić*, p. 240.

54. *Ibid*, pp. 238-39.

55. H. Hanak, *Great Britain and Austria-Hungary During the First World War* (London, 1962), p. 63.

56. *Paulovd*, pp. 333, 336.

57. *Letters of the Tsaritsa*, p. 392.

58. *ZRW*, "Russland und Rumänien," nos. 44, 45.

59. *MOEI*, 7:2, no. 672.

60. *Ibid*, 8:1, nos. 78, 148, 203, 276; 8:2, no. 553.

61. The Entente Powers allowed the date of Rumania's entry to be set back one week. Rumania promised not to fortify territory to be acquired in the Banat opposite Belgrade. A complete analysis of Russo-Rumanian diplomacy from August 1914 to August 1916 may be found in the study by Alfred Rieber, "Russian Diplomacy and Rumania," in *Russian Diplomacy and Eastern Europe, 1914-1917*, pp. 235-275.

62. A. Pingaud, *L'Histoire Diplomatique de la France Pendant la Grande Guerre* (3 vols., Paris, 1937-40), 2, 194-95.

63. *Paléologue*, 3, 169, 190; B. Gourko, *Memories and Impressions of War and Revolution in Russia* (London, 1918), p. 246. Gurko replaced Alexeev as Chief of Staff and was present throughout the Conference.

64. Semennikov, "Konferentsiia Soiuznikov v Petrograde," pp. 67-68.

65. War Cabinet Papers, "Allied (War) Conferences," (Cab. 28), I. C. Series, IC-16, Report of the Inter-Allied Conference at Petrograd, February 1-20, 1917.

66. *Paleologue*, 3, 190.

67. Marie, Queen of Rumania, *Ordeal, The Story of My Life* (3 vols., New York, 1934), 2, 144; V. N. Vinogradov, *Rumyniia v gody Pervoi Mirovoi Voiny* (Moscow, 1969), p. 199.

68. FO 371, "Balkans," no. 67303, March 26.

69. Desbaterile Adunării Deputatilor, 1916-1917, p. 15, cited *Vinogradov*, p. 198.

70. *Pravda*, January 20/February 2, 1918, p. 5, no. 464, March 29/April 11, 1917. In Jan.-Feb. 1918 during a period of hostilities between the Bolshevik regime and the Rumanian government, *Pravda* published a series of telegrams from Tsarist and Provisional Government archives to

demonstrate Rumanian treachery and greed. The 1918 *Pravda* citations below are from this collection.

71. *Ibid*, no. 371, March 7/20; FO 371, "Balkans," no. 64872, March 26.

72. *Pravda*, Jan. 20/Feb. 2, 1918, p. 5, no. 371, March 7/20.

73. *Ibid*, no. 566, May 5/18.

74. *Vinogradov*, p. 213.

75. FO 371, "Balkans," no. 113861, June 6 & minute by IBDI.

76. Izvestiia Odesskogo Frontovogo i Oblastnogo Sovetov, May 22, cited *Vinogradov*, p. 214.

77. The National Liberal Majority in the Chamber of Deputies was 93, in the Senate 35.

78. Miliukov, *Vospominaniia*, 2, 121. P. D. Kiselev served in the eighteen-thirties as Nicholas I's military administrator in the Danubian Principalities.

79. *Ezhegodnik Rech'*, 1914, pp. 10, 11; 1916, pp. 6, 10.

80. *Rech'*, March 23/April 5, p. 2.

81. *KiP*, 2, no. 350.

82. *Ibid*, 1, 495-96.

83. *Paléologue*, 3, 340.

84. *Vinogradov*, pp. 200, 211.

85. N. Avdeev et al., eds., *Revoliutsiia 1917 goda (Khronika Sobytii)* (6 vols., Moscow, 1923-30), 2, April 18/May 1, p. 47; *Pravda*, Jan. 18/31, 1918, p. 8, no. 534, April 22/May 5.

86. *Avdeev*, 2, 47; *Pravda*, Jan. 18/31, 1918, p. 8, no. 1611, April 12/25 & no. 512, April 13/26; *Izvestiia*, April 13/26, p. 2 & May 7/20, p. 4.

87. So described by the State Prosecutor Andrei Vyshinsky during Rakovsky's trial, *Report of the Court Proceedings in the Case of the Anti-Soviet "Bloc of Rights and Trotskyites"* (Moscow, 1938), p. 248.

88. Horst Lademacher, ed., *Die Zimmerwalder Bewegung: Protokolle und Korrespondenz* (2 vols., The Hague, 1967), 2, 86.

89. *Ibid*, 1, 104.

90. *Izvestiia*, May 7/20, p. 4.

91. *State Department Records relating to World War I and Its Termination, 1914-1929*, no. 763.72/4398, Vopicka (Jassy) to Lansing, May 4.

92. The meeting's official title in full was the Congress of Soviets of the Rumanian Front, the Black Sea Fleet and the Odessa Region.

93. I. G. Dykov, "Rumcherod i Bor'ba za Ustanovlenie Sovetskoi Vlasti na Rumynskom Fronte," *Istoricheskie Zapiski*, 57 (1956), 4; Petriaev, *Prolivy*, pp. 19, 20.

94. *Vinogradov*, p. 222; *Pravda*, Jan. 20/Feb. 2, 1918, p. 5, nos. 394, 787 & 8678 between July and September.

95. *Bor'ba Klassov*, no. 5 (1931), 86; *Izvestiia*, May 5/18, p. 4; *Russkie*

Vedomosti, May 2/15, p. 5.

96. Joseph Noulens, *Mon Ambassade en Russie Soviétique 1917-1918* (2 vols., Paris, 1931), 1, 96, 97.

97. As suggested in the title at least of a subsequent study of just this question: A. Bazarevsky, "De l'Entrée en Guerre de la Roumanie et les Inconvenients qui en resultèrent pour la Russia," *Les Alliés Contre la Russie* (Paris, 1927), p. 208.

98. *MOEI*, 6:1, no. 266; C. U. Clark, *Bessarabia, Russia and Roumania on the Black Sea* (New York, 1927), p. 127.

NOTES TO CHAPTER V

1. Adamov: *Aufteilung*, no. 285.

2. *Ibid*, no. 287. On April 12 Count Czernin expressed his government's readiness to conclude peace with Russia. The semi-official *Nord-deutsche Allgemeine Zeitung* endorsed the suggestion, underlining that there was nothing incompatible between the Austro-German program and the April 9 Declaration. *KiP*, 1, 482, fn. 1.

3. *Ibid*, 1, no. 166.

4. Adamov: *Aufteilung*, nos. 199, 207.

5. V. S. Vasiukov, *Vneshniaia Politika Vremennogo Pravitel'stva* (Moscow, 1966), pp. 109-110; *Aufteilung*, no. 290.

6. Sonnino Papers, "Arrivo," G-997, April 18.

7. FO 371, "Italy," nos. 35530, 37858, February 15 & 19.

8. War Cabinet Papers, "Allied (War) Conferences" (Cab. 28), IC-19; Sonnino Papers (Personal Files), "Conferenze degli Alleati 1917, St Jean de Maurienne."

9. Sonnino Papers, "Arrivo," G-1680, April 25.

10. *Ibid*, "Conferenze" where the Emperor's letters are discussed. Also *KiP*, 1, no. 325.

11. *Ibid.*

12. Adamov: *Aufteilung*.

13. Alexandre Ribot, *Lettres à un Ami* (Paris, 1924), p. 278.

14. *Le Temps*, April 22, p. 1.

15. Emphasis added. Italian press summaries in Mario Toscano, *Gli Accordi di San Giovanni di Moriana* (Milan, 1936), p. 290, fn. 123.

16. *Ibid*, pp. 292-93, fns. 124, 125.

17. FO 371, "Italy," no. 87601, April 29; Sonnino Papers (Personal Files), "Carteggio Sir James Rennell Rodd," April 29.

18. FO 371, "Italy," no. 87837, minute by the Permanent Under Secretary, Lord Hardinge of Penshurst, on a cable from Rodd.

19. For the Balfour mission generally and its work, see W. B. Fowler, *British-American Relations 1917-1918: The Role of Sir William Wiseman* (Princeton, 1969), pp. 25-30.

20. Adamov: *Aufteilung*, no. 294.

21. *Ibid*, no. 298.

22. V. S. Mamatey, *The United States and East-Central Europe, 1914-1918*

(Princeton, 1957), pp. 85ff.

23. Charles Seymour, ed., *The Intimate Papers of Colonel House* (4 vols., New York, 1926-28), 2, 130.

24. *Ibid*, p. 170 & fn.

25. House, Prime Minister Asquith, Grey, Lloyd George, A. J. Balfour, and the Lord Chief Justice Lord Reading.

26. Seymour, *Intimate Papers*, 2, 181.

27. *Ibid*, pp. 200-02; Charles Seymour, *American Diplomacy During The World War* (Baltimore, 1934), pp. 152-53.

28. Seymour, *Intimate Papers*, 2, 415. In 1930 House denied he had ever contemplated an increase of Russian territory in Europe or Asia, though he had been in favor of Russia's being allowed "at all times to have an outlet to the seas through the Dardanelles." While evidence eists to suggest a contrary view (fn. 24 above), Seymour felt that House did not press his opinions about Turkey and Russia for fear of breaking his understanding with Grey and driving Russia from the alliance. See H. N. Howard, *The Partition of Turkey, A Diplomatic History, 1913-1923* (Norman, 1931), pp. 136, 424, fn. 94.

29. Woodrow Wilson, *The State* (Boston, 1889), pp. 337-38.

30. Seymour, *Intimate Papers*, 3, 38.

31. *Fowler*, pp. 27, 28.

32. Seymour, *Intimate Papers*, 3, 42-44.

33. *Ibid*, pp. 48-49.

34. A. J. Mayer, *Wilson vs Lenin: Political Origins of the New Diplomacy, 1917-1918* (Cleveland, 1964), p. 330.

35. Seymour, *Intimate Papers*, 3, 51.

36. *Mayer*, pp. 330-31.

37. *Fowler*, p. 30.

38. Blanche Dugdale, *Arthur James Balfour* (2 vols., London, 1936), 2, 201.

39. Allan Nevins, *Henry White, Thirty Years of American Diplomacy* (New York, 1930), p. 339.

40. FO 371, "Italy," no. 101132, May 19; Sonnino Papers (Personal Files) "Carteggio Sir James Rennell Rodd," May 20; War Cabinet Papers, Cab. 28, IC-21.

41. *Ibid*, IC-22 where Lloyd George insists that Russia not be told "anything now."

42. Pingaud, *Histoire Diplomatique*, 3, 245.

43. R. W. Seton-Watson, *Masaryk in England* (Cambridge, 1943), p. 76.

44. *Ibid*, p. 86.

45. *The New Europe*, October 19, 1916, p. 1.

46. *Seton-Watson*, p. 87; Hanak, *Great Britain and Austria-Hungary*, p. 188.

47. *The New Europe*, April 52, pp. 15, 19.

48. *Ibid*, May 10, p. 116. Leeper worked in the Intelligence Bureau of the Department of Information and there helped draw up the Bureau's periodic reports on Russia and the Balkan countries.

49. *The Nation*, April 28, p. 86; *The Saturday Review*, April 21, p. 357; *Seton Watson*, pp. 83-90 *passim*.

50. *Mayer*, p. 164; H. N. Brailsford, *Turkey and the Roads of the East* (London, 1916), pp. 9-11; *The UDC*, Jan. 1917, C. R. Buxton, "The Settlement in the East of Europe"; March 1917, F. S. Cocks, "The Proposed Break-up of Austria and Turkey"; April 1917, E. D. Morel, "Russia, The Real and the Misrepresented"; and 'A Russian,' "The Truth About the Revolution in Russia" where Miliukov is discounted.

51. *The New Republic* (New York), April 21, p. 245.

52. *The Manchester Guardian*, May 5, p. 5.

53. J.F.N. Bradley, *La Légion Tchécoslovaque en Russie, 1914-1920* (Paris, 1965), p. 51; E. Benes, *Souvenirs de Guerre et de Révolution, 1914-1918* (2 vols., Paris, 1928), 1, 329.

54. Edward M. House Papers, "William G. Buckler File," April 27 & 30.

55. *Ibid*, July 1.

56. *Mayer*, p. 336.

57. L. E. Gelfand, *The Inquiry: American Preparations for Peace, 1917-1919* (New Haven, 1963), pp. 14, 18; R. L. Martin, *Peace Without Victory: Woodrow Wilson and the British Liberals* (New Haven, 1958), p. 139.

58. House Papers, Buckler File, April 27, May 8 & 11.

59. *Paléologue*, 3, 297.

60. *Mayer*, pp. 86, 88; *Krasnyj Arkhiv, 20* (1927), 6; Merle Fainsod, *International Socialism and the World War* (Cambridge, 1935), pp. 128-29.

61. *Paléologue*, 3, 297-99; M. Philips Price, *My Reminiscences of the Russian Revolution* (London, 1921), p. 20.

62. *Pravda*, October 21/November 3, 1912, cited Lenin, *Collected Works, 18* (1963), 368; *Pravda*, April 7/20, 1917, for his April Theses, text trans. *Browder/Kerensky*, 3, no. 1039.

63. *Den'*, April 7/20, p. 1; April 16/29, p. 2; April 23/May 6, p. 2; April 30/May 13, p. 2.

64. *Sukhanov/Carmichael*, p. 263; G. Tschudnowsky, "Schriften russischer Sozialisten über den Krieg," *Archiv für die Geschichte des Sozializmus und der Arbeiterbewegung* (Leipzig), 7 (1916), 65. As a Bolshevik prisoner Admiral Kolchak reported Plekhanov as having said in April 1917 that "to renounce the Dardanelles is the same as living with our throat squeezed in foreign hands. I consider that without [the Straits] Russia will never be able to live as she should want to." K. A. Popov, ed., *Dopros Kolchaka* (Leningrad,

1925), p. 60.

65. Irakli Tsereteli, "Reminiscences of the Russian Revolution: The April Crisis," *The Russian Review* (Hanover, N.H.), 14 (1955), 100-01.

66. *Paléologue*, 3, 310, 335-36.

67. R.H.B. Lockhart, *Memoirs of a British Agent* (London, 1933), p. 185.

68. *Paléologue*, 3, 313.

69. *Rech'*, April 20/May 3, p. 4 trans. *Browder/Kerensky*, 2, no. 964.

70. *Sukhanov/Garmichael*, p. 315.

71. *Tsereteli*, p. 104.

72. R. D. Warth, *The Allies and the Russian Revolution: From the Fall of the Monarchy to the Peace of Brest-Litovsk* (Durham, 1954), p. 59.

73. *Ibid*, p. 60; *Tsereteli*, 198, 199; *VVP*, April 22/May 5, p. 1; *Izvestiia*, April 22/May 5, p. 3.

74. *VVP*, April 26/May 9, p. 1; *Delo Naroda*, April 26/May 9, p. 3 both trans. *Browder/Kerensky*, 3, nos. 1075, 1076.

75. *Izvestiia*, April 29/May 12, p. 2.

76. *Sukhanov/Carmichael*, p. 334.

77. Chernov, *The Great Russian Revolution,* p. 201; Miliukov, *Vospominaniia,* 2, 370-371; *Sukhanov/Carmichael,* p. 338; V. B. Stankevich, *Vospominaniia, 1914-1919 gg* (Berlin, 1920), pp. 128-32; *Rech',* May 5/18, p. 3.

78. Nekrasov, L'vov and Tereshchenko generally sided with Kerenskii and three others to form the somewhat facetiously named "Left Seven" in the Cabinet.

79. *Rech'*, May 11/24, p. 2.

80. *Sukhanov/Carmichael*, p. 341.

NOTES TO CHAPTER VI

1. *Sukhanov/Carmichael*, p. 236

2. *Izvestiia*, May 7/20, p. 4. He evidently came to regret his eagerness to comment on this delicate subject. On May 10/23 *Izvestiia* reprinted without comment on a letter from Rakovsky where he emphasized his wish not to break his "Socialist neutrality" on a domestic Russian issue, p. 8.

3. *VVP*, May 6/19, p. 1 trans. *Browder/Kerensky*, 3, no. 1095.

4. *Russkie Vedomosti*, May 6/19, p. 3; *Birzhevie Vedomosti*, May 6/19, p. 1.

5. *Rech'*, May 9/22, p. 2.

6. May 6/19, pp. 1-2 trans. *Browder/Kerensky*, 3, no. 1101.

7. *Pravda*, May 6/19, p. 1.

8. *Rech'*, May 7/20, p. 4 trans. *Browder/Kerensky*, 2, no. 968.

9. *Sukhanov/Carmichael*, p. 337.

10. A. F. Kerensky, *The Catastrophe* (New York, 1927), p. 139.

11. Miliukov requested Izvol'skii's resignation on May 10 when the news of Paléologue's recall "stirred up strong pressure here for changes in our representation in France" to cite from the minister's telegram to Paris with the bad news. *Vasiukov*, pp. 131-32. Paleologue left Petrograd on May 16, being seen off at the Finland Station by S. D. Sazonov whose appointment to the London embassy lapsed with Miliukov's fall. *Paléologue*, 3, 342.

12. *Chernov*, p. 184.

13. Ignat'ev, *Russko-angliiskie Otnosheniia*, p. 146; *Buchanan*, 2, 117-18.

14. Sukhanov, *Zapiski*, 4, 73; V. Nabokov, "Vremennoe Pravitel'stvo," p. 46.

15. *Nabokov*, p. 63

16. Miliukov, *Istoriia*, 1, 167.

17. *Buchanan*, 2, 109.

18. *VVP*, May 9/22, p. 3 trans. *Browder/Kerensky*, 2, no. 969.

19. *Ibid.*

20. English text of the Appeal in Golder, *Documents*, pp. 340-43.

21. O. Gankin and H. Fisher, *The Bolsheviks and the World War: The Origin of the Third International* (Stanford, 1940), p. 956.

22. *Fainsod*, pp. 127ff.

23. 93 H.C. *Debates*, 5s, cols. 1625-36, 1666-67.

24. *Ibid*, cols. 1646-50.

25. *Ibid*, cols. 1652-53, 1704.

26. *Ibid*, cols. 1668-70.

27. *Ibid*, col. 1707.

28. *Ibid*, cols. 1714-15, 1731-35.

29. Edith Durham, a Radical, at first pro-Serbian, finally selected the Albanians as Europe's most deserving and oppressed small nationality. She was strongly anti-Russian and against individual Balkan nationhoods. F. W. Hirst, editor of the *Economist* until 1915, in 1916 he took over editorship of the weekly *Common Sense*, a journal favoring the preservation in some form of the Dual Monarchy.

30. House Papers, Buckler File, May 22, May 24.

31. *Ibid.* The Foreign Office followed up the suggestion of an American approach to Sofia but the response was discouraging. In the State Department's opinion the German hold on Bulgaria was too strong to be broken by any American initiative. FO 371, "Balkans," no. 115793, June 6; no. 117341, June 12.

32. Quoted in *Russkie Vedomosti*, May 21/June 3, p. 2.

33. *Il Messaggero*, April 26, p. 1.

34. E. & C. Woodhouse, *Italy and the Yugoslavs* (Boston, 1920), p. 140.

35. F. Rubbiani, *Il Pensiero Politico di Leonida Bissolati* (Florence, 1921), p. 226.

36. Sonnino Papers, "Arrivo," G-1136, May 2; G-1330, May 26; G-1437, June 1 where Imperiali (using the English words) complains of "a poisonous ass" on the *New Europe*'s editorial board, G-1479, June 5; G-1676, June 20; G-1680, June 20; "Partenza," G-700, May 11; G-717, May 15.

37. FO 371, "Turkey," nos. 87589, 95567, 102248, 104307 during April-May. On 104307, reporting Sonnino's assurances to Tereshchenko that "no spirit of conquest or domination inspired Italy's entry [into the war]," Hardinge minuted his surprise at "this rather bold statement from Rome."

38. Press summaries in Kirova, *Russkaia Revoliutsiia i Italiia*, p. 157.

39. FO 371, "Russia," no. 103988, May 22.

40. Great Britain, Historical Section of the Foreign Office, *Albania* (London, 1920), pp. 50-52.

41. Österreich-Ungarn, K.u.K. Ministerium des Äussern, *Zur Vorgeschichte des Krieges mit Italien* (Vienna, 1915), pp. 9-17, 21.

42. Seymour Cocks, ed., *The Secret Treaties and Understandings: Text of the Available Documents* (London, 1918), pp. 37-38.

43. G. F. Abbott, *Greece and the Allies, 1914-1922* (London, 1922), p. 4.

44. *Ibid*, pp. 50-55.

45. Adamov, *Griechenland*, nos. 19, 20.

46. *Ibid*, nos. 182, 186.

47. S. Cosmin, *L'Entente et la Grèce Pendant la Grande Guerre* (2 vols., Paris,

1926), 2, 136ff. Venizelos took care publicly to affirm his loyalty to the King, although he told the French minister this was a gesture to satisfy Britain and Russia. He was himself convinced that Constantine had sold himself "definitely and irrevocably"to Germany. *Ibid*, p. 288.

48. Adamov, *Griechenland*, nos. 298, 306, 307.

49. *Ibid*, nos. 216, 240, 273, 258, 312; *Letters of the Tsar to the Tsaritsa*, p. 229, *Letters of the Tsaritsa to the Tsar*, pp. 372, 393, 411, 412. The Empress began by concentrating on the King's woes ("poor, dear Tino") rather than on those of Greece itself ("it's a rotten country"). But she swung round eventually ("How dare we mix into a country's private politics . . . . It's an awful intrigue of Freemasons . . . .").

50. Adamov, *Griechenland*, no. 262.

51. Semennikov, "Konferentsiia Soiuznikov," p. 71.

52: Adamov, *Griechenland*, no. 340.

53. *Ibid*, no. 344.

54. *Ibid*.

55. *Journal Officiel*, Séances: Chambre, March 21, 1917, p. 784.

56. Adamov, *Griechenland*, no. 345.

57. *Le Temps*, March 31, p. 1.

58. Adamov, *Griechenland*, nos. 350, 351.

59. Toscano, *Gli Accordi*, p. 274; Sonnino Papers, "Conferenze degli Alleati 1917, St Jean."

60. *Pingaud*, 2, 328.

61. Adamov, *Griechenland*, no. 356; War Cabinet Papers, Cab. 28, IC-22.

62. So reported by the hostile Italian military attaché in Athens who wrote a book to record his indignation, Mario Caracciolo, *L'Intervento della Grecia nella Guerra Mondiale e l'Opera della Diplomazia Alleata* (Rome, 1925), p. 182.

63. Adamov, *Griechenland*, no. 353.

64. *Ezhegodnik Rech'*, 1916, p. 19ff.

65. *The Morning Post* (London), April 12, cited in the *New Europe*, April 19, p. 16.

66. *Ezhegodnik Rech'*, 1916, pp. 15-16.

67. Vasiukov, *Vneshniaia Politika*, pp. 116-17.

68. *Russkaia Volia*, March 9/22, p. 4.

69. Cited *ibid*, p. 2.

70. In sponsoring an independent Greek kingdom each of the three Protecting Powers had agreed not to put forward as candidates for the Greek crown members of their own royal houses. An offer to Queen Victoria's son, Prince Alfred, had been rejected in 1863.

71. A. F. Frangulis, *La Grèce et la Crise Mondiale* (2 vols., Paris, 1926), 1, 518.

72. Adamov, *Griechenland*, no. 357.

73. *Ibid*, no. 363.

74. *Pingaud*, 2, 329.

75. War Cabinet Papers, Cab. 28, IC-22; *Pingaud*, 2, 330.

76. Adamov, *Griechenland*, no. 366.

77. *Ibid*, no. 368; Sarrail, *Mon Commandement*, p. 262.

78. Adamov, *Griechenland*, no. 367.

79. *Ibid*, no. 369; J. Swire, *Albania, The Rise of a Kingdom* (London, 1929), p. 272; D. Lloyd George, *War Memoirs* (6 vols., London, 1933-36), 4, 2031.

80. *Pingaud*, 2, 332, 333.

81. *Frangulis*, 1, 527-28; War Cabinet Papers, *Minutes* (Cab. 23), WC-150, May 30, Appendix 1; Adamov, *Griechenland*, nos. 373, 377.

82. *Ibid*, nos. 382, 390, 394, 420; *Frangulis*, 1, 549. There were about 100 Russian troops involved in the deposition operation. They were sent afterwards to the Macedonian front. Sonnino Papers, "Arrivo," G-1807, July 2.

NOTES TO CHAPTER VII

1. *Frangulis*, 1, 558.
2. Allied replies trans. *Browder/Kerensky*, 2, nos. 972, 973, 974.
3. *Kirova*, p. 160.
4. Sonnino Papers, "Arrivo," G-1529, June 7; G-1549, June 10; "Partenza," G-923, June 10.
5. War Cabinet Papers, Cab. 23, WC-154, June 5.
6. *Kirova*, p. 160.
7. Three members of the Boselli Cabinet, including Bissolati, resigned from the Government on the grounds they had not been told of the forthcoming "protectorate." The crisis was eventually solved and the ministers restored without any change in the June 3rd proclamation.
8. *VVP*, May 31/June 13, p. 1.
9. *Rech'*, June 7/20, p. 3.
10. Adamov, *Griechenland*, no. 409.
11. *Ibid*, no. 399; *Kirova*, p. 164.
12. Adamov, *Griechenland*, nos. 400, 413, 416.
13. *Izvestiia*, June 4/17, p. 1.
14. Mary Hamilton, *Arthur Henderson* (London, 1938), p. 124; *Lloyd George*, 4, 1892-94; *Warth*, p. 71.
15. *Izvestiia*, May 30/June 12, p. 3 trans. *Browder/Kerensky*, 2, no. 981.
16. *Hamilton*, pp. 125, 128, 133.
17. *Ibid*, p. 129.
18. *Lloyd George*, 4, 1900.
19. They were, in addition to Labriola, I. Cappa, a member of the Republican Party and editor of the Milan *Secolo*, O. Raimondo, expelled from the Socialist Party when he joined the Masons, and D. Lerda.
20. She remained active in the Party through the October Revolution and became involved in Comintern activities. She left Russia in 1922 and was expelled from the Party two years later. For her work in the Socialist movement during the war, see *Fainsod*, pp. 153-56 & *passim*.
21. *Pravda*, May 18/31, p. 1.
22. Sonnino Papers, "Arrivo," G-1670, June 20.
23. *Rech'*, May 31/June 13, p. 3.
24. So he wrote in *Il Messaggero*, July 21, p. 1.
25. *La Stampa*, June 8, cited *Kirova*, p. 223.

26. Atti Parlamentari, Camera dei Deputati, *Discussioni*, June 20, pp. 13546-47.

27. *Pravda*, June 3/16, p. 2; Avdeev, *Khronika Sobytii*, 2, June 5/18, p. 252.

28. A. E. Ioffe, *Russko-frantsuzskie Otnosheniia v 1917 godu* (Moscow, 1956), p. 206.

29. *Ibid.*

30. *VVP*, June 23/July 6, p. 1.

31. *KiP*, 1, nos. 159, 160, 161 & fn. 2.

32. Sonnino Papers, "Arrivo," G-1237, May 14.

33. *Ibid*, G-1329, May 19.

34. *Den'*, May 14/27, p. 1.

35. *Pravda*, May 18/31, p. 1.

36. Sonnino Papers, "Arrivo," G-1383, May 28; G-1431, May 30.

37. War Cabinet Papers, Cab. 24, GT-284, May 24, "IBDI Report on Rumania."

38. Conservative opposition forced the eventual compromise to consist of the expropriation of a total of two million hectares (exclusive of Crown lands) and no loss of sub-soil (oil) rights.

79. *Russkaia Volia*, July 7/20, p. 3.

40. Sonnino Papers, "Arrivo," G-1724, June 19; *Pravda*, Jan. 20/Feb. 2, 1918, p. 5, no. 579, May 12/25.

41. Sonnino Papers, "Arrivo," G-1764, June 19 reporting information from the Russian minister in Jassy. .

42. *Russkaia Volia*, July 7/20, p. 3.

43. Sonnino Papers, "Arrivo," G-1635, June 28; *Pravda*, Jan. 20/Feb. 2, 1918, p. 6, no. 693, July 5/18.

44. *La Serbie*, May 27, p. 4.

45. *Ibid*, July 8, p. 4; *Russkaia Volia*, April 13/26, p. 2; *Birzhevie Vedomosti*, May 17/30, p. 1.

46. The antecedents of the Salonika trial loom large in the immediate pre-war history of Serbia. In 1903 a young army officer, Dragutin Dmitrievič-Apis, led the coup which expelled the Austrophile Obrenovič dynasty and replaced it with the Karadjordjevič King Peter. Thereafter Apis remained a potent factor in Serbian political life. In 1911 the society Union or Death, also known as the Black Hand, was formed. Apis soon became its President. The society demanded a hard line against Hapsburg expansion and Bulgarian irredentism in Macedonia; during the Balkan Wars it resisted Pašič's efforts to place that province under civilian rule. In 1913 Apis became head of the Intelligence Section of the General Staff, from which post he helped the Sarajevo conspirators in their murder of the Hapsburg heir. Once the war started Apis' star began to wane. In 1915 he

was transferred to a minor field command; on December 16, 1916, he and several others were arrested by Serbian authorities and charged with two capital offenses. The first was a conspiracy to betray the Government; the second a charge of attempted murder of the Prince Regent. Both were false. Pašić's full motives cannot be entirely known but it is likely they were prompted by a wish to re-assert control over the officer corps and eliminate dangerous opposition in the event of a negotiated Entente peace with the Dual Monarchy. See Luigi Albertini, *The Origins of the War of 1914* (3 vols., London, 1952-57), 2, 25-30 and R. W. Seton-Watson's review of M. Boghitschewitsch's "Le Procès de Salonique, 1917" in *The Slavonic (and East European) Review* (London), March 1928, pp. 703-06. A detailed Yugoslav study is in *Živanović* below.

47. M. Ž. Živanović, *Solunski Protses 1917* (Belgrade, 1955), pp. 535-37; Sonnino Papers, "Arrivo," G-1751, June 27.

48. *Živanović*, pp. 540-41.

49. Jovanović, *Dobrovolachki Korpus*, p. 179.

50. FO 371, "Balkans," no. 101349, May 18.

51. Sonnino Papers, "Arrivo," G-1245, May 14; *Živanović*, p. 541.

52. N. Gubskii, *Revoliutsiia i Vneshniaia Politika Rossii* (Petrograd, 1917), p. 20.

53. *Izvestiia*, June 22/July 5, p. 7; *Pravda*, June 23/July 6, p. 2; *Živanović*, p. 542; Mandić, *Fragmenti*, p. 245.

54. *Ibid*, p. 243; Sonnino Papers, "Arrivo," G-1685, June 19.

55. Vasiukov, *Vneshniaia Politika*, p. 313.

56. The British War Cabinet considered how it might boost Serbianmorale, "very much depressed about Sarrail." Ministers decided they had no objection to the Serbs acting in a way Sarrail did not like "or [which] might even contribute to bringing about his downfall." War Cabinet Papers, Cab. 23, WC-228, Sept. 5; Cab. 24, GT-1913 ud. for Cecil on Sarrail and the Pašić regime.

57. *Mandić*, p. 244; *Kirova*, p. 169; C. Jelavich, "Nikola P. Pašić: Greater Serbia or Jugoslavia?" *Journal of Central European Affairs* (Boulder), *11* (July 1951), pp. 138-39 for a brief account of the Corfu discussions.

58. *KiP*, 1, no. 208.

59. Kerensky, *The Catastrophe*, p. 195; Golovin, *The Russian Army*, pp. 267-82.

60. *Sukhanov/Carmichael*, pp. 432, 457.

61. *Russkoe Slovo* (Moscow), July 12/25, p. 3 trans. *Browder/Kerensky*, 3, no. 1187.

62. *Kerensky*, pp. 249-57; *Sukhanov/Carmichael*, pp. 486-92.

63. Ioffe, *Russko-frantsuzskie otnosheniia*, p. 207; *Vasiukov*, pp. 250-52.

64. War Cabinet Papers, Cab. 24, GT-1280, July 3.

65. So Ribot himself admitted, *Lettres*, p. 337.

66. War Cabinet Papers, Cab. 24, GT-831, ud.

67. His conclusions along these lines were presented in an undated draft "Some Notes on Peace Arrangements: The Balkans." War Cabinet Papers, Cab. 24, GT-2954; *PRFRUS*, 1917, "The World War," pp. 119-20.

68. *Kirova*, p. 171.

69. FO 371, "Balkans," no. 147411, July 26.

70. *Corriere della Sera*, July 24, p. 1.

71. C. Sforza, *Contemporary Italy, Its Intellectual and Moral Origins* (London, 1946), p. 173.

72. Sonnino Papers, "Arrivo," G-2046, July 24.

73. *Ibid*, G-1895, July 8; G-1912, July 11; G-1937, July 13; State Department Records, no. 763.72/5971 & 6012, July 26; A. Ribot, ed., *Journal de Alexandre Ribot et Correspondances Inedites, 1914-1922* (Paris, 1936), p. 166; Lady A. Gordon-Lennox, ed., *The Diary of Lord Bertie of Thame, 1914-1918* (2 vols., London, 1924), 2, 158; War Cabinet Papers, Cab. 28, IC-24.

74. Sonnino Papers, "Arrivo," G-2028, July 16; G-2048, July 20.

75. *Ibid*, G-1973, July 16; State Department Records, no. 763.72/5896; Sonnino Papers (Personal Files), "Carteggio Sir James Rennell Rodd," July 19; *PRFRUS* 1917, "The World War," pp. 144-45. The expression is Sharp's.

76. J. J. Pershing, *My Experiences in the World War* (2 vols., New York, 1931), 1, 117.

77. Sonnino Papers, "Conferenze degli Alleati 1917," Paris, July 25; p. 1.

78. *Ibid*, pp. 1-4, 15-18, 24; War Cabinet Papers, Cab. 23, WC-191a, July 20; Cab. 28, IC-24, 25a, July 25. There were approximately 630,000 Entente troops on the Macedonian front. Some 17,000 of these were Russian.

79. Ribot, *Journal*, p. 168, fn. 1.

80. *Lloyd George*, 5, 2551.

81. *Ioffe*, p. 207, fn. 3; *The Times*, July 26, p. 6.

82. Adamov, *Griechenland*, no. 438.

83. *KiP*, 1, no. 211.

84. K. Nabokoff, *Ordeal of a Diplomat* (London, 1921), pp. 127-30; Sonnino Papers, "Conferenze," London; War Cabinet Papers, Cab. 28, IC-25, August 7.

85. FO 371, "Turkey," no. 153074, July 31; Sonnino Papers, "Conferenze," London. The formula ran as follows: "If at any time the Russian Government formally signify their intention no longer to insist upon the territorial demands contained in [the 1915 and 1916 Asia Minor agreements], then this present agreement [St Jean de Maurienne] . . . shall be deemed to have lapsed except so far as the provisions of the said agreement designate

the spheres of interest and national aspirations of the parties thereto in the territories to which they refer; provided that if the Russian Government do not signify such intention before negotiations for peace with Turkey either separately or as part of a general peace are begun, then this agreement shall be binding upon the parties as though the Russian Government had consented to it." Original draft in English.

86. Ribot, *Journal*, pp. 170, 171 & fn. 1, 172.

87. War Cabinet Papers, Cab. 28, IC-25a, August 7; Ribot, *Lettres*, p. 340.

88. Ribot, *Journal*, p. 174, fn. 1; Cab. 28, IC-25d & 25e, August 8; Sonnino Papers, "Conferenze," London, August 8.

89. Ribot, *Journal*, pp. 174-75.

NOTES TO CHAPTER VIII

1. *Lockhart*, pp. 179-180.

2. *Sukhanov/Carmichael*, p. 374.

3. *Izvestiia*, July 23/August 5 trans. Browder/Kerensky, 3, no. 1203.

4. *Rech'*, July 23/August 5, p. 4.

5. July 26/August 8, p. 1 trans. *Browder/Kerensky, 3, no. 1210. List of the Second Coalition Ministry in ibid*, no. 1207.

6. Nabokoff, *Ordeal*, p. 116.

7. *PRFRUS*, 1917, "The World War," p. 150.

8. War Cabinet Papers, Committee of Imperial Defence—"Correspondence," (Cab. 17), G-179. Members of the Committee included Lloyd George, Chancellor of the Exchequer Bonar Law, the future Secretary for War Lord Milner, Lord Curzon and General Smuts.

9. *Ibid.*

10. *Warth*, pp. 123-30 for an account of the Allied embassies and Kornilov.

11. Sonnino Papers, "Arrivo," G-2398, Sept. 6; R.Sh. Ganelin, *Rossiia i S.Sh.A.1914/1917gg* (Leningrad, 1969), p. 351.

12. L. de Robien, *Journal d'un Diplomate en Russie, 1917-1918* (Paris, 1967), p. 138.

13. *Nabokoff*, p. 116.

14. *Rech'*, July 23/August 5, p. 4; *Izvestiia*, July 25/August 7, p. 5.

15. *VVP*, July 8/21, p. 1 trans. *Browder/Kerensky*, 3, no. 1185.

16. *KiP*, 1, 506, fn. 2.

17. See pp. 14-15.

18. *Mayer*, pp. 206-14 for a description of this debate.

19. *Journal Officiel*, Sèances—Chambre, p. 2168.

20. *KiP*, 1, nos. 352, 353, 354.

21. *Ibid*, no. 356.

22. *Ibid*, nos. 356, 357, 358, 359, 360 & fn. 4, 361.

23. Adamov, *Aufteilung*, no. 80.

24. In July 1919 this was precisely the British position against which Sonnino's successor Tomasso Tittoni appealed on the grounds that Russian consent in August 1917 was impractical "for the single reason that Russia had ceased to be an Allied state . . . and had lost the right to advance her interests in the alliance." E. L. Woodward, R. Butler, eds., *Documents on*

British Foreign Policy, 1919-1939, First Series, 4 (London, 1952), 22. Also Luigi Aldrovandi-Marescotti, *Guerra Diplomatica, Ricordi e Frammenti di Diario* (Milan, 1936), p. 374.

25. Sonnino Papers, "Arrivo," G-2392, Sept. 5.

26. Adamov, *Aufteilung*, no. 324.

27. Noulens, *Mon Ambassade*, 1, 40. But Carlotti lined up with Paléologue in supporting Miliukov against the preference of Thomas and Buchanan for Kerenskii. *Paléologue*, 3, 312.

28. *KiP*, 1, no. 212.

29. *Ibid.*

30. *Lockhart*, pp. 276, 282; *Buchanan*, 2, 187; *Ganelin*, pp. 34, 35 & *passim.*

31. *Rech'*, April 14/27, p. 1; *PRFRUS*, "The Lansing Papers, 1914-1920" (2 vols., Washington, 1939-40), 2, 336.

32. *KiP*, 1, no. 205. Tereshchenko had instructed that the government's statement be formally communicated to the Allies. Text of the statement in *VVP*, May 6/19, p. 1 trans. *Browder/Kerensky*, 3, no. 1095.

33. *PRFRUS*, 1917, "The World War," pp. 71-73; *Ganelin*, pp. 234-39.

34. May 30/June 12, p. 1 trans. *Browder/Kerensky*, 2, no. 977.

35. *PRFRUS*, 1918, "Russia" (3 vols., Washington, 1939-40), 1, 110.

36. Philip Jessup, *Elihu Root* (2 vols., New York, 1938), 2, 361, 366-67.

37. *KiP*, 1, no. 209.

38. *Ibid*, no. 213; Adamov, *Aufteilung*, no. 326; The Robert Lansing Papers (Library of Congress), "Desk Diaries," August 24, 1917.

39. Mamatey, *The United States and East-Central Europe*, p. 93 for Lansing's thoughts on a State Department memorandum on the future of the Slav nationalities of Austria-Hungary.

40. A. F. Kerensky, *The Catastrophe*, p. 323.

41. A. F. Kerensky, "The Policy of the Provisional Government of 1917," *The Slavonic (and East European) Review*, *11* (July 1932), 11.

42. A. F. Kerensky, *The Crucifixion of Liberty* (New York, 1934), p. 346.

43. A. F. Kerensky, *Russia and History's Turning Point* (New York, 1965), p. 433.

44. *Lockhart*, p. 180 (in 1931); to present writer in 1964.

45. *HAA*, "Der Weltkrieg," Part 2, no. 41, June 7.

46. Fischer, *Griff nach der Weltmacht*, pp. 563-69.

47. For the Sixtus von Bourbon—Parma mission and the Armand—Revertera, Mensdorff—Smuts and Smuts—Skrzynski encounters, Steglich, *Friedenspolitik*, pp. 15-58, 146-50, 249-52, 259-62.

48. *Ibid*, pp. 112-13; *PRFRUS*, 1917, "The World War," p. 157.

49. For Lloyd George and Bulgaria see pp. 90, 105, for Balfour on same, p. 51 and the Arthur J. Balfour Papers (British Museum), *17*, September 20,

1917, "Report on the Diplomatic Situation and the War" where he is pessimistic about a Balkan settlement.

50. FO 771, "Balkans," nos. 162107, 162621, 164838, 166883, 167389, 167426, 167852, 168090, 170695, 180915, 190499, 196738 between August 17 and October 12. Mr J. D. Gregory, Assistant Clerk at the Foreign Office and well versed in Balkan concerns, made the comment on Oustabashieff on 190499. He consistently discouraged speculation on Bulgarian readiness to do a deal with the Entente.

51. So reported by Bulgarian diplomats in Constantinople, Bulgaria: *Documents*, no. 1225 and by German representatives, *HAA*, "Die Türkei," No. 150, June 9.

52. *L'Echo de Bulgarie*, May 23, p. 2.

53. Bulgaria: *Documents*, no. 1243.

54. *L'Echo de Bulgarie*, July 6, p. 2; *Osmanischer Lloyd*, July 7, p. 3.

55. *Ibid*, Sept. 17, p. 1; Sept. 21, p. 3; October 10, p. 3.

56. *L'Echo de Bulgarie*, July 20, p. 1; July 25, p. 1; July 27, p. 1; July 30, p. 1.

57. *Ibid*, October 31, p. 1. For the Soviet program, see pp. 166-167.

58. Kh. Kabakchev, "Partiia tesnykh sotsialistov, revoliutsiia v Rossii i Tsimmerval'dskoe dvizhenie," *Oktiabr'skaia Revoliutsiia i Zarubezhnie Slavianskie Narody*, ed. A. Ia. Manusevich (Moscow, 1957), 10, 11, 19.

59. M. A. Birman, *Revoliutsionnaia Situatsiia v Bolgarii v 1918-1919 gg* (Moscow, 1957), pp. 45-46.

60. *PRFRUS*, 1917, "The World War," p. 604.

61. The exception was the mission in June of Henry Morgenthau and Felix Frankfurter. On Morgenthau's initiative and, apparently, with State Department approval, the two men travelled to Europe ostensibly to organize civilian relief work, but also, if possible, to sound out Ottoman officials on the chances of a separate Turkish peace. When they told Lansing from Madrid of their talks with some Entente officers they were quickly forbidden "to confer, discuss or carry messages relating to the international situation in Turkey or bearing upon a separate [Turkish] peace." *Ibid*, p. 129. The British received assurances from Wilson and Lansing that the mission was of slight consequence. Balfour Papers, *56*, June 12, 1917 (Spring Rice to Cecil); FO 371, "Turkey," nos. 104218, 114918, 138633. There is no evidence of a Russian involvement at any stage.

62. Seymour, *Intimate Papers*, 2, 415.

63. R. S. Baker, *Woodrow Wilson, Life and Letters* (8 vols., New York, 1927-39), 8, 379-80.

64. Robert Lansing Papers, "Desk Diaries," April 3. Panaretov's isolation in Washington caused his government some nervousness. On October 1 the Foreign Ministry denied rumors their minister was intriguing for a

separate peace and revealed it had had no contact with him for over a year. *L'Echo de Bulgarie*, Oct. 1, p. 1.

65. *Mamatey*, pp. 100, 102.

NOTES TO CHAPTER IX

1. FO 371, "Balkans," no. 169472, Sept. 8; War Cabinet Papers, Cab. 23, WC-229, Sept. 7.

2. *PRFRUS*, 1917,"The World War," pp. 208-214.

3. Kirova, *Russkaia Revoliutsiia i Italiia*, p. 184.

4. Sonnino Papers, "Arrivo," G-2078, July 26.

5. Stienon, *Le Mystère Roumain*, pp. 300-01.

6. Sonnino Papers, "Arrivo," G-2138, Aug. 7; G-2157, Aug. 7. In fact Kherson was (and is) on a branch line of the main Moscow-Odessa rail link.

7. *Ibid*, G-2238, Aug. 19.

8. Jane Degras, ed., *Soviet Documents on Foreign Policy* (3 vols., London, 1951-53), 1, 40.

9. Sonnino Papers, "Arrivo," G-2106, July 30; G-2120, Aug. 5; G-2165, Aug. 10; G-2363, Aug. 30; G-2445, Sept. 8.

10. *PRFRUS*, 1917, "The World War," p. 210.

11. Vinogradov, *Rumyniia v gody*, p. 219.

12. *Ibid*, p. 224; Dykov, "Rumcherod i Bor'ba," pp. 17-18 & fn. 91.

13. Sonnino Papers, "Arrivo," G-2569, Sept. 13; *Pravda*, Jan. 14/27, 1918, p. 2, no. 832, Aug. 24/Sept. 6; Jan. 20/Feb. 2, 1918, p. 5, no. 394, Sept. 25/Oct. 8.

14. *Ibid*, no. 8698, Aug. 12/25.

15. *Ibid*, nos. 394, 291, Sept. 30/Oct. 13; Sonnino Papers, "Arrivo," G-2790, Oct. 17.

16. FO 371, "Balkans," no. 204690, Oct. 16.

17. Clark, *Bessarabia, Russia and Rumania*, p. 127; *Russkie Vedomosti*, October 7/20, p. 2.

18. *Clark*, pp. 129-30; War Cabinet Papers, Cab. 24, GT-1520, July 25.

19. See p. 78.

20. *Pravda*, Jan. 14/27, 1918, p. 2, no. 398, June 10/23.

21. *Clark*, p. 142; Great Britain, Historical Section of the Foreign Office, *Bessarabia* (London, 1920), pp. 24-25.

22. Andrei Popovici, *The Political Status of Bessarabia* (Washington, 1931), p. 140.

23. S. M. Dimanshtein, ed., *Revoliutsiia i Natsional'nyi Vopros* (Moscow, 1930), pp. 189-90 for the General Secretariat statement in the Rada on September 28 on the need to guarantee the Ukrainian people full state rights

in its own land within a loose Russian framework.

24. In August Shcherbachev agreed that up to 40,000 Bessarabians might be enrolled in a reserve force. Its HQ were first in Odessa, then Kishinev. The Assembly (Sfatul Tsarii) came into being in November. *Bessarabia*, pp. 23-24; *Popovici*, pp. 130-31; *Clark*, pp. 145, 155-57; I. I. Dovgopolyi & N. D. Roitman, eds., *Iz Istorii Bor'by za Vlast' Sovetov v Moldavii (1918-1920): Sbornik Vospominanii Uchastnikov Grazhdanskoi Voiny* (Kishinev, 1964), pp. 25-28.

25. *Sukhanov/Carmichael*, p. 527; *de Robien*, p. 136; text of Kerenskii's address in *Browder/Kerensky*, 3, no. 1354.

26. *Izvestiia*, September 20/October 3, pp. 5-7.

27. *Ibid*, September 24/October 7, p. 4. Russia officially became a republic on September 1/14, *VVP*, September 3/16, p. 1.

28. List of the Third Coalition Ministry in *Browder/Kerensky*, 3, no. 1376.

29. *Sukhanov/Carmichael*, p. 534.

30. For Trotskii's speech *Browder/Kerensky*, 3, no. 1384, pp. 1728-30.

31. Golder, *Documents*, p. 647.

32. Fainsod, *International Socialism*, pp. 14-46 for the Stockholm sessions.

33. War Cabinet Papers, Cab. 24, GT-793, "IBDI Report on Stockholm & the Central Powers," ud.

34. *Ibid*, GT-827, May 21, "IBDI Report on Bulgaria."

35. *Izvestiia*, April 15/28, p. 2; *Pravda*, July 11/24, p. 3 for a strong "Narrow" attack on the "Broads" at Stockholm.

36. *HAA*, "Der Weltkrieg," No. 2c, Part 1, May 25 cited Lademacher, *Die Zimmerwalder Bewegung*, 1, 508, 510.

37. *Ibid*, pp. 508-09; list and dates of Stockholm delegations, *Fainsod*, p. 136, fn. 46.

38. *Izvestiia*, October 7/20, p. 2.

39. *Ibid*, p. 1.

40. *L'Echo de Bulgarie*, October 31 with press summaries.

41. *La Serbie*, October 28, p. 1; Sonnino Papers, "Arrivo," G-2868, October 27 for Carlotti on Spalajković and the Nakaz.

42. *Ibid*, G-2844, October 23; *PRFRUS*, 1917, "The World War," pp. 285-86; *Birzhevie Vedomosti* (Evening Ed.) October 17/30, p. 1; *Izvestiia*, October 20/November 2, p. 6.

43. *Birzhevie Vedomosti*, (Evening Ed.) October 1/30, p. 1.

44. Leon Trotskii, *The History of the Russian Revolution* (3 vols. in 1, New York, 1932), 3, 68-69 where he records the sarcastic observations of *Rech'* on the Nakaz.

45. *Vasiukov*, p. 442; Ignat'ev, *Russko-angliiskie otnosheniia*, p. 380.

46. Vremennyi Sovet Respubliki, Komissiia Po Inostrannym Delam, *Byloe* 6 (1918), no. 12 partially trans. *Browder/Kerensky*, 2, no. 996, p. 1131.

47. *Ibid*, pp. 1133-35.

48. *Byloe*, 6, no. 12, 20-21.

49. *Ibid*, 21-22; *VVP*, October 17/30, pp. 2-3.

50. *Rech'*, October 19/November 1, pp. 3-4 trans. *Browder/Kerensky*, 2, no. 999, pp. 1148-50.

51. *Izvestiia*, October 20/November 2, p. 3 trans. *ibid*, 2, no. 1003. The All-Russian Executive Committee of the Soviets of Peasants' Deputies had been set up following the first All-Russian Congress of Peasants' Soviets in May. The Peasants' Ex. Com. and that of the Soviets of Workers' and Soldiers' Deputies had been nominally united since the end of June. *Izvestiia*, June 19/July 1, p. 1. A Cossack delegation insisted it too should send a representative to Paris, *Birzhevie Vedomosti*, October 6/19, p. 5.

52. 98 H.C. *Debates*, 5s, col. 1189.

53. *Izvestiia*, October 17/30, p. 1.

54. Fischer, *Griff nach der Weltmacht*, p. 467.

55. 93 H.C. *Debates*, 5s, col. 1678.

56. House Papers, Buckler File, May 24.

57. Kerensky, *The Catastrophe*, p. 130.

58. House Papers, Buckler File, Buckler to House on November 3 quoting Lord Milner.

59. *Izvestiia*, October 17/30, p. 1.

60. *Ibid*, p. 2; *Rech'*, October 19/November 1, p. 4 trans. *Browder/Kerensky*, 2, no. 999, p. 1149.

61. *Ibid*, p. 1133.

62. de Robien, *Journal d'un Diplomate*, p. 336.

BIBLIOGRAPHY

The bibliography is organized in the following manner:

I. Manuscript Sources (including unpublished microfilm)

II. Governmental and Documentary Publications
 1. From Russian Sources
 2. From Entente Sources
 3. From Central Powers' Sources
 4. Other

III. Newspapers and Periodicals
 1. Russian
 2. Other

IV. Published Diaries, Memoirs, Letters and Biographies

V. General Works

VI. Monograph Studies

VII. Articles

I. Manuscript Sources

Arthur James Balfour Papers, British Museum, London.
Edward M. House Papers, Yale University Library, New Haven.
 The William G. Buckler File of correspondence between House and Buckler through 1917.
Robert Lansing Papers, Library of Congress, Washington, D.C.
 Included in these papers are Lansing's Desk Diaries.
Sidney Sonnino Papers (Microfilm)
 The following files: "Telegrammi in Arrivo," "Telegrammi in Partenza," "Carteggi Sir James Rennell Rodd, Barrere e Giers,"

"Conferenze degli Alleati."

Hauptarchiv des Auswärtigen Amtes (Microfilm)
The following sections: "Akten betreffend die Turkei," "Beziehungen zu Russland," "Bulgarien—Bulgarische Staatsmanner," "Der Weltkrieg."

Foreign Office Records, Public Record Office, London.
Within the section of General Correspondence (FO 371) the following files for 1917: "Balkans," "Russia," "Italy" and "Turkey."

State Department Records, National Archives, Washington, D.C.
The series "State Department Records Relating to World War I and Its Termination, 1914-1929" had a few items not already published in the *U.S. Foreign Relations* volumes.

War Cabinet Papers, Public Record Office, London.
The following files: Cab. 17—Committee of Imperial Defence *Correspondence*; Cab. 23—War Cabinet *Minutes*; Cab. 24—War Cabinet *Memoranda*; Cab. 28—*International Conferences*; Cab. 29—"P" (Peace) Series.

II. Governmental and Documentary Publications.

1. From Russian Sources:

Adamov, E. A. et al., eds., *Die Europäischen Mächte und die Türkei während des Weltkrieges: Die Aufteilung der Asiatischen Türkei*, Dresden, 1932. Originally published in Moscow as *Evropeiskie Derzhavy i Turtsiia vo vremia Mirovoi Voiny: Razdel Aziatskoi Turtsii*, Moscow, 1924.

———, *Die Europäischen Mächte und Griechenland während des Weltkrieges*, Dresden, 1932. Originally published in Moscow in 1922 as *Evropeiskie Derzhavy i Gretsiia v Epokhu Mirovoi Voiny.*

———, *Evropeiskie Derzhavy i Turtsiia vo vremia Mirovoi Voiny: Konstantinopol' i Prolivy*, 2 vols., Moscow, 1925.

Avdeev, N. N. et al., eds., *Revoliutsiia 1917 goda (Khronika Sobytii)*, 6 vols., Moscow, 1923-30.

Browder, R. P. & Kerensky, A. F. comps., *The Russian Provisional Government, 1917*, 3 vols., Stanford, 1961.

Degras, J., ed., *Soviet Documents on Foreign Policy*, 3 vols., London, 1951-53.

Dimanshtein, S. M., ed., *Revoliutsiia i Natsional'nyi Vopros*, Moscow, 1930.

Erusalimskii, A. S. et al., ed. & comp., *Mezhdunarodnie Otnosheniia v Epokhu Imperializma: Dokumenty iz Arkhivov Tsarskogo i Vremennogo Pravitel'stv 1871-1917 gg.* Series II (1900-1913), Vols. 18-20 published, each in two parts, Moscow, 1938-40.

Golder, F. A., ed., *Documents of Russian History, 1914-1917*, Gloucester, Mass. (reprint), 1964 (1927).

Gosudarstvennaia Duma, *Stenograficheski Ochety*, Third and Fourth Sessions, St Petersburg/Petrograd, 1908-1916.

Pokrovskii, M. N. et al., ed. & comp., *Mezhdunarodnie Otnosheniia v Epokhu Imperializma: Dokumenty iz Arkhivov Tsarskogo i Vremennogo Pravitel'stv 1871-1917 gg.* Series III (1914-1916), Vols. 1-10 published, 6-8 in two parts each, Moscow, 1931-38.

__________, *Das Zaristische Russland im Weltkriege*, Berlin, 1927. Originally published in Moscow and Leningrad in 1925 as *Tsarskaia Rossiia v Mirovoi Voine*.

Shchegolev, P. E., ed., *Padenie Tsarskogo Rezhima: Stenografischeskie Ochety Doprosov i Pokazanii dannykh v 1917 godu v Chrezvychainoi Sledstvennoi Kommissii Vremennogo Pravitel'stva*, 7 vols., Leningrad, 1924-27.

Semennikov, V. P., ed., *Monarkhiia Pered Krusheniem: Bumagi Nikolaia II i Drugie Dokumenty*, Moscow, 1927.

Stieve, F., ed., *Der Diplomatische Schriftwechsel Iswolskis 1911-1914*, 4 vols., Berlin, 1926.

__________, *Iswolsky and the World War*, London, 1926.

__________, *Iswolski im Weltkriege: Der Diplomatische Schriftwechsel Iswolskis aus den Jahren 1914-1917*, Berlin, 1925.

2. Entente Sources:

Boghitschewitsch, M. (Bogičević), ed., *Die Auswärtige Politik Serbiens, 1908-1914*, 3 vols., Berlin, 1928.

France, *Journal Officiel*: Débats Parlementaires (Chambre des Députés).

Great Britain, House of Commons—*Debates*, Fifth Series.

Italy, *Atti Parlamentari*, Legislatura XXIV—Camera dei Deputati.

Michel, Paul-Henri, ed., *La Question de l'Adriatique, Recueil de Documents*, Paris, 1938.

Woodward, E. L. & Butler, R., eds., *Documents on British Foreign Policy, 1919-1939*, 32 vols., London, 1946-65.

United States, Department of State, *Papers Relating to the Foreign Relations of the United States:*

(a) 1917, Supplement 2, "The World War," Washington, 1932.

(b) 1918, Supplement 1, "Russia," 3 vols., Washington, 1939-40.

(c) "The Lansing Papers, 1914-1920," 2 vols., Washington, 1939-40.

Central Powers' Sources:

Austria-Hungary, K.u.K. Ministerium des Äussern, *Zur Vorgeschichte des Krieges mit Italien*, Vienna, 1915.

__________, L. Bittner, H. Uebersberger & A. F. Pribram, eds., *Österreich-Ungarns Aussenpolitik von der bosnischen Krise 1908 bis zum Kriegsausbruch 1914*, 9 vols., Vienna, 1930.

Bulgaria, *Dnevnitsi (Stenografski) na XVII-to Obiknovenno Narodno Subranie*, 2 vols., Sofia, 1930.

__________, *Diplomaticheski Dokumenti po Uchastieto na Bulgariia v Evropeiskata Voina 1915-1918*, Sofia, 1921.

Germany, J. Lepsius, A. Bartholdy, F. Thimme, eds., *Die Grosse Politik der Europäischen Kabinette 1871-1914*, 53 vols., Berlin 1922-27, Vol. 18:2 (1924).

4. Other:

Lademacher, H., ed., *Die Zimmerwalder Bewegung: Protokolle und Korrespondenz*, 2 vols., The Hague, 1967.

III. Newspapers and Periodicals

1. Russian (political affiliation given where applicable):

Birzhevie Vedomosti. Conservative, business oriented.

Byloe, No. 6 (1918).

Delo Naroda. Organ of the Central Committee of the Social Revolutionary Party.

Den'.

Izvestiia. Organ of the Central Executive Committee of the Petrograd Soviet of Workers' and Soldiers' Deputies.

Novoe Vremia. Extreme Conservative.

Pravda. Organ of the Central Committee of the Bolshevik Party.

Rabochaia Gazeta. Menshevik.

Rech'. Organ of the Constitutional Democratic Party.

Russkie Vedomosti (Moscow).

Russkaia Volia.

Vestnik Evropy. Monthly.

Vestnik Narodnogo Kommissariata Inostrannykh Del (Moscow), No. 4-5 (1920).

Vestnik Partii Narodnoi Svobody, No. 2 (1917). Official Cadet gazette.

Vestnik Vremennogo Pravitel'stva. Official gazette of the Provisional Government.

Zhurnaly Zasedanii Vremennogo Pravitel'stva. Record of Cabinet transactions.

2. Other:

The Times (London)
The Manchester Guardian
The Daily Chronicle
The Daily Mail
The Daily News
The New Europe
The Nation
The New Republic (New York)
The Saturday Review
The U.D.C.
Le Temps
Il Giornale d'Italia
Il Messaggero
Corriere della Sera
La Serbie (Geneva)
Deutscher Geschichtskalender für 1917 (Leipzig) Nos. VI:1, VI:2, VII:1, VII:2.
L'Echo de Bulgarie (Sofia) with summaries of the Bulgarian press.
Osmanischer Lloyd (Constantinople) with summaries of the Turkish press.

IV. Published Diaries, memoirs, Letters and Biographies

Aldrovandi-Marescotti, L., *Guerra Diplomatica: Ricordi e Frammenti di Diario*, Milan, 1936.

Baker, R. S., *Woodrow Wilson, Life and Letters*, 8 vols., New York, 1927-1939.

Benes, E., *Souvenirs de Guerre et de Révolution, 1914-1918*, 2 vols., Paris, 1928.

Buchanan, Sir G., *My Mission to Russia and Other Diplomatic Memories*, 2 vols., London, 1923.

Charykov, N. V., *Glimpses of High Politics, Through War and Peace, 1855-1929*, New York, 1931.

Chernov, V., *The Great Russian Revolution*, trans. & ed. by Philip Mosely, New Haven, 1936.

Dovgopolyi, I. I. & Roitman, N. D., eds., *Iz Istorii Bor'by za Vlast' Sovetov v Moldavii (1918-1920 gg.), Sbornik Vospominanii Uchastnikov Grazhdanskoi Voiny*, Kishinev, 1964.

Dugdale, B., *Arthur James Balfour*, 2 vols., London, 1936.

Erzberger, M., *Erlebnisse im Weltkriege*, Berlin, 1920.

Gordon-Lennox, Lady A., ed., *The Diary of Lord Bertie of Thame 1914-1918*, 2 vols., London, 1924.

Gourko, B., *Memories and Impressions of War and Revolution in Russia*, London, 1918.

Hamilton, M., *Arthur Henderson*, London, 1938.

Jessup, P. C., *Elihu Root*, 2 vols., New York, 1938.

Kerensky, A. F., *The Catastrophe*, New York, 1927.

——————, *The Crucifixion of Liberty*, New York, 1934.

——————, *Russia and History's Turning Point*, New York, 1965.

Knox, Major General Sir A., *With the Russian Army 1914-1917*, London, 1921.

Kokovtsov, V. N., *Out of My Past, The Memoirs of Count Kokovtsov, Russian Minister of Finance 1904-1914*, Stanford, 1935.

Lloyd George, D., *War Memoirs*, 6 vols., London, 1933–36.

Lockhart, B., *Memoirs of a British Agent*, London, 1933.

Mandić, A., *Fragmenti za Historiju Ujedinjenja*, Zagreb, 1956.

Marie, Queen of Rumania, *Ordeal, The Story of My Life*, 3 vols., New York, 1934.

Miliukov, P. N., *Vospominaniia*, posthumously ed. by M. M. Karpovich & B. El'kin, 2 vols., New York, 1955.

Nabokoff, K., *Ordeal of a Diplomat*, London, 1921.

Nekliudoff, A. V., *Diplomatic Reminiscences Before and During the World War*, trans. by Alexandra Paget, London, 1920.

Nevins, A., *Henry White, Thirty Years of American Diplomacy*, New York, 1930.

Noulens, J., *Mon Ambassade en Russie Soviétique, 1917-1919*, 2 vols., Paris, 1933.

Paléologue, M., *An Ambassador's Memoirs*, trans. by F. A. Holt, 3 vols., London, 1924–25.

Pares, Sir B., *My Russian Memoirs*, London, 1931.

Pershing, J. J., *My Experiences in the World War*, 2 vols., New York, 1931.

Price, M. Philips, *My Reminiscences of the Russian Revolution*, London, 1920.

Ribot, A., *Lettres à un Ami*, Paris, 1924.

——————, ed., *Journal de Alexandre Ribot et Correspondances Inedites, 1914-1922*, Paris, 1936.

Riha, T., *A Russian European, Paul Miliukov in Russian Politics*, Notre Dame, 1969.

Robien, L. de, *Journal d'un Diplomate en Russie, 1917-1919*, Paris, 1967.

Rosen, R. R., *Forty Years of Diplomacy*, London, 1922.

Sarrail, M., *Mon Commandement en Orient, 1916-1918*, Paris, 1920.

Savinsky, A. A., *Recollections of a Russian Diplomat*, London, 1927.

Sazonov, S. D., *Vospominaniia*, Paris, 1927.

Schelking, E. de, *Recollections of a Russian Diplomat: The Suicide of Monarchies*, New York, 1918.

Seton-Watson, R. W., *Masaryk in England*, Cambridge, 1943.
Seymour, C., ed., *The Intimate Papers of Colonel House*, 4 vols., New York & Boston, 1926-28.
Shipov, D. N., *Vospominaniia i Dumy o Perezhitom*, Moscow, 1918.
Stankevich, V. B., *Vospominaniia, 1914-1919*, Berlin, 1920.
Sukhanov, N. N. [Himmer], *Zapiski o Revoliutsii*, 7 vols., Berlin, 1922-23.
————, ed., abridged & trans. by Joel Carmichael as *The Russian Revolution 1917*, New York & London, 1955.
Tomić, J. N., ed., *Jugoslavija u Emigratsii: Pisma i Beleshke iz 1917*, Belgrade, 1921.
Vulliamy, C. E., ed., *The Letters of the Tsar to the Tsaritsa and of the Tsaritsa to the Tsar, 1914-1917*, Hattiesburg, 1970.

V. General Works

Albertini, L., *The Origins of the War of 1914*, trans. by Isabella Massey, 3 vols., London, 1952-57.
Carnegie Endowment, *Report of the International Commission to Inquire into the Causes and Conduct of the Balkan Wars*, Washington, 1914.
Cocks, S., ed., *The Secret Treaties and Understandings: Text of the Available Documents*, London, 1918.
Corbett, Sir J. S., *History of the Great War Based on Official Documents: Naval Operations*, 5 vols., London, 1920-31.
Great Britain, Historical Section of the Foreign Office, *Albania, Bessarabia*, London, 1920.
Khvostov, V. M., ed., *Istoriia Diplomatii*, 3 vols., Moscow, 1959-65.
Langer, W. L., *European Alliances and Alignments, 1871-1890*, 2nd. ed., New York, 1962.
Lenin, V. I., *Collected Works*, 4th ed., 45 vols., trans. Y. Sdobnikov, Moscow, 1960-70.
Macartney, C. A., *The Hapsburg Empire, 1790-1918*, London, 1968.
Miliukov, P. N., *Istoriia Vtoroi Russkoi Revoliutsii*, 3 vols., Sofia, 1921-23.
Pingaud, A., *L'Histoire Diplomatique de la France Pendant la Grande Guerre*, 3 vols., Paris, 1937-40.
Report of the Court Proceedings in the Case of the Anti-Soviet "Bloc of Rights and Trotskyites," Moscow, 1938.
Sforza, C., *Contemporary Italy, Its Intellectual and Moral Origins*, trans. Drake & Denise De Kay, London, 1946.
Swire, J., *Albania, The Rise of a Kingdom*, London, 1929.
Trotsky, L., *The History of the Russian Revolution*, 3 vols. in 1, trans. by Max

Eastman, Ann Arbor, ud. The original English language edition appeared in 1932.

VI. Monograph Studies

Abbott, G. F., *Greece and the Allies, 1914-1922*, London, 1922.

Ancel, J., *L'Unité de la Politique Bulgare, 1870-1919*, Paris, 1919.

Birman, M. A., *Revoliutsionnaia Situatsiia v Bolgarii v 1918-1919 gg*, Moscow, 1957.

Bradley, J.F.N., *La Légion Tchécoslovaque en Russie, 1914-1920*, Paris, 1965.

Brailsford, H. N., *Turkey and the Roads of the East*, London, 1916.

————, *Macedonia, Its Races and Their Future*, London, 1906.

Caracciolo, M., *L'Intervento della Grecia nella Guerra Mondiale e l'Opera della Diplomazia Alleata*, Rome, 1925.

Carlgren, W. M., *Iswolsky und Aerenthal vor der bosnischen Annexionskrise, Russische und österreichisch-ungarische Balkanpolitik 1906-1908*, Uppsala, 1955.

Clark, C. U., *Bessarabia, Russia and Roumania on the Black Sea*, New York, 1927.

Cosmin, S. [S. P. Phocas-Cosmetatos], *L'Entente et la Grèce Pendant la Grande Guerre*, 2 vols., Paris, 1926.

Cvijić, J., *Grundlinien der Geographie und Geologie von Mazedonien und Altserbien, nebst Beobachtungen in Thrazien, Epirus und Nordalbanien*, Gotha, 1908.

Danilov, Iu. A., *La Russie dans la Guerre Mondiale, 1914-1918*, trans. by A. Kaznakov, Paris, 1927.

Denikin, A. I., *Ocherki Russkoi Smuty*, Paris, 1921.

Diakin, V. S., *Russkaia Burzhuaziia i Tsarizm v Gody Pervoi Mirovoi Voiny 1914-1917*, Leningrad, 1967.

Djordjević, M. P., *Srbija i Jugosloveni za vreme Rata 1914-1918*, Belgrade, 1922.

Fainsod, M., *International Socialism and the World War*, Cambridge, 1935.

Fischer, F., *Griff nach der Weltmacht: Die Kriegszielpolitik des kaiserlichen Deutschland 1914/1918*, Dusseldorf, 1962.

Fowler, W. B., *British-American Relations 1917-1918: The Role of Sir William Wiseman*, Princeton, 1969.

Frangulis, A. F., *La Grèce et la Crise Mondiale*, 2 vols., Paris, 1926.

Ganelin, R. Sh., *Rossiia i S.Sh.A. 1914/1917 gg*, Leningrad, 1969.

Gankin, O. & Fisher, H., *The Bolsheviks and the World War: The Origin of the Third International*, Stanford, 1940.

Gelfand, L. E., *The Inquiry, American Preparations for Peace, 1917-1919*, New Haven, 1963.

Golovin, N. N., *The Russian Army in World War I*, Hamden, 1969. Originally published in 1931.

Gubskii, N., *Revoliutsiia i Vneshniaia Politika Rossii*, Petrograd, 1917.

Hanak, H., *Great Britain and Austria-Hungary During the First World War*, London, 1962.

Hauser, O., *Deutschland und der englisch-russische Gegensatz 1900-1914*, Gottingen, 1958.

Helmreich, E. C., *The Diplomacy of the Balkan Wars, 1912-1913*, Cambridge, 1938.

Howard, H. N., *The Partition of Turkey, A Diplomatic History 1913-1923*, Norman, 1931.

Iashchenko, A., *Russkie Interesy v Maloi Azii*, Moscow, 1916.

Ignat'ev, A. V., *Russko-angliiskie otnosheniia nakanune Oktiabr'skoi Revoliutsii, fevral'-oktiabr' 1917 g.*, Moscow, 1966.

Ioffe, A. E., *Russko-frantsuszkie otnosheniia v 1917 godu*, Moscow, 1956.

Jovanović, I. et al., comps., *Jugoslovenski Dobrovolachki Korpus u Rusiji 1914-1918*, Belgrade, 1954.

Kirova, K. E., *Russkaia Revoliutsiia i Italiia, mart-oktiabr' 1917 g.*, Moscow, 1968.

Kuhne, V., *Les Bulgares Peints Par Eux-Mêmes*, Paris, 1917.

Lewis, B., *The Emergence of Modern Turkey*, 2nd. ed., London, 1968.

Mamatey, V. S., *The United States and East-Central Europe, 1914-1918, A Study in Wilsonian Diplomacy and Propaganda*, Princeton, 1957.

Manteyer, G. de, ed., *Austria's Peace Offer, 1916-1917*, London, 1921.

Martin, R. L., *Peace Without Victory, Woodrow Wilson and the British Liberals*, New Haven, 1958.

Mayer, A. J., *Wilson vs. Lenin, Political Origins of the New Diplomacy*, Cleveland & New York, 1964.

Meininger, T. A., *Ignatiev and the Establishment of the Bulgarian Exarchate*, Madison, 1970.

Mileff, M., *La Bulgarie et les Détroits*, Paris, 1927.

Miliukov, P. N., *Balkanskii Krizis i Politika A. P. Izvol'skogo*, St Petersburg, 1910.

__________, *God Bor'by*, St Petersburg, 1907.

Mühlmann, C., *Oberste Heeresleitung und Balkan im Weltkrieg 1914-1918*, Berlin, 1942.

Papadopoulos, G., *England and the Near East, 1896-1898*, Salonika, 1969.

Paulová, M., *Jugoslavenski Odbor, Povjest Jugoslavenske Emigratsije za Svetskog Rata od 1914-1918*, Zagreb, 1924.

Petriaev, A. M., *Prolivy*, Petrograd, 1917.

Philipson, C. & Buxton, N., *The Question of the Bosphorus and the Dardanelles*, London, 1917.

Popovici, A., *The Political Status of Bessarabia*, Washington, 1931.

Popov, K. A., ed., *Dopros Kolchaka*, Leningrad, 1925.
Radeff, S., *La Macédoine et la Renaissance Bulgare au XIX Siècle*, Sofia, 1918.
Radoslawoff, V., *Bulgarien und die Weltkrise*, Berlin, 1923.
Rubbiani, F., *Il Pensiero Politico di Leonida Bissolati*, Florence, 1921.
Russian Institute, Columbia University, *Russian Diplomacy and Eastern Europe, 1914-1917*, New York, 1963.
Seton-Watson, R. W., *The War and Democracy*, London, 1914.
Seymour, C., *American Diplomacy During the World War*, Baltimore, 1934.
Smith, C. Jay, *The Russian Struggle For Power, 1914-1917*, New York, 1956.
Steglich, W., *Die Friedenspolitik der Mittelmächte 1917-1918*, Wiesbaden, 1964.
Stienon, C., *Le Mystère Roumain et la Défection Russe*, Paris, 1918.
Sumner, B. H., *Russia and the Balkans, 1870-1880*, Hamden, 1962. First published in 1937.
Thaden, E. C., *Russia and the Balkan Alliance of 1912*, University Park, 1965.
Toscano, M., *Gli Accordi di San Giovanni di Moriana*, Milan, 1936.
Trumpener, U., *Germany and the Ottoman Empire, 1914-1918*, Princeton, 1968.
Uebersberger, H., *Österreich zwischen Russland und Serbien: Zur südslawischen Frage und der Entstehung des Ersten Weltkrieges*, Cologne, 1958.
Vasiukov, V. S., *Vneshniaia Politika Vremennogo Pravitel'stva*, Moscow, 1966.
Vinogradov, V. N., *Rumyniia v gody Pervoi Mirovoi Voiny*, Moscow, 1969.
Wade, R., *The Russian Search For Peace, February-October 1917*, Stanford, 1969.
Warth, R., *The Allies and the Russian Revolution: From the Fall of the Monarchy to the Peace of Brest-Litovsk*, Durham, 1954.
Wilkinson, H. R., *Maps and Politics, A Review of the Ethnographic Cartography of Macedonia*, Liverpool, 1951.
Wilson, Woodrow, *The State*, Boston, 1889.
Woodhouse, E. & C., *Italy and the Yugoslavs*, Boston, 1920.
Zakharov, M. N., *Nashe Stremlenie k Bosforu i Protivodeistvie emu Zapadoevropeiskikh Derzhav*, Petrograd, 1916.
Živanović, M. Ž., *Solunski Protses 1917*, Vol. 243 of Posebna Izdanja, Belgrade, 1955.

VII. Articles

Bazarevsky, A., "De l'Entrée en Guerre de la Roumanie et les Inconvénients qui en resultèrent pour la Russie," *Les Alliés Contre La Russie*, Paris, 1927, 230-237.
Dykov, I. G., "Rumcherod i Bor'ba za Ustanovlenie Sovetskoi Vlasti na Rumynskom Fronte," *Istoricheskie Zapiski* (Moscow), 57 (1956) 3-34.
Hutchinson, J. F., "The Octobrists and the Future of Imperial Russia as a

Great Power," *The Slavonic and East European Review, L,* No. 119 (April 1972), 220-237.

Jelavich, C., "Nikola P. Pašić: Greater Serbia or Jugoslavia?" *Journal of Central European Affairs* (Boulder), July 1951, 133-152.

Kabakchev, Kh., "Partiia tesnykh sotsialistov, revoliutsiia v Rossii i tsimmerval'dskoe dvizhenie," *Oktiabr'skaia Revoliutsiia i Zarubezhnie Slavianskie Narody*, ed. A. Ia. Manusevich, Moscow, 1957.

Kerensky, A. F., "The Policy of the Provisional Government of 1917," *The Slavonic (and East European) Review*, X, (July 1932), 1-19.

Krasnyi Arkhiv (Moscow), "Konstantinopol' i Prolivy," 6 (1924), 48-76; "Politicheskaia Situatsiia v Rossii nakanune Fevral'skoi Revoliutsii," 17 (1926), 3-35; "Diplomatiia Vremennogo Pravitel'stva v Bor'be s Revoliutsiei," 20 (1927), 3-38; "Dnevnik P. N. Miliukova," 54-55 (1932), 3-48; "Russkaia Parlamentskaia Delegatsiia zagranitsei v 1916 godu," 58 (1933); "Materialy otnosiashchiesia k istorii anglo-russkogo soglasheniia 1907 goda," 69-70, (1935), 3-39.

Miliukov, P. N., "Konstantinopol' i Prolivy," *Vestnik Evropy* (Petrograd), January 1917, 354-382; February 1917, 227-260; April-June 1917, 525-548.

__________, "Diplomaticheskaia Istoriia Voiny," *Ezhegodnik Rech'* 1915, 43-121.

__________, "Obshchestvennoe Mnenie, Parlamenty i Pravitel'stva Soiuznikov," *Ezhegodnik Rech'* 1915, 176-290.

__________, "Proiskhozhdenie Voiny," *Ezhegodnik Rech'* 1915, 1-42.

__________, "Territorial'nye Priobreteniia Rossii," *Chego Zhdet Rossiia Ot Voiny?*, Petrograd, 1915, 49-62.

__________, "Tseli Voiny: Sud'ba Germanii, Avstro-Vengrii, Turtsii," *Ezhegodnik Rech'* 1916, 29-128.

__________, "Vstuplenie Neitral'nykh Gosudarstv," *Ezhegodnik Rech'* 1915, 122-175; 1916, 29-128.

Mosely, P. E., "Russian Policy in 1911-1912," *Journal of Modern History* (Chicago), March 1940, 69-86.

Nabokov, V., "Vremennoe Pravitel'stvo," *Arkhiv Russkoi Revoliutsii* (Berlin), 1 (1922), 9-96.

Nekliudov, N. A., "Predskazanie Russkoi Revoliutsii," *Arkhiv Russkoi Revoliutsii*, 1 (1922), 257-259.

Popov, I., ed., "Perepiska Miliukova i Tereshchenko s Poslami Vremennogo Pravitel'stva," *Bor'ba Klassov* (Moscow), 5 (1931), 84-88.

Rubinshtein, N., "Vneshniaia Politika Kerenshchiny," *Ocherki Po Istorii Oktiabr'skoi Revoliutsii*, ed. by M. N. Pokrovskii, 2 vols., Moscow, 1927, 2, 349-450.

Seton-Watson, R. W., Review article of *Le Procès de Salonique 1917* by M. Boghitschewitsch (Bogičević), *The Slavonic (and East European) Review*, 6 (1928), 703-711.

Tschudnowsky, G., "Schriften russischer Sozialisten über den Krieg," *Archiv für die Geschichte des Sozialismus und der Arbeiterbewegung* (Leipzig), 7 (1916), 60-94.

Tsereteli, I., "Reminiscences of the Russian Revolution: The April Crisis," *The Russian Review*, 14 (1955), 93-108, 184-200, 300-321; 15 (1956), 37-48.

INDEX